A STRANGER IN TIBET

Kawaguchi, dressed as a Tibetan monk, in Darjeeling
after his first trip.

A Stranger in Tibet

The Adventures of a Wandering Zen Monk

SCOTT BERRY

KODANSHA INTERNATIONAL
Tokyo and New York

Photo and illustration credits
Tohoku University, Faculty of Arts and Letters (Matsumoto
Eiichi, photographer): pp. 54, 126, 186, 209, 257, 271, 285
Birendra Pratap Singh: pp. 58–59, 81, 93
Pema Thapkey: p. 41
Ganesh Photo Lab, Kathmandu: pp. 235, 263

Jacket photo
Scott Berry

Publication of this book was assisted by a grant from the
Japan Foundation.

Distributed in the United States by Kodansha International/
USA Ltd., 114 Fifth Avenue, New York, New York 10011.
Published by Kodansha International Ltd., 2-2, Otowa 1-
chome, Bunkyo-ku, Tokyo 112, and Kodansha International/
USA. Copyright © 1989 by Kodansha International Ltd. All
rights reserved. Printed in Japan.
ISBN 4-7700-1391-4 (in Japan)
First edition, 1989

Library of Congress Cataloging-in-Publication Data

Berry, Scott, 1945-
  A stranger in Tibet.

  Bibliography: p.
  1. Kawaguchi, Ekai.   2. Scholars, Buddhist–
Japan–Biography.   I. Title.
BQ968.A8957B47   1989   294.3'927'0924 [B]   88-81849
ISBN 0-87011-891-9 (U.S.)

Contents

Acknowledgments

Researching a book in four countries inevitably involves debts of gratitude to more people than can be properly thanked, but the following are a few of the most memorable.

In Thak Khola, Govindaman Serchan of Tukche (who unfortunately died before publication of this book) and his wife were extremely generous and helpful, as was the well-known Bhakti Hirachan in Marpha. Again in Tukche, Manoj Kumar Tulachan of the Himali Lodge certainly deserves mention for providing some of the best meals along a well-catered trail. The Syang Lama, the most important religious figure in the region, was also generous with his time, telling us tales, in Nepali simple enough for me to follow, about Padmasambhava.

In the Kathmandu Valley I am indebted to Ganesh Vajra, the unofficial Fifth Chiniya Lama, who gave me the benefit of his knowledge of family tradition, of the stupa at Boudha, and the various Rana palaces. Norbu Lama of Kathmandu confirmed for me Kawaguchi's writing skills in Tibetan. Jim Goodman, a long-term resident who knows as much about Kathmandu and the Newaris as any non-Nepali, provided some unusual insights into life in the valley. And special thanks go the the Tibetan and Nepali artists, in particular Pema Thapkey and Birendra Pratap Singh, whose work does so much to enhance this book.

I deeply regret that the uncertainty of the political situation in Tibet makes it impossible to thank by name the people who helped me there.

In Japan, Kawaguchi's two surviving nieces, Miyata Emi and Uehara Sumi, were kind enough to share some of their memories with me, and Mrs. Miyata read over the last chapter, suggesting several corrections and additions. My old friend Hayakawa Akio, a history teacher by profession, dug up some obscure facts of Japanese history for me. I would also like to thank the three generations of Hattoris at the Hanno Kannonji, the eldest of whom studied Tibetan under Kawaguchi. Okuyama Naoji of Tohoku University and Takayama Ryuzo of Osaka University offered both encouragement and useful criticism, as did Pema Gyalpo of the Tibet Cultural Center. In Stephen Shaw I was fortunate to discover an ideal editor of the kind that Kawaguchi himself lacked.

My wife, Naoko, was responsible not only for removing some excesses from the manuscript but for providing much of the original inspiration, as well as the drawings with the chapter headings. Our two daughters, Maya and Anna Mei, helped us to make friends with people we might otherwise not have met in India, Nepal, and Tibet, and were the best possible traveling companions.

Though every effort has been made to avoid errors of fact, it is still possible that some have crept in, and responsibility for them rests solely with me. One controversial point may be the romanization of Nepali and Tibetan words. I have tried to use the most conventional spellings I could find for common words, place names, and personal names, but often there seems to be little agreement about what is "correct." An example is that the ceremonial greeting scarves used by Tibetans are commonly romanized as variously as *kata*, *khatag*, or *khatagh*. Occasionally, when no other reference could be found, I have had to fall back on the spellings used in *Three Years in Tibet*, as with the river Chemayungdung-gi-chu, or the names of some of Kawaguchi's friends.

Note: Japanese names (except in some quotations) are given in the Japanese order, with the surname first.

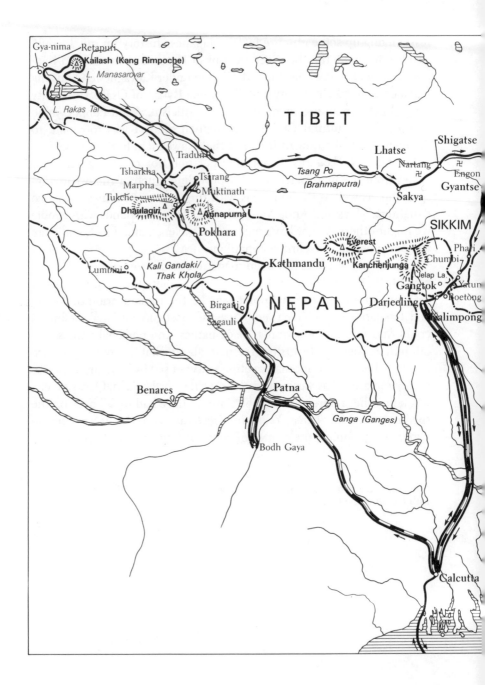

Gya-nima Retapuri
Kailash (Kang Rimpoche)
L. Manasarovar
L. Rakas Tal

TIBET

Shigatse
Lhatse   Nartang 卍
Tsang Po   Engon
(Brahmaputra)   Gyantse
Tradum
Tsharkha   Tsarang
Marpha   Muktinath   Sakya
Tukche
Dhaulagiri △ △ Annapurna   SIKKIM
Pokhara   Phari
Everest   Chumbi
Lumbini   Kali Gandaki/   Kanchenjunga Jelap La Yatun
           Thak Khola   Kathmandu   Gangtok Toetong
                                   Darjeeling Kalimpong
           Birganj   N E P A L
           Sagauli

Benares   Patna

                        Bodh Gaya   Ganga (Ganges)

                                              Calcutta

THE FIRST JOURNEY

—— K.'s route

0   100   200 miles

L. Lham Tso

卍 Reting

Kichu

Lhasa   卍 Ganden

Khamba La

...mi-la

L. Yamdruk Tso

Karo La

BHUTAN

INDIA

The Inspiration

On July 4, 1900, in one of the great unheralded moments in the history of exploration, a young Japanese Zen monk named Kawaguchi Ekai crossed from Nepal into Tibet at a spot so obscure that even today no one is quite sure where it was. He was already the first Japanese to have visited Nepal. He now became the first to enter Tibet.

His trip would be hardly less remarkable today, more than eighty years later, for while much of Tibet and Nepal are now commonly visited by tourists, the parts of Nepal with which he was most familiar are still strictly forbidden to outsiders. He was able to go there, as well as to Tibet, not because he had contrived to get permission or led an armed expedition, but because he spoke Tibetan so fluently and had adapted so completely to the Tibetan way of life that he was able to travel in disguise. His journey was the result of long, if haphazard, planning and preparation, hard work, and no small amount of luck; for he had set off from Japan two and a half years before with the firm goal of reading, and if possible collecting, the Tibetan translations of the Mahayana Buddhist scriptures, but not yet knowing a word of Tibetan and with only the vaguest idea of how he was going to attain his goal.

* * *

By 1900 Tibet was one of the few places in the world to have successfully frustrated that curious breed of men willing to risk life, limb, and reputation in order to discover the sources of rivers, the locations of mountains, and the secrets of forbidden cities. A handful of determined Western explorers, scholars, and missionaries had reached its borders and made forays into the heartland, but none (with the exception of one Englishman so eccentric that he did not even want to be there) had even caught sight of the great monastic centers or the mysterious capital of Lhasa in almost two hundred years; for Tibet and the Tibetans wanted nothing to do with the outside world.

It had not always been so. Once, the Tibetans had welcomed any and all who could successfully challenge their forbidding terrain, and were for a time particularly fond of missionaries, being under the impression that these Christians were as open-minded as they were themselves and shared a similar passion for religious debate for its own sake. They were perhaps encouraged in this belief by a remarkable Jesuit named Ippolito Desideri who in the seventeenth century lived in the Sera monastery (where Kawaguchi was later to live for over a year) and studied the Tibetan language and religion thoroughly enough to be able to discourse with the monks as an equal. Though he won the respect of the Tibetans, he seems to have won few debates (and fewer converts), and the behavior of later, less remarkable missionaries was to erase the good impression he had made.

The ban on foreigners came originally not from the Tibetans themselves but from the insular Chinese, who at a time when they were strong enough to enforce their dubious claim that Tibet was part of the Middle Kingdom, imposed their own closed-door policy on Tibet. Since the terrain made it so difficult to get in anyway, this was an easy enough measure to uphold, and in the end it was the fate of China itself at foreign hands that convinced the Tibetan government that the policy was after all valid. For not long after China's doors had been prized open, that once proud country found itself at the mercy of foreign powers, while the same was true of Tibet's other giant neighbor, India, to the south. Meanwhile, tiny but independent Nepal, assisted by its mountains and jungles, simply closed its own doors. The Tibetans decided during the nineteenth century to follow Nepal's lead and continue a policy they had not chosen for themselves.

Most people, of course, need only to be told that something is forbidden and they will rush to try it, so a form of unofficial race (which has been readably chronicled by Peter Hopkirk in *Trespassers on the Roof of the World*) developed to be the first foreigner into Lhasa. The rules were far from clear, and the real winners were more often

2

than not simply ignored by the other contestants. Thomas Manning, for example, was a bizarre British sinologue who actually managed to reach Lhasa from Calcutta in the early nineteenth century. But his goal had been forbidden China itself, and—totally unaware of the significance of his trip—he was disconcerted to find himself turned back at what he regarded as no more than an uncivilized outpost of the Chinese Empire. His journal was not published until many years after his death, and even then he was generally ignored by later travelers.

In the 1860s a succession of "Pundits," Indian spies of Himalayan origin trained by the British in secret surveying techniques, began a series of extensive Tibetan journeys, some of which should rank high in the annals of exploration. One even lived out his disguise so well that, turning up in Lhasa penniless, he was able to support himself in his supposed trade for a year there before continuing on to Koko Nor. But the Pundits were "natives," and besides they were operating in secret. Europe cared nothing for non-Caucasian explorers and perhaps for this reason ignored the first Japanese to gatecrash both Nepal and Tibet— especially as his journey put all previous European attempts to shame. Kawaguchi's *Three Years in Tibet* was published in Madras in 1909 and shortly afterward in London. Though read and appreciated by a select few, it seems to have passed rather quickly into obscurity, and was not reprinted until 1979, and then only in a limited edition of a thousand copies in Kathmandu.

Kawaguchi was at any rate an unlikely figure. Sometimes charming but often infuriating, occasionally brilliant but frequently bungling, scholarly and learned but at the same time hardheaded and intolerant (as well as being possibly the only vegetarian explorer on record), he traveled alone, often destitute and on the point of starvation, stumbled his way to the most complete exploration of the mysteries of Tibet to date, and in the end let his prejudices largely negate his accomplishments.

But then Kawaguchi was a trailblazer in more ways than one. Japan has not been noted for its explorers simply because during the great age of exploration it was forbidden by law to enter or leave Japan, which itself became the object of European and American curiosity. It was not until after the Meiji Restoration in 1868 that the Japanese began to take their first tentative steps abroad, and these were directed toward the West. By the time the Japanese, following their imperialist mentors, began to focus their attention on East Asia, there was little left of the world that had not been explored and mapped. The colonization of Africa was in full swing, the sources of the world's great rivers had all been traced, India and parts of Southeast Asia were subject to the British, Indonesia to the Dutch, and Indochina to the French. China was being carved up by anyone who could stake a claim—including, of course, Japan.

Kawaguchi was born two years before the Meiji Restoration and was thus chronologically a child of the new age. Yet in most ways he was not a modern man at all but a throwback to a much earlier age of high adventure in the cause of knowledge and the Buddhist faith. There is reason to believe that he thought of himself, not as a Japanese version of Sir Richard Burton or Sven Hedin, but more along the lines of the great Chinese pilgrims who brought Buddhism from India to China in the fifth and seventh centuries.

At the same time, there is an element of farce that is never far from the surface in Kawaguchi's travels, and had he not had the ability—rare enough in explorers—to laugh at himself, he would have been a very sad figure indeed. As it is, the reader of *Three Years in Tibet* often finds himself looking forward to the next unlikely situation in which the incompetent explorer will land himself. Again and again he forgets directions or simply loses his way and walks around in huge circles. Lost and alone, he coughs up blood, is prostrated by convulsions, and is robbed of all his possessions and food without ever, it seems, losing his underlying cheerfulness. It was just as well that his first experience of this kind came in midsummer (although, involving as it did a hailstorm at fifteen thousand feet, it was bad enough even then), for he was able to work out a method of "spiritual conquest over bodily ailment" that would serve him well in the more difficult times to come. This method was simply to force his frozen and exhausted body to cling to life through meditation, and in the process he was to compose some of his best poetry. What this could not help him with was the succession of lusty Tibetan ladies who unaccountably made assaults on his prized vow of celibacy.

In 1900, when he secretly left one forbidden land for another, Kawaguchi was thirty-four years old, lean and tough—if a trifle frail-looking—and accustomed to living on one frugal vegetarian meal a day. He had spent the entire previous year in disguise in a culturally Tibetan village called Tsarang in the little-known semi-independent kingdom of Lo, between Nepal and Tibet, and there at an altitude of nearly twelve thousand feet had kept himself in shape by running up and down mountainsides with a load of rocks on his back (the villagers, who at this point took him for a Chinese monk from Lhasa, thought this was some sort of mortification of the flesh). After two and a half years of hard study he spoke Tibetan well enough to pass as a native if he had to, had learned to live without bathing for months on end, and was confident of his health and physical strength. He was now ready for the central part of his great adventure.

But where had he come from, this scholarly wanderer? What was the inspiration that had driven him from the seemingly quiet, comfortable, and secure life of a parish priest or a sequestered scholar in Japan here to these barren, frozen lands? To answer these questions we must return to the harbor town of Sakai, near Osaka, in a Japan almost as closed and insular as Tibet itself.

* * *

By birth Kawaguchi Sadajiro (he was to change his name on ordination) was fated to be nothing more exciting than a bucket and barrel maker. As with most crafts in Japan, this is an exacting and highly developed trade. The finished products are beautiful and finely made, are useful for everything from aging saké to making pickles, and are about the last thing one can imagine our hero spending his life among. Yet he was the first-born son, and eldest sons in Japan had a strong responsibility to succeed in the family tradition.

His father had a reputation for honesty and hard work, and was deeply religious in an uncritical and unquestioning way characteristic of simple, hardworking people. His mother was from a family that had once been doctors to great lords but had fallen on hard times, and her marriage was clearly a step down in the world. She was a well-educated woman, which was unusual for the wife of an artisan, and this was to be important to all her five children, as she instilled in her four sons and one daughter a deep love of learning that was to be rather a trial to her illiterate husband.

In most ways his childhood was typical, though he was known as a quiet and sensitive child, particularly after an incident that occurred when he was only three years old and that seemed to affect him deeply. For when his father's brother died, it became the boy's duty (according to tradition) to light his uncle's funeral pyre, an overwhelming experience of death close up for a child of that age. Until the age of twelve he attended elementary school, after which his father decided reasonably enough that further education would be of little use. But the boy's appetite for knowledge had been aroused, and there could be no turning back. Two years later, presumably with the discreet encouragement of his mother, he began to attend night school after work, and would often read far into the night (a habit he retained: long afterward he described himself painfully deciphering some text by the light of three incense sticks). Yet, though this early stimulus remained with him throughout his life, acquiring knowledge would always be a struggle—against his family, against Zen tradition, and ultimately against the language and climate of Tibet.

The first sign that there was anything really unusual about this young craftsman came when at the age of fifteen he read the life of the Buddha and was so inspired that he decided to try to live for three years by "*shojin* vows," which required strict vegetarianism, celibacy, and abstinence from alcohol. The vegetarianism must have caused considerable inconvenience to the household, since a seaside family in Japan lives essentially on rice, fish, and shellfish, and most Japanese automatically assume that a "vegetarian" will eat fish. But he was, after all, the eldest son in a country where sons in general command unwarranted respect, and his doting mother bought a separate cooking pot in which she prepared his meals so that his food would not be contaminated by meat or fish.

But this was more than simply a boyish prank, and Sadajiro himself was more than just a bookish adolescent prig. The Japanese generally feel that anyone who can polish off a large bottle of saké (about four pints) in an evening is a fair tippler, and Sadajiro, at fifteen, was known

6

for this ability. And while a cynic might argue that the morning after almost half a gallon of saké would be enough to make anyone take vows, it would hardly be enough to make one stick to them for the rest of one's life. Later, in Tibet, Kawaguchi would somewhat surprisingly admit to early "experiences" with women as well.

Finding enough time to study was still a problem, though for a while he reached a compromise with his father, being allowed more hours of study in return for going to bed earlier so that he could put in a good day's work. But when he announced his intention to leave home and become a monk, he encountered all the opposition that tradition could muster. In Tibet he would discover a country where it was a matter of pride for a family when its sons joined monasteries, but it was otherwise in Japan—particularly during the early Meiji era, when Buddhism was being downplayed in favor of a more nationalistic emperor-centered version of Shinto—and especially when an eldest son was involved. It must then have been a source of particular chagrin for Sadajiro to see two of his younger brothers join monasteries while he himself had to stay behind, making buckets and keeping accounts. Yet in the end, though we know no details, his father seems to have given in, and one can only sympathize with this simple artisan who found himself burdened with a son whose taste for learning did not extend to the craft in which he was apprenticed.

The next watershed in Sadajiro's life came at the age of nineteen, when he left home. He was well aware that this was the age at which the Buddha himself had determined to give up worldly life to seek the truth. He now decided to extend his vows up to ten years and embarked on several adventures that in some ways foreshadowed his later experiences. There was first an escapade as a draft resister, which could have landed him in serious trouble. Up to this point eldest sons had been exempt from military service, but a new law made them fair game for Japan's rising military aspirations. Sneaking off to Tokyo, Kawaguchi developed an elaborate plan for waylaying no less a person than the emperor himself, at the racecourse, to voice his objections. Luckily for all concerned, he was tracked down by family friends before putting this plan into action.

Not long afterward he went away for a week to meditate in a forest,

7

living off nothing but pine needles. He tells us that they were bitter at first but that by the end of the week he had come to quite enjoy them. And while he felt that he had benefited from the experience, it also had the effect of reinforcing his growing belief that meditation without knowledge was of little use. In this he was in conflict with Zen doctrine, with its anti-learning bias and reliance on meditation and sudden revelation. Here we see the seeds of his own later anti-sectarianism, for his personal beliefs combined study and meditation in a way no existing Japanese sect did.

The next few years follow an erratic course, with a spell at Doshisha University in Kyoto, employment as a teacher in his hometown of Sakai, hard times and a case of beri-beri, wanderings from temple to temple, studies at the Tetsu Gakukan in Tokyo, English lessons from a missionary who tried to convert him to Christianity, and Pali lessons from a man who tried to convert him to Theravada Buddhism. His most influential teacher during this period was Nanjo Bun'yu, a pioneering Sanskritist who had spent eight years at Oxford, where he had learned of the existence of Tibetan sacred texts rumored to be unusually faithful to the Sanskrit originals; and Kawaguchi, who could already read Chinese, now seems to have begun studying Sanskrit. One's impression is of a restless mind searching here and there for whatever would satisfy it.

Then comes a strange little interlude back in Sakai when at the age of twenty-five he celebrated ten years of living according to *shojin* vows by letting them lapse and going on a small binge, indulging in saké and shellfish. But shortly thereafter we find him in Tokyo, finally being formally ordained at the Gohyaku Rakanji ("the Temple of Five Hundred Buddhas"), and again taking up the non-compulsory vows. He also changed his name from Sadajiro to Ekai Jinko ("Ocean of Wisdom, Wide Virtue"). It appeared that he was settling down, especially as he enrolled again at the Tetsu Gakukan (literally "the hall of philosophy," and later Toyo University), an institution that had been set up expressly to keep the virtues of old Japan from disappearing in an age of rapid Westernization. But a month later he made the mistake of accepting the rectorship of the large and important Gohyaku Rakanji, where he had been ordained.

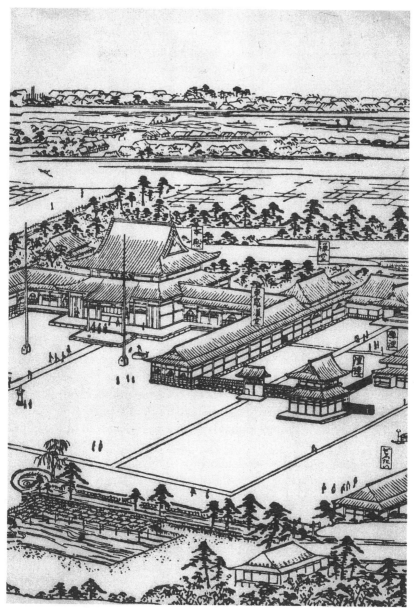

The old Gohyaku Rakanji.

The old temple has long since been replaced by high-rise apartments, but wood-block prints show a wealthy and active-looking institution. The rector's duties involved collecting and administering funds, officiating at funerals (most Japanese associate Buddhism only with death and the expensive rites that go with it), seeing that the leaking roof was repaired, and looking after the upkeep of the gate, walls, and grounds. These duties left little time for meditation and less for study, and Kawaguchi probably found them about as satisfying as making buckets. He discovered, however, that the only way to get out of the job was to renounce his monastic ties, which he eventually did a little more than a year after ordination, in a huff over alleged immorality among the hierarchy. For this impetuous gesture he was rewarded by being banned from staying at any temple belonging to the sect. In fact, as we trace his life in the period that follows, it is often difficult to tell just when Kawaguchi was a monk and when he wasn't, though his conduct was always governed by vows stricter than those adhered to by most official monks. In a nation of "organization men," Kawaguchi was beginning to discover that he just did not fit in.

His intention on leaving the Gohyaku Rakanji had been to go to the head temple of the Obaku sect (Obakusan, or Mampukuji, near Kyoto) and live there in seclusion—though it seems naive of him to have expected to be welcomed by a hierarchy whose behavior had so scandalized him that he had renounced his ordination. Here, Kawaguchi undoubtedly hoped to resolve the paradox that had long troubled him—that of a Zen monk (on and off, at least) convinced of the importance of the kind of study that Zen largely rejected. For at the temple of Obakusan was a collection of the Chinese *Tripitaka* known for its large, clear print (indeed, the only one in Japan apparently that could be read without injury to the eyes). And his ambition, in the long run, after working his way through it, was to translate the difficult classical Chinese into more accessible Japanese.

Now it must not be supposed that reading this huge canon is like reading the Bible or the Koran. The Chinese *Tripitaka* is a collection of about sixteen hundred separate works which, with typical Buddhist tolerance, include not only approved texts but virtually any writings thought worth preserving by Chinese Buddhists at any time. It contains translations from Pali of the ancient Theravada works, translations from Sanskrit of the Mahayana scriptures (sometimes several different versions of the same thing), as well as works that originated in China.

The Obaku Zen sect did not reach Japanese shores until 1655 and was the last sect of Chinese Buddhism to arrive. Unlike the others it retained a good deal of its original character: at Obakusan, prayers were recited in Ming-dynasty Chinese, the monks wore Chinese ceremonial hats, and even the vegetarian food was prepared in the Chinese style. The first thirteen abbots came from China—an unusual example of cultural interaction during the insular Edo period—and it was during this time that the *Tripitaka* was printed. Kawaguchi was able to read it since he had taken up the study of Chinese at the age of fifteen, and while he never appears to have achieved any real competence in the spoken language, he was soon reading the most complicated classics (this is, of course, far less difficult for a literate Japanese than for a European, since the characters that form such an important part of the Japanese writing system are Chinese in origin).

But if Kawaguchi expected peace and seclusion in this huge temple complex in the hills east of Kyoto, he was to be sadly disappointed. First of all he had a struggle just to be allowed in, and then he stepped right into the thick of the sort of unseemly squabble among monks that he was later to so deplore in Tibet. While he was always careful in his translated writing to avoid any criticism of Japan or Japanese Buddhism, it would seem that the unpleasantness at Obakusan was an important factor in his decision to leave Japan.

Judging from what he allowed to be published in English, Kawaguchi must have felt that events over the next three years were best forgotten, and here we need look only at their general outline. It seems that the previous abbot of Obakusan and his associates had run the temple into debt by misappropriating funds and directing them to their own use. He had left the monastery once to try a political career, but had been so unsuccessful that he was now trying to stage a comeback at Obakusan in order to cover his personal debts with more temple funds. Even worse from Kawaguchi's standpoint, the former abbot and his followers were openly keeping mistresses, and visiting monks were shocked to see diapers hanging to dry in the temple precincts where women were supposedly forbidden.

Kawaguchi was inevitably drawn into the controversy between the "worldly" and "spiritual" factions there, as he could hardly be expected to remain comfortably indifferent to such goings-on. He was worried moreover that, with the debts the temple was incurring, it would soon cease to exist. In practice, being only on the fringe of this community, he had no right to be involved at all, but he got around this by being accepted as the follower of an established resident, and even obtained a formal position in the temple office. He now proceeded to write tracts and make speeches, and apparently aroused such strong feelings in the small world of the monastery that he received death threats. But in the end the return of the high-living abbot was blocked, though a number of his followers were allowed to remain and Kawaguchi was forced to resign his position. He was, however, allowed to stay on at the temple as long as he restricted himself to his studies. This of course had been his object from the beginning, and he seems to have been wounded by the accusation that he himself was making a play for the abbacy.

Knowing how restless and unfocused his progress had been so far, it comes as no surprise perhaps that Kawaguchi, now free to immerse himself in ancient scriptures, soon found fault with even these, for the Chinese texts he examined seemed far from adequate. The problem with reading Buddhist works in Chinese is that not only the words but the very concepts have often been translated from an Indian to a Confucian/Taoist context more congenial to Chinese thought. Kawaguchi really felt he needed to look at the originals. Yet most of the Sanskrit texts had been destroyed, though some had been taken to Nepal and Tibet for safekeeping, during the Muslim invasions of India. With most of the originals gone, the best translations were said to be locked away in the monasteries, and language, of Tibet—presumably because pre-Buddhist Tibetan culture had no sophisticated concepts of its own to substitute for those received. The idea of searching these out first occurred to Kawaguchi at Obakusan.

The attraction of this idea to someone of his unconventional temperament is obvious. He had tried running a temple and found it irksome. He did not approve of his superiors. He had tried being a recluse and had found himself embroiled in an unseemly power struggle. On the other hand, he enjoyed physical challenges (like that week spent living off pine needles) as well as intellectual ones. The dangers involved in a trip to forbidden Tibet would be so great that he could ask no one to share them. This was something he would have to do alone, far from account keeping, routine funeral services, and temple intrigues. The inadequacy of the Chinese texts is the sort of excuse he might well have invented had it not already existed.

But if he was serious about it he would be obliged to learn yet another difficult language from scratch, and then face a clandestine journey into the unknown. This he seemed willing to take on, for the decision he made was to keep him out of Japan for seventeen of the next eighteen years. As a solitary wandering scholar Kawaguchi was to find his vocation at last.

Darjeeling

Kawaguchi never went about anything in a normal way. An explorer might reasonably be expected to go around collecting men and matériel for an expedition. Kawaguchi's main concern on the eve of departure was with karma—his own and that of friends and former parishioners. And once again we are confronted with the oddities of a personality that was completely out of step with the times and determined to let nothing stand between itself and its purpose.

Indifferent to wealth and possessions in an age of burgeoning materialism, he turned down any going-away presents he was offered and instead exacted pledges from friends and acquaintances of abstention from alcohol and tobacco. He had already rejected offers of large sums to help him start his own temple, for his admirers thought his Tibetan venture sheer madness and uniformly predicted disaster. But he knew his own mind and was having none of their attempts to keep him in Japan. To Tibet he would go, and in so doing he would shame some of his more worldly friends into a little righteousness. He proudly informs us that he collected about forty pledges in Tokyo, and with his typically understated humor tells us that "many" even stuck by them. He was perhaps proudest of having convinced several friends who were ardent fishermen to give up their hobby and burn their nets. There was also a restaurateur whose establishment specialized in "poultry dinners," but who was persuaded to go into another business. Kawaguchi was convinced that the good he had done in saving the lives of so many "finny and feathered creatures" was instrumental later in protecting him during his own encounters with danger.

The strength of Kawaguchi's beliefs, his outspokenness, and his intolerance are all brought out in his account of how he induced one of his fishing friends to give up his hobby. He had found this former parishioner distraught over the recent death of his three-year-old child.

"Do you really find it so hard to bear the death of your child?" asked the monk rather heartlessly. "What would you think of a person who dared bind and kill a beloved child of yours and roast and eat its flesh?"

"Oh! Devilish! The devil only could do that; no man could!" answered the understandably horrified friend.

"You are a fiend then, at least to the fishes of the deep," replied Kawaguchi, driving his point home in a way that even he admitted might be in bad taste. But in the end the fishing nets were burned. As many other episodes suggest, Kawaguchi was never one to let convention get in his way when he felt strongly about something, and he probably would have made a thoroughly bad parish priest had he stuck to it.

It must also be understood that in deciding on this journey Kawaguchi was firmly at odds with the prevailing interests of his day. As late as the time of his birth, Japan remained almost as isolated from the outside world as the Tibet he now hoped to visit, and the great reform movement known as the Meiji Restoration which took place when he was two years old began as a movement to oust the foreigners who had forced a limited opening of Japan in the 1850s. Yet it soon became something quite different, for the Japanese were shrewd enough to realize that if they were to compete with the West they could do it only by playing the West's own game. Thus, when Japan did decide to open up, it did so with typical single-mindedness, and by 1897 the country had for thirty years been thirstily and uncritically absorbing everything Western from dance steps to diet.

Of course cultural importation was nothing new to Japan. What was new was that this island nation now looked beyond China for inspiration, beyond a continent from which so much had been taken in the past but whose power was now spent. Despite a modest Buddhist revival among scholars and clergy toward the end of the century, the vast majority of the population looked forward to an industrialized, mechanized, and militaristic future—not back to the dusty temples and faded philosophies of an earlier age. The men Kawaguchi approached for pledges wore Western suits and hats, and the new Japanese military machine had already had a successful go at Japan's old mentor. To propose, then, like Kawaguchi, to cross the Himalayas to remote Tibet, not to trade or to spy out a military advantage but simply to gaze into the dim past, must have seemed to his contemporaries both foolish and irrelevant.

Not long before his departure a commemorative photograph was taken of Kawaguchi in full monk's regalia alongside two of his brothers, and a glance at this picture (unfortunately unavailable for reproduction) might help enlighten us further as to why everyone was predicting disaster. The young man with his freshly shaven pate certainly looks more like the popular cartoon monk Ikkyu-san than he does an intrepid explorer, but there is something else as well. Photographs of Kawaguchi taken later in life show a fairly benevolent-looking individual wearing a slightly bemused smile, the smile of a man who has come to terms with himself and the world. But the face staring starkly back at us from this early photo has a touch of the fanatic about it. He seems to burn with some inner fire, and when he told people in all seriousness, "If I die, well and good; it will be like a soldier's death in a battle-field, and I should be gratified to think that I fell in the cause of my religion," we can well imagine he was taken seriously.

His spiritual preparations had taken his mind off more mundane matters, and it seems only on the brink of departure that he realized he was broke. Though until now he had pointedly turned down all farewell presents in favor of pledges, he suddenly found it necessary to hastily accept five hundred yen (about $250 in those days). Seldom has an explorer set off with a lighter purse, or with so hazy an idea of what he was actually going to do.

* * *

He seems in fact not to have thought about this problem at all until he reached Singapore. After all, few Japanese or Westerners even today have much idea of what to expect of Tibet—then, it was a total mystery. Having left Japan with no more than a sketchy notion of confronting the roof of the world head-on, he spent his time aboard ship, not planning, but preaching to the passengers and crew and happily discussing religion with a Japanese-speaking English missionary. In Singapore he was abruptly informed by the Japanese consul that he had two choices: he could lead an armed expedition or he could go as a beggar. This advice was undoubtedly meant to discourage the unlikely explorer and send him scurrying home, but in the event it was ignored.

> I answered Mr. Fujita [the consul] to the effect that being a Buddhist priest, as I was, the first of the methods that he had mentioned was out of the question for me, and that my idea at the time was to follow the second course; although I was far from having anything like a definite program for my journey. I told him further that I intended to wander on as the course of events might lead me. I left the Consul in a very meditative mood.

More likely, he left him thoroughly annoyed. Consuls have always hated having travelers like Kawaguchi turn up on their doorstep.

But he is soon gone, and reappears in Calcutta in August, at the height of the steamy monsoon, a time of year that is guaranteed to fray the nerves of travelers and residents alike. Yet our monk does not even mention the weather, though he does pause to marvel at the giant fireflies he observes from the train window on the undoubtedly uncomfortable three-day ride to Siliguri at the foot of the Himalayas.

And here we might pause ourselves to look ahead briefly, for there is something curiously contemporary about Kawaguchi's trip from here on. If his itinerary sounds vaguely familiar, it is because it combines the dreams and the reality of so many young people from Europe, America, and Japan today. Consider for a moment. He leaves Calcutta as quickly as possible and sets out for the highland refuge of Darjeeling. There he stays for a year and a half of study before going on a pilgrimage to Bodh Gaya, the site of the Buddha's enlightenment—then largely in a state of neglect but now the festive site of the exiled Dalai Lama's annual sermons. From Bodh Gaya he follows what has become one of the most well-trodden paths in the world: to the Nepalese border at Birganj, and on to Kathmandu. In the Kathmandu Valley he stays at the great stupa of Boudhanath, then as now the center of Tibetan activity in the valley, and proceeds to Pokhara. At Pokhara he pauses for a few days before setting off for the upper reaches of the Kali Gandaki Valley, today probably the most popular trek in Nepal. But at Kagbeni, north of Jomsom,

17

the reconstructable portion of his trip ends for a while, for he was to spend a year in Lo—the forbidden "Mustang" that every trekker dreams of sneaking into—and subsequently enter Tibet via equally forbidden Dolpo. In Tibet, however, the modern traveler can rejoin him: with considerable difficulty at Mt. Kailash, or with a good deal less in Lhasa or at the Sera monastery at the foot of the mountains just north of Lhasa.

Yet in 1897 this journey was quite unknown, and even Kawaguchi's approach to it was ultimately far less casual than that of most of today's travelers. He may have decided to go as a beggar, but he was not going unprepared. While other explorers of the day were spending large sums of money outfitting themselves, stocking up on provisions, engaging translators, and embarking with unwieldy caravans, Kawaguchi decided instead to store up as much as possible inside that formidable brain of his. This meant not only learning a new language but equipping himself with everything from proper modes of behavior to the latest Lhasa gossip.

And this is why his first stop was Darjeeling, where he was to devote a year and a half to basic preparations. Instead of spending money he would spend time. Once he had begun his great adventure he was certainly in no hurry to end it, and the way he dawdles purposely at the beginning and the end of his journey brings to mind other explorers from other lands. There was England's Sir Richard Burton, for example, who had a habit of throwing away his chances of glory by lagging behind with his Arab friends while his rivals in London stole his thunder. Or the even more striking example of the enigmatic Swiss Burckhardt, who set out in 1809 to look for the source of the Niger, traveled for years disguised as an Arab, paid a surreptitious visit to Mecca, and thought of so many excuses to extend his trip that he finally died before ever returning to Europe—or getting anywhere near the source of the Niger. Kawaguchi was in fact to see his homeland only once in the next eighteen years, when he returned there in 1903–1904 to publish a series of newspaper articles and collect the Japanese Buddhist texts that he had promised to the Rana prime minister of Nepal.

Here we begin to see in Kawaguchi some of those peculiar qualities which one finds in the best of Japanese eccentrics, for the Japanese have a tradition of eccentricity similar to that of the British—though neither eccentricity nor rebellion are encouraged for their own sake, as they often are in Britain. A Japanese eccentric, however, is expected to cultivate his particular idiosyncrasy in the same way as the Japanese do everything else: wholeheartedly. It does not matter much if no measure of success is achieved (and it can be a positive advantage if the eccentric dies in the process): what matters is the effort. In this sense Kawaguchi was wholly Japanese.

*　*　*

Darjeeling, seven thousand feet up in the Himalayan foothills, famous for its tea plantations, its healthy air, and the parties thrown by the British who went there to escape the heat of the plains, was also the home of one of the finest scholars and explorers of Tibet the age had yet produced. History has failed to remember him, but it was because of him that Kawaguchi went to Darjeeling.

He was a Bengali named Surat Chandra Das. His being Indian, in fact the last of the great Pundits, prevented the British from ever giving him his due, beyond rewarding him with the post of headmaster of the Tibetan High School in Darjeeling. On the other hand, his work as a British agent seems to have made it impossible for his fellow Indians, right up to the present, to see in him anything more than a collaborator. Yet the Tibetan-English dictionary he was compiling when he met Kawaguchi is still in print (indeed it has recently been reissued in Japan and India) and remains a standard work of reference, so that today Chandra Das's name is probably best known among Western followers of Tibetan Buddhism who have to struggle with difficult translations.

Kawaguchi hoped to become Das's pupil and the two seem to have hit it off, though initially the visitor had little but his enthusiasm to recommend him. He had yet to prove himself either as a traveler or a linguist, and one suspects that no one was more surprised than Das when almost five years later the exhausted monk appeared on his doorstep after a two-year sojourn in Tibet, and proceeded to very nearly die of the only serious illness he suffered on his entire trip.

Surat Chandra Das is the first of a series of colorful friends

Surat Chandra Das.

Kawaguchi was to make along the way. Surprisingly, perhaps, it was not to holy men and scholars that he seemed attracted, but to spies, rogues, vow-breakers, and womanizers. Since Kawaguchi is often at pains to hide his own humanity from his reader, it is through these friends that, in some ways, one can get closest to knowing what sort of man he must have been.

A number of writers have pointed out that Das is supposed to have been the original for Hurree Babu in Kipling's *Kim*; and though it is difficult to connect the robust, mustachioed Bengali gentleman revealed in both his photographs and his impeccable—if somewhat stilted—Victorian prose with the fat, puffing, umbrella-wielding "verree fearful man" speaking mangled Babu English that we find in Kipling, a glance at Das's own accounts of his travels does suggest a man who suffered rather than enjoyed his journeys, and who often wondered just what he was doing in the unlikely situations in which he frequently found himself. On beginning a journey he exhibits none of the carefree joy one usually associates with the born traveler, but only fear of death in the snows and "faint hope" that he will ever see his home again. At the end of the first day of his second trip to Tibet, far from glorying in the freedom of a night spent in the wilderness, he complains of being unable to sleep due to the "unevenness of the ground, the insects creeping over me, the prickly points of bramble and weeds penetrating the thin rug on which I lay, and a shower of rain. . . ." An almost audible sigh escapes from the page. Later he grumbles about leeches spoiling his afternoon nap, and his first concern at the end of every day's march is always to procure some local beer: either *murwa* (made from millet), or *chang* (made from barley). An encounter with a man-eating tiger, which for Kawaguchi would become the occasion for a poem, merely provokes in Chandra Das a "quaking heart."

Yet like Kipling's Babu he must have concealed a good deal of courage beneath his conventional exterior. He was, after all, a spy, and had the Tibetan government learned what he was really up to on his visits it would have made short work of him, and he could have expected no assistance from his British employers. That he was well aware of what his fate was likely to be is indicated by the way he dwells on several rather nasty punishments he either heard about or observed while he was in Tibet. As it happened, he was not found out until after he had returned to India, but, as a result, a number of his Tibetan friends were punished (including one of the country's most distinguished scholars, who was executed by drowning) and a wave of paranoia swept Tibet, leading to much stricter vigilance at the borders and causing Kawaguchi untold difficulties twenty years later.

The scholar/spy certainly extended every courtesy to the aspiring explorer and helped him along in his studies, both by finding him teachers and generously offering to pay his board, for the Japanese monk was, as he himself put it, "not too well stocked with the wherewithal." He arrived in Darjeeling with about three hundred yen (a little over $150), and this was to last him seventeen months—though without Das's help he would have been hard put to it to hold out for more than half a year.

On the other hand, whether out of jealousy or sincere concern for his Japanese friend's well-being, Das made every effort to discourage him from his plan of entering Tibet. There is also a possibility that he had been ordered to keep an eye on this unorthodox character. The Japanese were now becoming a significant military power in Asia. After they had joined in the humiliation of China their expansionist tendencies were only too obvious. Just because Kawaguchi appeared to be a monk was no reason he could not also be a spy: hadn't Chandra Das himself gone to Tibet in the guise of a Sikkimese holy man? Though it has long been suspected that Kawaguchi *was* working for somebody, in the end no real evidence has turned up to support this, and he was probably too incompetent to have been much good as a spy even if it had not gone against his beliefs. Nevertheless, the suspicion was certainly justified, for in 1901, nine months after Kawaguchi's own arrival in Lhasa, a genuine Japanese agent called Narita Yasuteru did show up in Lhasa for two weeks. Like Kawaguchi, he was disguised as a Chinese, and both were unaware of the other's presence; but Narita was little the wiser about anything when he left the city.

Perhaps because he himself suffered the hardships of travel so acutely, it was difficult for Das to imagine the frail-looking little monk surviving at all. For Das, the journey itself was a kind of penance, a trial to be endured only because it could lead eventually to years of secure and comfortable academic work. He was probably baffled by a traveler like Kawaguchi for whom the trip had its own rewards. Indeed, when we later read of shoulder-deep river crossings in sub-freezing weather, solitary nights in the snow, coughing up blood from altitude sickness when lost and without shelter, encounters with bandits, and days on end without food, we are left in little doubt that Das himself would not have survived Kawaguchi's trip. At any rate, he never abandoned his efforts to dissuade his Japanese student, and long afterward a letter from Das to Kawaguchi, a last-ditch attempt to convince him to give up which reached him in the Nepali town of Marpha, would have the ironic effect of forcing the wavering monk into a decision to continue.

* * *

Kawaguchi has little to say about Darjeeling in his writings. He spent a year and a half there, but it was merely a training ground. Perhaps because his friend Chandra Das tried so hard to persuade him to stay rather than attempt the perilous journey onward, he seems to have deliberately closed his mind to the fascination of the town—for Darjeeling is an attractive place at whatever level it is approached.

Dominated by Kanchenjunga, the world's third highest mountain, Darjeeling sits atop a spur that gives it one of the finest views of any

22

town in the Himalayas; yet Kawaguchi, who was by no means immune to mountain scenery, does not even mention the view except later to compare it unfavorably with Pokhara. In other ways as well he gives an unorthodox picture of the town. Where an Englishman's account would have made the predictable references to drinks at the club, to fellow residents at the many English-style cottages that peer out of the mist, the best parties of the season, perhaps a dalliance with the wife of another Sahib left behind to grill on the plains, and of course a stroll on the Chowrasta and the Mall, our monk mentions little besides temples and language lessons. Oddly, or perhaps simply out of prudence, he never brings up the undercurrent of intrigue always present in Darjeeling, of which he must have been aware (associating as he did with one of its central figures), for England and Russia were now well into their "Great Game," with dominance of Asia as the prize.

Because of its proximity to Tibet and Sikkim—and because it has been a winter retreat for wealthy Tibetans for as long as it has been a summer retreat for the British—Darjeeling has always been one of the most convenient places in India to study the language and culture of Tibet, and has thus attracted more than its share of offbeat scholars. The saddest story is probably that of the Hungarian Csoma de Körös, often considered the father of Tibetan studies, who died there in 1842.[1] Hoping to find in the Tibetans some clue to the mysterious origins of the Hungarian people, he spent years studying on the western borders of Tibet around Ladakh, but was never able to get past the watchful border guards there. He then came to Darjeeling in order to make another attempt from the other side, but in the lowland approaches contracted a fever (possibly the same type that Kawaguchi was to pick up on his way out of Tibet) and died at Darjeeling, which ironically had been established as a health station, before realizing his cherished dream.

Resident at the same time as Kawaguchi and Chandra Das was Dr. L. Austine Waddell, a British physician as well as amateur archaeologist and anthropologist who had unearthed the site of the Buddha's birthplace at Lumbini in Nepal, and who in Darjeeling studied Tibet's religion in his spare time by the unusual expedient of buying a temple, monks and all, and instructing the inmates to carry on business as usual. His famous book, *The Buddhism of Tibet or Lamaism*, until recently a standard work on the subject, is noteworthy not only for its careful and exhaustive scholarship but for bigotry and intolerance that far surpass Kawaguchi at his worst. Kawaguchi, as we shall see, often felt he had to defend his faith by running down the Tibetans and what he saw as their outlandish version of Buddhism; Waddell condemns the Tibetans out of pure racial snobbery.

They seem to have been unaware of one another, for of course they moved in rather different circles. Kawaguchi's world would have been that of the bazaars and the Tibetan temples from the point of view of a simple scholar monk: a foreigner, to be sure, since he still wore the robes of a Japanese priest, but one without the racial inhibitions that so constrained the British rulers (it was George Orwell who pointed out that the life of a Sahib was one long struggle not to be laughed at). Waddell, the Victorian Burra Sahib, would have moved in the decorous atmosphere of the clubs and tea rooms with scenes of Salisbury Cathedral on the walls, and he would only have looked at the other life around him as a scientist looks at tiny organisms through a microscope.

Yet what is surprising is that, except for a grudging acknowledgment by Waddell in a preface that someone called "Babu Suratchandra Das" has written a book and done some translations, Waddell and Das never mention one another in their writings. Here we have two of the greatest Tibetologists of their day, both employed by the same government, living within a mile or two of each other and sharing several friends and acquaintances; yet neither has left any evidence of knowing his opposite number or his work. Prudence? Both were, after all, spies of sorts, but much of their work was public enough. Perhaps each simply had his own reasons for not liking the other. Das had made two secret trips to Tibet in the early 1880s, while Waddell was forced to content himself with eventually entering Tibet under force of arms as part of the widely criticized British invasion under Colonel Francis Younghusband in 1904 (Younghusband, who generally went out of his way to see the best in people, gives us an insight into Waddell's difficult personality by referring to him as a "miserable old woman"). Or perhaps it was pure snobbery on Waddell's part, and reaction to it on

Das's. The latter may have been a great scholar/spy and the head-master of the local Tibetan school at a salary of six hundred rupees a month, but he was still a "native" and could under no circumstances have been invited to the club.

Kawaguchi was of course under the same racial restrictions, but he gives no indication of either noticing or minding, for he had more interesting things to think about. There was first and foremost the formidable task of learning Tibetan. While he always maintained that Tibetan was a more difficult language than English, there are some remarkable, if superficial, similarities between Japanese and Tibetan which are likely to make the Japanese speaker feel at home in the early stages of his studies. These affinities are there because in each case the languages have been influenced by both Sanskrit and Chinese. Tibetan and Japanese, for example, both have Chinese-based number systems which are so similar as to sound like dialects of one another. Both languages also share corresponding systems of humble and honorific address in which the speaker always places himself in a definite relationship with the person he is addressing or talking about. And since the written syllabaries in both languages are ultimately based on Sanskrit (and were developed at about the same time in the eighth or ninth centuries A.D.), the vowel sounds are almost identical and are learned in the same order.

So far so good, but fairly early on Tibetan begins to show what it is really made of. English speakers are accustomed to a written language that bears a fairly close resemblance to the language as spoken; but spoken and written Tibetan are in practice different things. This may be a common stumbling block of Asian tongues, but it is a stumbling block nonetheless. Because it has retained archaic spellings, Tibetan is full of silent letters that were at one time pronounced. The letters are grouped in syllables and are not only strung out left and right but piled on top and hung underneath as well, their forms and pronunciations sometimes changing according to where in the syllable they appear; in extreme but by no means uncommon cases, syllables of five letters will have only one pronounced. This is about as logical as if "a draughthorse brought to slaughter" were not an exception but the rule in English, and it has led to such a tortured system that Western scholars and writers usually have to romanize everything twice: once according to the spelling and once according to the pronunciation. Works on Tibet are thus full of illuminating little asides like "(Tib. *Hjam-dpal*: pron. *Jampay*)" or "(Tib. *sPrul-sku*: pron. *tulku*)" or even "(Tib. *bKa' brug pa*: pron. *Kargyupa*)." St. Francis Xavier is credited with accusing the Devil himself of having devised the Japanese language to hinder the spread of the gospel. Kawaguchi might well have echoed him concerning Tibetan.

But instead, with characteristic energy, he simply tucked up his robes and got down to work. His first teacher, a personable old Mongolian monk at the Ghoom monastery a few miles south of Darjeeling, and a friend of both Waddell and Das, proved to be a disappointment. He and Kawaguchi were at first excited to discover that their names (Serab Gyatso and Ekai) had the same meaning ("Ocean of Wisdom") in their respective languages. But the lessons soon developed into one of those missionary encounters that seemed to plague Kawaguchi. It appeared that every time he tried to learn a language, his teacher tried to convert him to his own religion or sect; it had already happened in Japan with English and Pali, and now it was happening in India with Tibetan. Though he himself was hardly innocent of preaching, Kawaguchi could never stand being preached to, and instead of just trying to get the most out of the situation he would rebel. After a frustrating month Chandra Das arranged for him to live with the family of a married Tibetan priest called Lama Shabdung so that he could pick up the colloquial language, which would be vital to the success of his trip. At the same time he began studying more systematically at the Government High School.

Ever since the Meiji Restoration, and particularly since World War II, Japan has proved a monumental frustration to foreign language instructors, and conventional wisdom has it that, with the possible exceptions of the Americans and the British, the Japanese are the world's worst language students. Yet this is not entirely fair. The Japanese may not be conspicuously successful at English (largely because it is so disastrously taught in their schools), but they often outperform their Western counterparts when it comes to learning Asian languages. Still, Kawaguchi was after more than simple communication. He needed to be convincing not just as a native speaker but as an educated native speaker. And he went about the task with both energy and the kind of imagination that contemporary linguistic theorists would have us believe they had invented. Here is an example of his remarks on language learning:

> It is a well known thing that the best way to learn a foreign language is to live among the people who speak it, but a discovery—as it was to me—that I made while at Shabdung's was that the best teachers of everyday language are children. As a foreigner you ask them to teach you their language; and you find that, led on by their instinctive curiosity and kindness, not unmingled with a sense of pride, they are always the most anxious and untiring teachers, and also that in their innocence they are the most exacting and intolerant teachers, as they will brook no mispronunciation or mis-accent, even the slightest errors. Next to children, women are, I think, the best language teachers. . . . Six or seven months after my installment in the Shabdung household, I had become able to carry on all ordinary conversation in the Tibetan tongue, with more ease than in my English of two years' hard learning, and I regard Tibetan as a more difficult language than English. . . . That progress was the gift of my female and juvenile teachers. . . .

In the Japanese edition of his book he goes on to describe how he would sit with the children, carefully watching the way they used their lips, tongues, and teeth, as he worked toward perfect imitation. Frequently, just when he thought he had got the hang of it, he would make a complete mess of things, and he felt that the good-natured laughter that greeted his failures was another reason why he progressed so quickly.

Here we also have the first of our celibate monk's curious references to women. This one is innocent enough, but later in his travels he seems constantly to fall out of mortal danger almost literally into the arms of some beautiful maiden, and later chapters of *Three Years in Tibet* bear titles like "A Beautiful Rescuer" and "A Himalayan Romance."

* * *

And so one can imagine him, a young monk, close-cropped and with a clean-shaven face—for he had yet to grow the beard that was to become his trademark—sitting on the floor at his Tibetan folding desk on the outskirts of Darjeeling or walking to and from the Government High School, his head so busy with the vagaries of the Tibetan language that he probably seldom noticed or had time to gaze toward Kanchenjunga, which lay between him and his goal. It must have been a pleasant time for him. "I lived as though back in my boyhood, attending school in the morning, and doing my lessons at home in the company of the children of the family in the afternoon." For the first time since his own childhood he could study without interference from parents, parishioners, leaking roofs, or interfering abbots.

The area in which he lived is to this day called "Lhasa Villa" in memory of Chandra Das's famous house, which has long since disappeared—along, it seems, with any memory of its owner. Less than an hour's walk from the center of Darjeeling, it enjoys a view of tea-enshrouded slopes and a deep valley extending all the way to the foot of Kanchenjunga. It must have been a quiet place, ideal for study, especially with a family. In the evenings, once his Tibetan was good enough, Kawaguchi would sit amidst the scroll paintings and the carved wooden tables decked out in red, blue, and gold, drinking Tibetan buttered tea and listening to his host tell stories of old Tibet. From him he would have heard of the vast, windswept plains inhabited only by demons, and of the conquest of these demons by the Tantric mystic Padmasambhava, of mountaintop monasteries, of hermits who walled themselves up for life, and of saints who, after dying, took up their duties again in a new incarnation. For while he was learning the language he was also learning the obscure history, topography, and culture of that hidden country, and it is to these that we too must now turn if Kawaguchi's adventures are to make any sense to us.

---

1. It was de Köros, in fact, who discovered for the West the existence of the Tibetan manuscripts Kawaguchi was now after, and this knowledge came to Japan—as we have seen—by way of Oxford.

Of Demons and Mystics

Two factors have always dominated life in Tibet: the cold and the sheer emptiness. Professor Guiseppe Tucci, one of this century's most active explorers and scholars of Tibet, sums up the latter nicely when he says that "man is truly overwhelmed by nature's pitiless vastness."

Most of Tibet is located on a high, exposed plain where little or nothing grows. It is a land where sparse life clings precariously to the rare footholds afforded by nature. It has always been almost devoid of inhabitants, and the miracle is that this windy plateau fifteen times the size of Great Britain has even been able to support the three or four million people who have lived there at any given time; for the odds against life, and particularly something so frail as human life, are high.

Not that it is desperately cold all the time. The midday sun in summer can be very hot indeed, though the air temperature seldom exceeds 68° F and a cloudy, rainy summer's day can be bleak. It is not unusual to find snow on important passes even in August. Summer nights are chilly, and winter by the standards of most of the world can only be described as nightmarish. Getting warm then is always a problem, for while the population is sparse, trees are in no great supply either (it is simply too high in most places) and there is thus virtually no fuel except for the dried dung of that ubiquitous beast of burden the yak—and even this must be very carefully conserved. Under the circumstances it is hardly surprising that the Tibetans have always looked upon water as something best used to make tea or beer with, and most certainly not something to immerse the body in. The daily hot bath so essential to the Japanese never quite caught on here. Rather, the

Tibetans traditionally regarded Mongolians, who were said to bathe three times in their lives (the day they were born, the day they married, and the day they died), as eccentrically fastidious.

Some farming is done in the more protected valleys, and a summer barley crop is grown by settled villagers along the rivers, but most Tibetans have always depended on their animals, as well as a bit of opportune trading, to keep them alive. Butter and meat are two important staples; yak's wool is braided into ropes and woven into tents and blankets. Life has always been lived right on the edge of survival, and vegetarianism is simply a luxury beyond the scope of the environment, no matter how devout as Buddhists the people may be.

It should not surprise us that such an environment and way of life have produced a hardy and independent people. Nor should it surprise us, when we consider the terrain, the hostile winds, and sudden storms, that these people should have a healthy respect for the spirits of the land. It was in fact the power of these spirits that directly shaped the Buddhism that eventually took hold here, and we shall have occasion to look at them, and at the remarkable man who overcame them, a little later.

Long before Buddhism made its appearance, there was an indigenous religion in Tibet called the Bon, which was based on the fear and control of demons and spirits. Its priests were shamans who went into a trance to communicate with the spirit world. Shamanism is, of course, by no means uncommon in the world today and has survived even in industrialized Japan, but in Tibet at this time it had reached the position of a state religion. Like most shamanistic faiths it developed rites for exorcising demons and curing sickness—its most drastic cure involving an actual journey to the world of the dead to try to bring back the spirits of those seriously ill. But the most important rites were reserved for the dead, to make sure they stayed where they belonged and did not return to torment the living.

This faith, as might be expected, had its dark side. Animal sacrifices were common, and every three years a great ceremony was held during which donkeys, horses, and even human beings were sacrificed. Though we have no way of knowing if the Tibetans were, as they themselves contend, cannibalistic before the establishment of Bud-

dhism, it seems likely that in a warlike, meat-eating society which practiced human sacrifice as well there may have been at least some ritual
cannibalism. There is even evidence to support this in some of the rites
observed by Tibetan Buddhists involving little human-like figures,
called *torma*, made of dough and stuffed with tiny models of internal
organs and a red fluid representing blood.

Tibet may not have been a particularly gentle or humane society in
the sixth century when it got its first good look at Buddhism, but its
southern neighbor, India, where Buddhism had originated and prospered for over a thousand years, was arguably the most civilized country on earth. Yet Buddhism first came to Tibet not from India—the
Indian influence would come later—but from Nepal and China, and by
this time had already undergone a series of mutations, for Buddhism is
one of the world's most adaptable religions. This attribute has always
been at once the faith's greatest strength and weakness: strength
because it has facilitated its dissemination and made it more attractive to people of varying backgrounds; weakness because the original
teaching has sometimes been watered down, obscured, or occasionally
even lost altogether. The sixth century was by coincidence to see the
initial spread of Buddhism to the two lands where in the end it probably diverged most sharply from the original teachings: Tibet and Japan.

* * *

The original doctrine, in fact, can scarcely have held much popular
appeal. It owed its inception to a young nobleman in a small north-
Indian state in the sixth century B.C. who took up an option open to Indians of all castes, classes, and backgrounds: that of taking to the road
with begging bowl and staff to seek the truth. This particular prince,
however, was unusual in several respects, as this journey to discover
the secrets of birth, death, and suffering was not often undertaken by
the young and wealthy; nor was the search often crowned, as in this
case, with earth-shaking success. Yet the stark way to salvation that was
revealed to the prince-turned-ascetic (who came to be known as the
Buddha, or Enlightened One) would in time be embraced by millions
and would provide Hinduism with its only serious challenge for the
next fifteen hundred years. (The Hindu Brahmans were, incidentally,

to emerge victorious in this strangely peaceful struggle by the rather devious expedient of incorporating Buddhism's more attractive elements into their own beliefs and then bringing the Buddha into their own pantheon as an incarnation of Vishnu.)

Though the Buddha's way did attract adherents, it was by no means an easy path to follow, promising through the extinction of desire and suffering, not everlasting bliss, but the extinction of the very self, which in any case was held to be illusory. It was, it seemed, a path for saints and not for common men. Buddhahood was an infinitely remote attainment, remaining, even for those most spiritually advanced, a destination many lives away. The original teaching has been called, rightly or wrongly, deeply pessimistic, and it is indeed doubtful that the Buddha meant to found a religion at all.

Over two hundred years later, a huge area of northern India, stretching from present-day Afghanistan to Bengal, found itself united under the rule of a king named Ashoka, often considered the greatest ruler in India's history. Yet he was not a warrior king. Molding the many former kingdoms into an empire had been largely the work of his grandfather, accomplished by such typical means as mass slaughter and enslavement. According to legend, however, Ashoka's exposure to the death and suffering caused by his own conquest of a neighboring state so shocked him that he himself took up the Dharma, or the Buddha's way, and actively promoted it with the dual purpose of soothing his conscience and providing a unifying spiritual force to help keep his vast empire together. It is often asserted that had it not been for Ashoka, who popularized the teachings for the first time by endowing temples, collecting the scriptures, instituting festivals, and generally making the doctrine more accessible, Buddhism would never have taken hold as a popular religion. The scriptures were written down in the Pali language, current in Ashoka's time, and taken by his son to Ceylon, where they have survived to the present day.

Meanwhile, two currents of thought had begun to develop and, by about the first century A.D., had formed separate branches of the faith. The first, which stuck closely to the original message, stressed individual effort toward enlightenment. This is what would later be called Theravada or Hinayana Buddhism. Hinayana means "the Lesser

"Vehicle," as opposed to the other system of belief, the Mahayana or "Greater Vehicle." The implication is not that Hinayana is inferior to Mahayana, but that it holds out less hope of enlightenment.

The difference lies principally in the revolutionary notion of the Bodhisattva, which softened the rather harsh outlook of the Theravada. A Bodhisattva is a being capable of Buddhahood who voluntarily puts this off in order to be reborn into the world of suffering and assist other suffering beings on their way to enlightenment. The idea of compassion is central here, and lest the Buddha himself be thought selfish for having grabbed his own enlightenment and run out on everyone, it was pointed out that in past lives he too had gone through countless Bodhisattvahoods. Thus the concept of the Bodhisattva opened the way to an influx of new spiritual elements—besides broadening the religion's popular appeal. And it is Mahayana Buddhism, as one might expect, that exhibits the most variety, having eventually spread to China, Tibet, Korea, Vietnam, and Japan, where it adopted the characteristics of each country.

Yet the complexity began in India itself, for though Ashoka's empire fragmented politically after his death, the great flowering of Indian culture begun in his reign continued. Buddhism and Brahmanism embarked on a long and in some ways almost brotherly rivalry that was characterized by debate and tolerance rather than by violence and conversion by the sword. This rivalry was to change dramatically both faiths. The original simplicity of Buddhism became overlaid with a large measure of doctrinal subtlety in order to be able to take issue with the infinitely more complex Brahmanist tenets. Thus the Mayahana has the prolonged conflict with the Brahmans to thank in part for its development, and during this period some of the farthest reaches of doctrine began to be explored as Buddhism gradually absorbed the older Tantric traditions, which had been practiced for centuries on the fringes of Hinduism.

These Tantric traditions had as their basis not only that enlightenment was possible but that it was possible in one lifetime (as opposed to working one's way up through a long cycle of deaths and rebirths), given the proper discipline. There is a heavy undercurrent of magic and mysticism in this branch of the Mahayana—which is in fact sometimes thought of as a third and separate stage in the development of Buddhism known as the Vajrayana: "the Diamond or Thunderbolt Vehicle." Though Kawaguchi belonged to the Mahayana tradition, he was to reject many of its doctrines—particularly Vajrayana doctrines—in the most violent manner. Yet the majority of the texts for which he was searching were written in Sanskrit during the time of the development of the Vajrayana.

It was partly as a reaction to the intellectual trappings and folk beliefs accumulated by the Mahayana that a reform movement founded by an Indian monk named Bodhidharma, who wandered into China in the fifth century, gained ground there and was later transported to Japan. Known as Chan in Chinese and Zen in Japanese, this movement sought to cut through all the layers of interpretation that had grown up over the centuries and return to fundamental principles. Bodhidharma's four propositions were quite specific.

A special transmission outside the scriptures;
No dependence upon words and letters;
Direct pointing to the soul of man;
Seeing into one's own nature.[1]

But though its founder was an Indian, Chan went on to become the most characteristically Chinese form of Buddhism, embracing in particular Taoist humor and ambiguity ("The Tao that can be expressed is not the true Tao"). It has even been called a Chinese revolt against Buddhism. Nor did the four propositions prevent Zen from developing its own distinctive scriptures and art, but these are austere, unvarnished, and any obscurity is an attempt to bypass rather than challenge the intellect, so that ultimately Zen came to represent the antithesis of Tantric Buddhism with its elaborate secret doctrines and equally complex artistic tradition. Tantric Buddhists tend to offer great respect to images and paintings, while a Zen master once made a point of burning a statue of the Buddha to keep warm. As much as Kawaguchi might at times disagree with certain aspects of Zen, particularly its aversion to book learning, the very fact that he came from a tradition so far removed from Tibet's Tantrism seemed to put him on a collision course with that country right from the beginning.

34

* * *

The Buddhism that was to shape and be shaped by the character of the Tibetan people first arrived there as a by-product of aggressive militarism and expansion under King Srontsan Gampo in the sixth century. A well-known figure in Tibetan history, Srontsan Gampo seems to have just missed wider historical recognition, for like Genghis Khan he took a population of scattered nomads under independent-minded chieftains and welded them into a formidable army that at once began striking out in all directions. But his human resources were limited; and though he made forays into China and India, and captured and held much of Turkestan and Nepal, the inadequacy of his forces, combined with the formidable barrier of the mountain passes that had to be crossed to get anywhere at all, kept the Tibetan Empire on a far smaller scale than the Mongol Empire of some centuries later.

One of the areas brought under the sway of Tibet at this time was the Kathmandu Valley, the heart of present-day Nepal and an important Buddhist center said to have been visited by Ashoka and his daughter, who left a number of reminders behind. To cement his supremacy, Srontsan Gampo requested, and was given, the hand of the Nepalese princess Bhrikuti in marriage. Bhrikuti, a devout Buddhist, refused to begin an alliance with this wild barbarian king without taking both Buddhist images and monks along with her; and the Nepalese court presumably encouraged her in this, hoping that her faith might teach their ferocious neighbors a little compassion. Srontsan Gampo, for his part, seemed open enough to new ideas to build a temple for her in his newly established capital of Lhasa. It also seems possible that he had heard the story of Ashoka and looked on the new faith as a means to reinforce his own regime by toppling the Bon priests from power.

For the Bon priests certainly needed putting in their place politically, however loyal the king may still have been to their spiritual guidance. Priests, in his experience, had a way of easing themselves into power and clinging to what they gained, and some of the doctrines of the Bon had become—to say the least—an inconvenience from his point of view. A good example was the custom of the time for kings to step aside (or, if they were obstinate, to be killed) as soon as they had a son who had reached the age of thirteen and could ride a horse. One need hardly ascribe altruistic motives to a monarch wishing to change that sort of custom, while, equally, one can understand the entrenched clergy's interest in maintaining the status quo, since they were able to exert their greatest influence over adolescent kings.

Having married his Nepalese princess, Srontsan Gampo now went after the greater prize of a bride from the Chinese imperial family. The recently inaugurated T'ang dynasty at first brushed him off. The Tibetan king replied with an invasion involving enough rape and pillage to convince the Dragon Throne that it was better to give up one princess and a little pride than have the whole country overrun by savages.[2] It would seem that the lessons the Nepali Buddhists were hoping to convey were a little slow in taking hold.

The Chinese princess, Wen Ch'ing, was also a Buddhist, and also brought her own images and entourage of monks with her. She, too, of course had to have her own temple, and in attempting to build it the king unwittingly stirred up the first direct conflict between the new faith and the ancient demons of the land: the temple kept falling down, until it was discovered that there was an underground lake at the very spot chosen for it. The obstinate princess liked this site, however, and in this instance at least the Buddhists prevailed, for they managed to transport the lake spirit all the way to western China, where it manifested itself as the huge inland sea called the Koko Nor—drowning many people and inundating villages in the process. Yet the temple, known as the Jokhang, or Tsuglahkhang, remains today at the center of both the city of Lhasa and the Tibetan Buddhist faith.

Thus, while Tibetan history credits Srontsan Gampo with being an incarnation of Chenrisig, the Bodhisattva of Compassion, what facts we have seem to suggest that his motives for admitting Buddhism into Tibet were almost entirely opportunistic. Yet the Tibetans feel a close personal connection with their historic figures, and their affection for this marriage and the consequent introduction of Buddhism is shown in the way they remember the two wives as incarnations of the Green and White Taras, female Bodhisattvas revered as embodying the active and motherly aspects of compassion.

What followed these alliances was the first great cultural age of

Tibet, though since at this point there was little indigenous culture to build on, it depended exclusively on influences imported from outside, and its scope remained relatively narrow and centralized. Artisans, builders, and painters came from Nepal, monks and scholars from India and China. Tibetan scholars for the first time traveled abroad—to both India and China, but especially to India, with its centuries-old university tradition. These universities had originally been simply places where monks waited out the monsoon season until they could again take to the road to preach, teach, and attend the sick; but they had developed into some of the greatest institutions of learning the world has ever seen. At Nalanda, the largest and most famous, which was at the time far older than Oxford and Cambridge are today, there were over ten thousand students, three huge libraries, and eight colleges, and the standard of learning was high. And later, when monasteries began to be established in Tibet, it was the great Indian universities on which they were modeled.

One of the Tibetan scholars took upon himself the task of adapting a current north-Indian alphabet to the oddities of the Tibetan language, making it possible for the first time to write things down in Tibetan. This led not only to translations being made of Sanskrit works but to the Bon beginning to develop a written canon of its own. And this, in turn, is the point at which one notices the older faith beginning to borrow from Buddhist teachings, which suggests that though its priests were still in control of most of the population outside the capital, they were already worried about the rising influence of Buddhism. Whether they hoped to head off and subvert the foreign faith by offering something so similar that no one would see the point of changing sides, or whether there were among the Bon priests those who were willing to accept the truth wherever they might find it, is not known. What is known is that this was the start of a period of exchange that lasted centuries. Tibetan Buddhism, like its Japanese counterpart, would be influenced by older beliefs and the character of their adherents, while the Bon took on so much from Buddhism that today a stranger can visit a Bon temple and see no superficial difference from a Buddhist one.

During the next hundred years or so the fortunes of the Dharma in Tibet fluctuated but never really made a great deal of headway—and probably none at all outside the capital. The problem was those demons. The average Tibetan farmer or nomad was not interested in metaphysical debate but in how to live most successfully with his un-friendly environment, and the Bon was obviously best qualified to help. Its priests had long since come to a satisfactory arrangement with the spirits of the land, so why risk raising the devil with something new? The difficulties experienced in building the Jokhang for Princess Wen Ch'ing should have provided a good enough example. If the demons were to lose their temper over some religious controversy in far-off Lhasa, who would suffer for it?—the common man, of course, who might suddenly find his village at the bottom of a lake, or his tents and yaks swallowed up by an earthquake. Buddhism had as yet done nothing to convince the general populace that it was capable of, or even interested in, dealing with the Underworld.

A glance at these demons is instructive, and we know a fair bit about them because when they were finally subdued they were neither slain nor banished but converted to become protectors of the Dharma, so that under Buddhism they survived as awesome yet benevolent spirits. There was, for example, Jamun the Eminent Enemy, whose specialty was crushing people between mountains. The White Dakini of the Glaciers and the Twelve Earth Goddesses dealt in thunderbolts and moving mountains, while Sham-po was a great white yak the size of a mountain whose nostrils produced blizzards and whirlwinds. Particu-larly treacherous was a huge white reptile which was as high and as long as a chain of hills but which might suddenly turn up anywhere. So here we have in mythical form what must have been the principal fears of everyday life, and stripped of their colorful names they make an eminently practical list: earthquakes, electric storms, landslides, bliz-zards, and losing one's way in the mountains.

Three generations after Srontsan Gampo there was fresh and very strong evidence of just how displeased these demons were with the in-troduction of a new religion that ignored them. First the empire crumbled as military fortunes began to wane. Turkestan with its rich cities along the Silk Road was lost, with a corresponding drop in revenue for the kingdom. In 703 Nepal rebelled and chased the Tibetans back across the Himalayas. The royal family was still attempting to use Buddhism to curtail the power of the Bon, and with Nepal now hostile it turned again to China. In spite of military setbacks, the Tibetan king managed to arrange a marriage with another Chinese princess, who also came complete with monks and images to lead a full-scale Buddhist revival. But her arrival was followed by a smallpox epidemic which not only ravaged the population but killed the new queen herself.

What more proof was needed? Following a popular outcry, both Indian and Chinese monks were expelled, and the Bon, now reinforced by a written canon, was in a stronger position than ever.

There was, however, to be one last and ultimately successful attempt to establish the Dharma under King Trison Detson in the mid-eighth century, and the protagonists were two of India's most remarkable men. They were both associated with Nalanda, and though they represented two opposing currents of thought in the Indian Buddhism of the day, they seem to have known, liked, and respected one another, as they worked together toward a common goal. The first, named Santarakshita, was a learned and gentle scholar. He came from a long tradition of careful study, debate, and tolerance. He represented reason, knowledge, and compassion. There was no magic about him, and in Tibet he never stood a chance.

His mission was a nightmare, as he was beset by almost all our above-mentioned demons. He eventually made his way to Lhasa, which by then had been the capital for about a hundred years. Just outside the city is a large rock outcropping, the Red Hill, on which the Potala palace of the Dalai Lamas now stands. In those days it was occupied by a much smaller palace, where Santarakshita stayed under the king's protection. But the king could only protect him from hostile forces in this world, and one day when he was preaching on the Red Hill in full view of everyone the White Dakini of the Glaciers and the Twelve Earth Goddesses summoned one of their sudden storms, and the palace itself was struck by lightning.

The Dharma's defeat could hardly have been more obvious and embarrassing, and a lesser man than Santarakshita might have given up altogether. But this setback convinced him, not that the Dharma should surrender, but that it should change tactics. If demons were the enemy, then what was needed was a demon slayer.

* * *

Here enters one of the most enigmatic and flamboyant characters in all Asian history, and it is unfortunate that Kawaguchi chose him as his particular nemesis without ever making any real attempt to understand him, for his somewhat hysterical opinions on the demon-slaying Padmasambhava—who is universally admired in Tibet as the patron saint of the country—cast doubt on his reliability as an observer, and were to earn him the distrust and dislike of many Tibetans.

Not that Padmasambhava is an easy character to understand, and there is certainly nothing saintly in the conventional sense about him. The aura of hero-worship that commonly surrounds such figures makes it hard to separate legend from reality. As the pioneering British Tibetologist Evans-Wentz said of him early in this century: "His less critical devotees generally regard the strange stories told of him . . . as being literally and historically true; the more learned interpret them symbolically. And the anthropologist observes that the historic Padmasambhava, like the historic King Arthur, is barely discernible amidst the glamour and legend of myth."

That he actually existed, and was evidently a man of exceptional charisma, seems beyond dispute, but even the Buddha, who is alleged to have predicted his coming, has added to the riddle of Padmasambhava's life. Some have thought that the prediction meant he would appear in twelve years' time, others in twelve hundred years (which is "historically" accurate), and Tibetan historians have tended to place him at virtually any propitious point in that span of time. The confusion is reinforced by the variety of names he accumulated in Tibet, where deities and illustrious figures of Indian origin usually retain their Sanskrit designations as well as acquiring Tibetan ones. Thus the character we already know as Padmasambhava (Sanskrit for "Lotus Born") is more commonly thought of as Guru Rimpoche (a combination of Sanskrit and Tibetan meaning "Precious Teacher"), Lobon Rimpoche (*lobon* is Tibetan for "teacher"), Padma Chugne (a Tibetan translation of "Padmasambhava"), or sometimes Urgyan Rimpoche, after his birthplace. He also has eight forms, each with its own title.

The eight forms of Padmasambhava. The two female figures
are his Indian and Tibetan consorts.

But much of the obscurity can perhaps be blamed on the Tantric tradition itself, of which Padmasambhava was the foremost practioner at the time, and whose esoteric practices are easily misinterpreted. Books that promise a ready understanding of it are even less realistic than those promising mastery of a foreign language in three weeks. The sexual element in it, for example, is often overemphasized by Western writers, though it is merely one facet of the rigorous mental and physical discipline required to attain enlightenment in a single lifetime—the goal of Tantrism. It is only mentioned here because Kawaguchi's judgment on the subject was so clouded, and few followers in fact engage in its more advanced techniques. Put briefly, the idea is to conquer pleasure, to prove oneself in full control of and thus superior to the forces that hold normal human beings in their grip. Though intercourse may at times be performed during meditation by couples who have practiced together and between whom a strong spiritual bond exists, this is something taken up only after years of preparation and training. Ejaculation by the male is taboo, but if it should occur he should have such total control over his muscles as to be able to retract his semen. Thus as part of the training one learns to suck in liquids through the penis, and advanced practitioners are said to be able to separate milk and water in this way.

Nonetheless, it is obvious that without discipline Tantrism can degenerate into something less than spiritual. This is a danger that Tibet's Tantric Buddhism has faced again and again, and the way in which it has been confronted and overcome is central to an understanding of later Tibetan history.

But this is to jump ahead, and it is Padmasambhava's story that now concerns us. His birth was miraculous, as indeed it had to be, for the whole point of his coming was that the Buddha, having been born of woman, was not "pure" enough to teach the Tantras. Only someone born of a lotus would be worthy of this task. Naturally enough, he came from an area where miracles were common: Uddayana, or Urgyan, which lay somewhere to the northwest of today's Kashmir, or possibly in Swat on the Pakistani side of the border. About a century before the Guru's birth, Hsuan-Ch'uang, one of those widely traveled Chinese monks who provided part of the inspiration for Kawaguchi's journey, noted that "the people are in disposition somewhat sly and crafty. They practice the art of using charms. The employment of magical sentences is with them an art and a study." The region was also known to Marco Polo, who said of its inhabitants:

> They have an astonishing acquaintance with the devilries of enchantment, inasmuch as they can make their idols speak. They can also by their sorceries bring on changes in the weather, and produce darkness and do a number of things so extraordinary that no one without seeing them would believe them. Indeed this country is the very source from which idolatry has spread abroad.

This last sentence would suggest that the Venetian knew something of Padmasambhava's reputation.

One day, legend has it, the king of Urgyan discovered a beautiful ten-year-old boy seated in a lotus in the Indus River, and being childless he took the boy home to be raised in the palace as his son and heir. The story of his early life has much in common with that of the Buddha, who was also raised as a prince and gave up the comforts of a privileged position to become a wandering ascetic. The manner in which Padmasambhava took his leave of worldly life, however, shows him to have been a very different sort of person from the gentle Prince Siddhartha. The young man who would become the Buddha slipped away at night. Padmasambhava, having found his own attempts at a quiet departure blocked, chose the unusual expedient of getting himself banished for committing public murder: of a man, a woman, and a child whom he killed from a distance, standing on the palace roof in front of the assembled citizenry (his victims apparently had harmed Buddhism in present or past lives).

The next few years were spent undergoing an unusual form of education in cemeteries and cremation grounds, where he is said to have met and learned to deal with every sort of demon or spirit imaginable. In between these lurid experiences he visited the great centers of learning, where he received a more orthodox education, and it is even believed that the sages of old manifested themselves to teach him all they had known.

Padmasambhava seems to have become a legend and folk hero in his own time, and the tale of how he lured the princess Mandrava away from the kingdom of Sohor to be his spiritual consort would be a grand romance were it not that the entire purpose of their alliance was to conquer rather than to indulge passion. Mandrava was a "peerless princess who could find no partner worthy of her beauty and her intellect"—until she met the Guru and recognized in him the companion that karma had chosen for her. Her father and her suitors were understandably displeased when she went off to meditate with this wild holy man in a cremation ground, and the couple were seized and condemned to be burned alive at the stake. But the fire turned to water and the stake to a lotus on which Padmasambhava and Mandrava could be seen seated in meditation.

The Guru's greatest fame in India came from his skill in the combined arts of magic and debate. It will be remembered that at this time the Buddhists and the Brahmans were engaged in a long series of debates whose outcome could be very serious, for entire communities of monks were put up as wagers—and forced to convert, if their side lost, to the winner's faith. Indeed these debates seem to have provided one of the great spectacles of the day, taking on the guise of major sporting events. But there had been some significant defeats for the Dharma; in fact, for some years now Buddhism had been slowly succumbing to a resurgent Hinduism, and the monks of Nalanda now called on Padmasambhava to answer the challenge. They were confident enough of their own debating ability, but Brahman magic had lately proved stronger, and it is probably an indication of the degeneracy of the times that so much store should have been set by it.

Here Padmasambhava apparently scored one of the last great victories for the Dharma in India. Almost simultaneously, however, poor Santarakshita was struggling against similar forces in heathen Tibet, and, appealing to the one man he felt was capable of dealing with them, he invited the Guru to tackle this more daunting task. His journey there—along the same route that Kawaguchi was to follow twelve hundred years later—took him via Parping, just outside the Kathmandu Valley (where the caves in which he meditated are still revered), and up the valley of the Kali Gandaki River. On the way he subdued demons wherever he met them.

44

In Lhasa there was a brief controversy with King Trison Detson over who should bow to whom, but the Guru simply caused a lightning bolt to set the king's clothes on fire and so received a hurried bow. He then set about his task. At Samye, southeast of Lhasa, where demons had been making the ground shake and preventing the construction of a temple, he ended the earthquakes and began constructing what was to become Tibet's first monastery—an impressively symbolic series of buildings representing nothing less than the traditional Buddhist view of the universe and incorporating in its great hall architectural styles from Tibet, India, and China. Santarakshita joined him there, and almost immediately the work of translating the Pali Theravada scriptures and the Sanskrit Mahayana scriptures into Tibetan began.

Then, leaving the scholars behind in the sanctuary he had created for them, Padmasambhava set off with Mandrava and a newly acquired Tibetan consort, Yeshe Tsogyal (who later wrote his biography). Traveling all over the country, he pacified the many demons he encountered, often turning them into *Dharmapala*, or "protectors of the Dharma," and saw to the founding of monastic communities.

* * *

In the end, how are we to evaluate Padmasambhava? Should we even try? Isn't it perhaps better simply to let his story stand? For while his detractors have called him a fornicator, drunkard, murderer, charlatan, and worse (and Kawaguchi was to become one of his greatest critics), the Guru himself would probably have denied none of it, but merely bemoaned the ignorance that allowed people to see so far and no farther. In fact he seems to have foreseen the difficulty that future generations might have with him, and perhaps he had Kawaguchi in mind when he answered a friend's criticism of the way he lived by saying: "Inasmuch as this fellow is ignorant . . . I should pardon him."

One thing, nevertheless, does seem certain: however we interpret his life, and whatever we may think of him, there was probably no one else in the eighth century with the charismatic presence to have converted Tibet, and had it not been for Padmasambhava there would have been no Buddhist Tibet for Kawaguchi to explore.

1. From *Zen Buddhism* by Christmas Humphreys.

2. In a curious reinterpretation of history, the Chinese today base their claim to Tibet on this humiliation and the resulting marriage.

Kathmandu

But whether he would ever get there now seemed questionable, for toward the end of 1898 Kawaguchi suddenly announced that he had come to his senses. He had, after all, achieved his goal of mastering the Tibetan language in a year and a half, so why should he risk his life among a people that did not want him there? Chandra Das had been right all along. The only sensible course of action was to go home, where he could live safely as a respected scholar. He could read Tibetan books just as well there, and in far more comfort than in Tibet itself. Accordingly, on January 5, 1899, he went to Calcutta, ostensibly to get a ship home.

In fact he had no intention of abandoning his project, but it was impossible for him to leave openly from Darjeeling for Tibet. There were three border crossings that were feasible from Darjeeling, but all were heavily guarded. It was only too well known that there was a Japanese monk in town studying the Tibetan language in the hope of going to Tibet, and the moment he headed north any number of acquaintances would have rushed to the border posts to turn him in for a likely reward.

Chandra Das thought Kawaguchi should simply present himself at one of these border posts and admit to the guards that he was a Japanese who wanted to study Buddhism in Tibet; "but I had reasons for thinking little of this suggestion," Kawaguchi remarks dryly, and the reader is left to wonder if perhaps his Bengali friend hoped thus to put a quick end to the escapade.

Since he could not set out directly from Darjeeling, Kawaguchi was left with the choice of trying to find his way to his destination through one of two other forbidden countries: Nepal or Bhutan. No Japanese was known to have visited either nation before, but Nepal had about it the further attraction that within its borders was Lumbini, the birthplace of the Buddha. There was also said to be a complete collection of the Mahayana texts in Sanskrit somewhere in the country.

Entering Nepal in 1899, however, was a very different proposition from what it is today. The least of one's problems was that the train stopped at Sagauli, a day's walk south of Birganj, that mosquito-ridden lowland town on the Nepalese frontier. The real problems were not physical but political. After having large chunks of their newly acquired empire wrested away from them by the British a century before, and coming uncomfortably close to being colonized themselves, the Nepalese were very wary of foreigners of all sorts. True, the British had managed to place a Resident in Kathmandu, but he often complained of being a virtual prisoner, and the Nepalese had expressed their displeasure at his presence by locating the Residency on land that was not only waterless but infested with demons. The Resident's task anyway was less diplomatic than concerned with recruiting the famous Ghorka fighting men, who the pragmatic British had decided were more useful as friendly mercenaries than as enemies. Otherwise it was only Indians, Tibetans, and the occasional Chinese with a good reason for being there who were allowed into Nepal. Since Tibetan and Chinese monks occasionally passed through the country on their way to and from the pilgrimage sites of India, it was Kawaguchi's hope that, disguised as one of these, he would have no difficulties. In the event he had none, but this was largely due to a phenomenal stroke of luck.

Calcutta was a good place to throw his pursuers off the scent, and here Kawaguchi seems to have changed his Japanese dress for the maroon robes of a Tibetan monk, the same costume that a Chinese monk living in Lhasa would have worn. He then went by train to Gaya, the nearest station to Bodh Gaya, site of the Buddha's enlightenment 2400 years before, which he found in a rather shocking state of neglect (its restoration was something he worked for later in life). Here he fulfilled an ambition by spending a night at the very scene of the enlightenment.

The feeling I then experienced was indescribable: all I can say is that I sat the night out in the most serene and peaceful ecstasy. I saw the tell-tale moon lodged, as it were, among the branches of the Bodhi-tree, shedding its pale light on the "Diamond Seat," and the scene was superbly picturesque, and also hallowing, when I thought of the days and nights the Buddha spent in holy meditation at that very spot.

Kawaguchi seems to have been under the impression that this was the tree beneath whose branches the Buddha had made his spiritual discovery. In fact it was a descendant. A cutting from the original tree had been taken to Ceylon in the time of Ashoka, and later, when the original died, a piece of the now flourishing Ceylonese tree was brought back and replanted on the site. Anyway, it was the feeling that was important. While at Bodh Gaya he was entrusted with a miniature silver pagoda supposed to contain a relic of the Buddha, and a volume of scriptures written on palm leaves, intended as presents for the Dalai Lama from a Ceylonese monk. He then took a train for Sagauli.

On arriving at Sagauli he made a characteristic decision. From here on his English would be useless, as would his Tibetan until he got to a Tibetan-speaking area, "so it became a necessary part of my Tibetan adventure to stop awhile at Sagauli and make myself a master of working Nepalese." Kawaguchi was nothing if not thorough. But it was at this point that luck, or karma, intervened.

Though he had spent only a brief time in Calcutta, he had used that time well, and somehow had made the acquaintance of a Nepali government official called Jibbahadur. It is unfortunate that he does not tell us just how or under what circumstances this meeting took place, for the outcome was a letter of introduction to a close friend of Jibbahadur's. We can only surmise that Kawaguchi was already in disguise, since it would seem that the letter referred to him as what he would now claim to be for several years: a Chinese monk who had long resided in Lhasa and was presently on his way home from a pilgrimage.

The man to whom Jibbahadur had written was no less a personage than the abbot of Boudhanath, a Buddhist holy spot particularly revered by Tibetans about four miles outside Kathmandu. His name was Buddha Vajra, and he was the second in a line known as the Chiniya Lamas. He and Jibbahadur had a blood-brother relationship of a kind peculiar to Nepal and referred to as *meet*. Kawaguchi explains it as follows:

> I may observe here that in Nepal ... the word friend conveys a much deeper meaning, probably, than in any other country. To be a friend there means practically the same thing as being a brother, and the natives have a curious custom of observing a special ceremony when any two of them tie the knot of friendship between them. The ceremony resembles very much that of a marriage, and its celebration is made an occasion for a great festival. . . . It is only after the observance of these formalities . . . that any two Nepalese may each call themselves the friend of the other.

In fact there are several words for "friend" in the Nepali language, but *meet* is by far the most significant of them. After the ceremony, special honorific language is used between two *meet*, whereas normal friends would address each other in familiar terms. Wives and children are expected to treat a husband or father's *meet* with the same respect they would show to his elder brother, and a favorite theme of Nepali folklore and children's stories is that of *meet* helping each other out of difficult situations. The relationship has been made much use of in Nepali history, particularly by Prithvi Narayan Shah, the first king of the present dynasty, who unified Nepal in the eighteenth century. Many of his allies were bound to him through *meet* relationships, and as these were regarded with rather more respect than an ordinary treaty would have been, a great deal of useless bloodshed was avoided.

The day after he arrived in Sagauli, Kawaguchi observed a party of three gentlemen with shaven heads and swathed, like himself, in the burgundy robes of the Tibetan priesthood getting off the train. This, he thought, would be a good time to try out his disguise. If he were able to travel in their company he would undoubtedly have an easier time of it at Birganj. So he went up and introduced himself as a Chinese, and faced the first of many similar grillings he was to undergo over the coming years.

"You speak Chinese, of course?" then asked the gentleman. My reply in the affirmative caused him at once to talk to me in quite fluent Chinese, which put me in no little consternation in secret. Compelled by necessity I ventured calmly: "You must be talking in the official Peking dialect, while I can talk only in the common Foshee tongue, and I do not understand you at all." He was not to let me off yet. Says he next: "You can write in Chinese, I suppose." Yes, I could, and I wrote. Some of my characters were intelligible enough to my guests, and some not, and after all it was agreed that it was best to confine ourselves to Tibetan.

China must be one of the few countries in the world where one can convincingly get away with claiming to be a native without speaking the language, and the two reasons why this is so are revealed in the quotation. The various dialects of Chinese are as mutually unintelligible as the various languages of Europe, but the written language is the same everywhere and is held in great respect. Thus, to a literate Chinese, a good command of the latter makes more of an impression than any deficiencies in speech. Even so, Kawaguchi can be counted lucky in his travels not to have run into anyone from "Foshee."

But why, here on the plains of northern India, was he suddenly confronted with a Chinese-speaking monk? The strange fact is that Kawaguchi had stumbled across the Chiniya Lama—the very man to whom he had a letter of introduction. As the lama explained soon afterward, his father, the first to bear this title, had "come from China and gone back there," but before returning he had married a Nepali woman and founded the line of "Chiniya Lamas" by fathering a son, to whom he taught his native language.[1]

By the time Kawaguchi had discovered all this in the course of conversation, he was thoroughly enjoying himself sitting in a little roadside resthouse (these shanties with bamboo poles and straw roofs were the only accommodation available for travelers rich or poor in Sagauli) and supporting his story by filling in the lama and his two companions on the latest Lhasa gossip, which he had picked up from Lama Shabdung in Darjeeling. It was then decided that they should travel together "afoot instead of on horseback, so that we might better enjoy one another's company, and perchance, also, the grand scenery on the way."

And suddenly everything is going very well indeed. The young monk has just tested his disguise and found it almost flawless, with the result that he is "no longer a stranger and a solitary pilgrim, but a guest, a companion, to a high personage of Nepal." Besides, there is no more glorious time of year than January on the north Indian plains: the crisp, cool nights and clear, sunny days are enough to lift the heart of even the most jaded traveler.

But most of all, even today when it is so commonly done, it is impossible to be immune to the thrill of entering Nepal, of climbing the foothills of the Mahabarat Range and glimpsing in the distance the highest mountains in the world. Imagine then what it must have meant to Kawaguchi to penetrate where no Japanese had ever before set foot. During his second night inside the border, at a place called Bichagori, he heard the sound of a tiger roaring nearby, and his enthusiasm burst forth in a way quite foreign to poor Das's "quaking heart." For he promptly composed the following poem:

> The night sleeps still and calm,
>   The moon shines bright,
> What ho!—so loud a roar
>   The stillness breaks,
> Vibrating—ah! It is a tiger fierce!
>   In ripples rough his roar terrific throws
> The surface even of the mountain stream.

(It is only fair to mention here that Kawaguchi's poems read much better in Japanese. They were put into English verse by an Indian friend, Professor Jamshedi N. Unwalla, M.A., from Kawaguchi's own free prose translations.)

A couple of days later, from the Chandragiri Pass above Thankot, Kawaguchi had his first sight of the Kathmandu Valley. After a motorable road was built in the 1950s this trail has ceased to be used, and it is a shame, for from it one could see the city of Kathmandu and the two huge stupas of Swayambunath and Boudhanath, all backed by the Himalayan panorama.

But before we allow him to enter this enchanted valley we should step back for a moment and take a look at an earlier, historical landscape.

* * *

In a northwestern corner of the Kathmandu Valley, not far from the present city, stands Swayambu Hill. Said once to have been an island, it is now the highest hill within the valley, and upon it sits its second largest stupa, a place so holy that it has attracted pilgrims from as far away as Mongolia. Behind this prominent site, and connected to it by a spur, is a lower hilltop and at its western end is a much smaller stupa. Few visitors come here, and even if they do they probably take no notice of it, for apart from one day during the winter when students pay a visit to pray for success during the school year, it is largely neglected. This stupa is the valley's main shrine to Manjusri, the Boddhisattva of Wisdom, and it is odd that he is not more honored here, since the valley is said to owe its very existence to him—and to his sword.

According to a legend borne out by geological evidence, the Kathmandu Valley was once a lake. On an island in this lake was a blue lotus containing the eternal flame of the Primordial Buddha—the one who came before all others and from whom all others are sprung;[2] and when Manjusri came to worship this flame, he decided to make it easier for mankind to do likewise by draining the lake. So his sword, normally used not for acts of violence but for cutting through knotty problems, was put to work cutting what are known as the Chobar Gorges in the south of the valley, and through which the valley is still drained.

No one knows precisely when people began to settle in what was now the largest reasonably flat expanse of land in the mountains, but it is generally agreed that the Newaris are the valley's original inhabitants, and it is to them that Nepal owes its glorious artistic tradition. The Chinese pilgrim Hsuan-Ch'uang, who has already described for us Padmasambhava's Urgyan, visited the valley in the year 637 (only a few years before Princess Bhrikuti departed for Tibet) and left behind this description:

Manjusri, the Bodhisattva of Supreme Wisdom.

The kingdom of Nepal . . . is in the middle of the snowy mountains. Its soil abounds in fruit and flowers and the climate is cold. The inhabitants are of a hard nature, and neither good faith nor justice appeals to them, but they are gifted with a very considerable skill in the arts. . . . The houses are of wood, painted and sculptured; the people are fond of bathing, of dramatic representations, of astrology, and bloody sacrifices. . . . Irrigation—practically and scientifically applied—makes the soil of great value. Buddhism and Brahmanism flourish in the principal temples, which are wealthy and well supported. Numerous monasteries shelter the

Buddhist priests. Commerce prospers and trade is well organized and directed.

What is striking here is how little, in every respect but one, the valley has changed over the last thirteen hundred years. The only difference, assuming that Hsuan-Ch'uang was not simply being ethnocentric, is in the character of the people: few visitors today would describe the Newaris in negative terms.

Until quite recently "the kingdom of Nepal" was synonymous with the Kathmandu Valley, and from about the thirteenth to the eighteenth centuries it was ruled by a family called the Mallas, a high-caste Hindu family which nonetheless encouraged the arts and religion of the largely Buddhist Newaris. For most of this period the valley was in fact divided into at least three rival kingdoms ruled by cousins from the three centers of Kathmandu, Patan, and Bhaktapur. They were often at war—a rather gentle form of warfare by modern standards in which few people were killed—but more important was the peaceful rivalry they carried on in art and architecture, and it is monuments from Malla times that so fascinate visitors today, as each kingdom tried to outdo the other in splendor. So much did this Malla splendor depend on the skills of the Newaris, and so active was the Mallas' patronage of them, that early Western historians often mistakenly referred to them as the "Newar kings." In practice the Newaris seem to have always lived in, but never ruled over, the Kathmandu Valley.

One curious Newari custom that continued to flourish and even gained new impetus under the Mallas was the worship of a young girl as Virgin Goddess, or Kumari, thought to be a living embodiment of the goddess Taleju, patroness of the royal family. One of her most interesting aspects is that, though she is chosen from the Buddhist Sakya caste of goldsmiths, she becomes the embodiment of a Hindu goddess, and thus symbolizes the unity—or at least the lack of enmity—between the two communities.

The Royal Kumari of Kathmandu was to play an important part in the demise of the Mallas and the birth of the present Shah dynasty. When Prithvi Narayan Shah, the first king of the dynasty that still rules and the man who unified Nepal from his small kingdom of Gorkha, finally made his way into Kathmandu after many years of trying, he did so right in the middle of the huge Indrajatra festival which takes place every autumn. An essential part of the festival is that the Royal Kumari should give the king a blessing by placing a red mark, or *tika*, on his forehead to ensure his successful rule in the coming year. And it was just at this point, with all his soldiers primed with drink for the pulling of Kumari's chariot, that King Jayaprakesh Malla heard of Prithvi Narayan's approach and fled in panic. Instead of carrying out a massacre, however, Prithvi Narayan simply stepped into the king's place and peacefully secured his legitimacy with a *tika* from Kumari, then ordered the festival to continue.

It was an auspicious start to a new dynasty, and indeed it was only through the strength born of unity that Nepal was able to fight off the Honourable East India Company and avoid being absorbed into British India. Though Nepal did lose a good deal of territory, most of it anyway was of recent acquisition, and when a treaty was finally signed with the British (at Sagauli in 1816) Nepal took the shape we know today. Yet the real power of the Shahs was to be brutally overthrown one night seventy years later when an ambitious army officer named Jung Bahadur Rana massacred every member of the royal family—and every other rival he could find—who showed any ability, leaving the country as devoid of able administrators as of pretenders to the throne. But Jung Bahadur was more than just a butcher, and he had the foresight to retain the monarchy, though for the next hundred years the king would be in thrall to the Rana prime ministers who effectively ruled the country.

This was roughly the political situation that Kawaguchi found in 1899. It appeared to him that the country had two kings, and he thoroughly confuses things by calling them the king *de facto* and the king *de jure*, while in practice the situation was not unlike one illustrated by Japanese history, where for two and a half centuries a powerful military clan prevailed over an emperor who remained purely a figurehead. Yet, while Rana Kathmandu, like Tokugawa Edo, was closed to the outside world, it reflected the kind of superficial Westernization that was to reach Japan only after it emerged from its seclusion.

For once Jung Bahadur had secured power he traveled to Europe, a custom that was continued by his successors. From there they brought back some of the most bizarre tastes imaginable, for they loved the trappings and glitter of the European aristocracy without in the least understanding or caring what lay behind them. Thus from the floor of the Kathmandu Valley arose—as one later traveler called them—"palaces like Metro-Goldwyn lavatories." Many of these neo-classical monstrosities are still around, and beside the graceful and harmonious brick, wood, and tile architecture of the Malla period they strike a jarring note. Most at least are outside the old city of Kathmandu and so do not clash too badly, but the old Hanuman Dhoka palace had to suffer the indignity of having the unsightly Ghadi Baitak added to it. One can only stand back in awe at the monumental bad taste that placed this building immediately opposite the charming Kumari Ghar (the Royal Kumari's home and temple) and adjoining a square containing some of Kathmandu's finest multi-roofed temples.

The Ranas and the royal family also sported elaborate European uniforms, but none of this Westernization went beyond the surface. They remained conservative high-caste Hindus and were certainly not prepared to import any progressive ideas along with the luxury—much less think up any of their own. Even colonial India was far ahead of Nepal in education and medicine. Somebody had to pay for all the glitter, and the country was milked for all it was worth (in the next chapter we shall see how the revenue from the salt trade in the distant Thak Khola Valley found its way into the coffers of the Ranas). The Newari arts were stifled and nearly died, and for the first time Buddhism was actively oppressed.

* * *

But Kawaguchi was to see little of all this, at least on this, his first of three visits to Nepal. He was very wary still, and as fascinating as Nepal might be, his goal remained Tibet and he was unwilling to risk any chance of exposure when he had only just begun. He seems to have spent almost all his time at Boudhanath—the valley's largest stupa, whose origins deserve a brief digression.

According to *The Legend of the Great Stupa*, it was built by a woman who raised chickens for a living, and who "copulated with four different men, all of them of low caste, and ... bore a son by each of them: the first son was born of a stablehand, the second of a swineherd, the third of a dogkeeper, and the fourth of a poultryman." Despite her lowly occupation and the presence of four illegitimate offspring, the woman prospered, deciding eventually to use her hard-won profits to erect a building to house "the Mind of all the Buddhas." Her project might never have got anywhere had she not sought permission from the king, who—impressed by her business acumen and piety—gave her leave to build a stupa on a plot of land no bigger than an ox's hide. The woman's plans, however, were on a more ambitious scale, and she cunningly cut the hide into narrow strips, encircled an acre or two, and set to work. Fearing that some of their own wealth would have to go toward outdoing her, others tried to put a stop to this, but the king would not go back on his word; and persistence was rewarded by the completion of Nepal's grandest Buddhist monument. More significant for Tibet, however, its moving spirits were reincarnated as important figures in the establishment of Buddhism there, and it is this that has made the site a focal point for northern pilgrims.

Even today Boudha is at its best in winter, and Kawaguchi's arrival coincided with the great winter migration. The high Tibetan plateau

Boudhanath (with the Chiniya Lama's house and temple on the far right).

58

and the higher regions of northern Nepal become so cold that those of the inhabitants who can do so escape to the more congenial lowland climate, where they are free to pursue two of their favorite activities: trading and making pilgrimages—in the case of the poorest, coupled with begging. Kawaguchi's description of the scene could as well have been written in the 1980s as in the 1890s:

> Every year between the middle of September and the middle of the following February ... crowds of visitors from Tibet, Mongolia, China, and Nepal come to this place to pay their respects to the great temple. The reason why they choose the most apparently unfavorable season for their travel thither is because they are liable to catch malarial fever if they come through the Himalayan passes during the summer months. By far the greatest number of the visitors are Tibetans, of whom, however, only a few are nobles and grandees, the majority being impecunious pilgrims and beggars, who eke out their existence by a sort of nomadic life, passing their winter in the neighborhood of the tower and going back to Tibet in the summer.

Although, after the closing of the Nepal-Tibet border by the Chinese in 1959, this annual pilgrimage was confined for many years to Nepali Bhotias (Buddhists who are culturally Tibetan) and Tibetan refugees, it is now back again in full force as farmers, nomads, and city dwellers

flock there on the way to India every winter for the teachings of the Dalai Lama at Bodh Gaya. For a few weeks they crowd the circuit around the stupa, chanting, spinning prayer wheels, drinking *chang,* bargaining over whole carcasses of dried meat, and generally turning this corner of the Kathmandu Valley into a miniature Tibet. The smells of rancid yak butter, incense, dung fire smoke, putrefying mutton—the smells of Tibet itself—pervade all, and everywhere one sees the smiles of a people who are at home wherever there is room to stretch out and make a cup of salted, buttered tea.

It was to the poorest of these pilgrims that Kawaguchi now turned for information, and we can imagine him sitting in the warm winter sunshine at the base of the stupa in earnest conversation with these disreputable and dirty, but deeply religious, characters. Now that his disguise was working, he intended to find out all he could about how to reach his goal.

And here the account given in *Three Years in Tibet* differs substantially from the story told by Kawaguchi's nephew Akira in his biography of his uncle. For Kawaguchi himself states emphatically that the abbot of Boudhanath remained ignorant of his real identity. Yet Akira's account (and he of course had access to his uncle's private journals) states just as emphatically that he took his host into his confidence and received active assistance from him. This agrees with the tradition in the Chiniya Lama's family that the abbot "helped a Japanese monk go secretly to Tibet." It thus seems likely that even ten years later, in 1909 when the translation was published—after this secret visit and two later open ones—Kawaguchi felt it necessary to protect his friend by implying that he had been an unwitting dupe. For the latter was not only abbot of the stupa and headman of the village surrounding it, but an official interpreter to the government of Nepal, and should have been duty-bound to report a disguised intruder.

What Kawaguchi needed was a route that was so little used as to allow him to enter Tibet unnoticed. This was more difficult than it sounds, even in the days before electronic surveillance and rapid communications. Given the nature of the border—the Himalayan range— those places where a crossing is physically possible are limited to cols, the approaches to which are easily guarded. For the past several hundred years the Tibetans had been keeping watch on these very spots, using what Kawaguchi calls "challenge gates," and in the twenty years since Chandra Das's escapade their vigilance had increased. Even Tibetans had to be in possession of an official pass—and prepared to bribe the guards as well—in order to go back and forth. In other words, he was looking for a way into Tibet so secret that even his host might not know about it.

What was striking, however, was that even with all these difficulties there were obviously lots of poor Tibetan pilgrims at Boudha who had neither pass nor money. "Encouraged by these considerations, I took to befriending the Tibetan mendicants, of whom there was then a large number hanging about ... and my liberality soon made me very popular among them." But at first all he could find out was that they generally managed by "imploring a passage with prayer and supplication" at some checkpoint inside the country after sneaking across the frontier. This he deemed too dangerous.

"My persistent efforts finally brought me, however, their reward. I ascertained that by taking a somewhat roundabout way I might reach Lhasa without encountering the perils of those challenge gates." His "somewhat roundabout way" was a four-hundred-mile detour on foot to Lake Manasarovar and Mt. Kailash via the kingdom of Lo, the small semi-independent border province that is still forbidden to outsiders. No, Kawaguchi was not one to let minor problems stand in his way.

It was just the presence of Kailash and Manasarovar that gave him the pretext he needed, for had these two holy spots not been there—and they are two of the holiest sites in the world for Hindus and Buddhists alike—he would have had no excuse whatsoever, respectable Chinese monk that he was supposed to be, for taking such a circuitous and bandit-infested route to Lhasa. As it was, keeping up certain pretenses between them, he was now able to go to his host and say:

> "Having come thus far, I should always regret a rare opportunity lost, were I to make a stork's journey from here to Lhasa, and thence to China. The Chinese Text speaks of Mt. Kailāsa (Tib. *Kang Rinpo Che*) rising on the shore of Lake Mānasarovara (Tib. *Maphamyumtsho*). I want to visit the sacred mountain on my way

home. So I should be very much obliged to you if you would kindly get men to carry my luggage for me."

The answer he got was reminiscent of Chandra Das. The route was pathless (as indeed it was) and full of marauding robbers (as it also was), and going that way would be inviting death. All the better. Kawaguchi loved replying to such attempts at discouraging him with comments like "I should consider myself well repaid if I met death while on a pilgrimage to a holy place."

If this conversation took place at all, it was certainly for public consumption, and presumably in the presence of others. Still, Kawaguchi's last comment must have been a relief to the lama: friends though they were, there was potentially serious trouble to be had from this Japanese monk, and if he did in fact die along the way his death would be both convenient and meritorious. And so it was that in early March 1899 Kawaguchi set out from Boudha in some state, mounted on a white horse ("a gift from my fatherly friend") and accompanied by three servants—two men and an old woman—as well as a man to oversee them. This would be the most elaborate entourage of his entire trip, and he was soon to learn the disadvantages of traveling in this way.

He followed the old route to Pokhara, one taken today only by local villagers and by foreigners wanting to do an obscure trek. In those days, he tells us, the caste system was so rigidly enforced that non-Hindus were not even allowed inside a Hindu house, and so he slept out in the forest or under the eaves of people's homes. From Trisuli Bazaar he looked longingly north toward the Tibetan border at Kyirong, only five days' journey away, a popular and heavily guarded crossing.

Like most modern visitors he was enchanted by Pokhara. "Pokhara looked like a town of villas at home, the site being chosen for the beauty of its natural scenery. . . . In all my travels in the Himalayas I saw no scenery so enchanting. . . ." He also found it the cheapest place in Nepal, and he stayed there for six days in order to have a tent made (it cost him twenty-five rupees). He then headed northwest on what is now a familiar hiking course. This would take him along the old trade route up the Kali Gandaki River and through one of the country's most romantic valleys, where in the end he was to stay for more than a year.

The view from Pokhara.

1. As of this writing, the post is empty. The Fourth Chiniya Lama, Punya Vajra (the third son of Buddha Vajra), passed away in 1982. The next in line died before being installed. At present the eldest male of the family, Ganesh Vajra, performs the ceremonial functions of the Chiniya Lama while awaiting confirmation from the royal palace.

2. Known to Tibet's older sects as Samantabhadra, he is usually represented as a blue, naked figure, sometimes in union with a pure white consort. The reformed Gelupa sect calls him Dorje Chang, and its images of him, also blue, are elaborately clothed and bejeweled. As Dainichi, he is important to Japan's Esoteric Shingon sect.

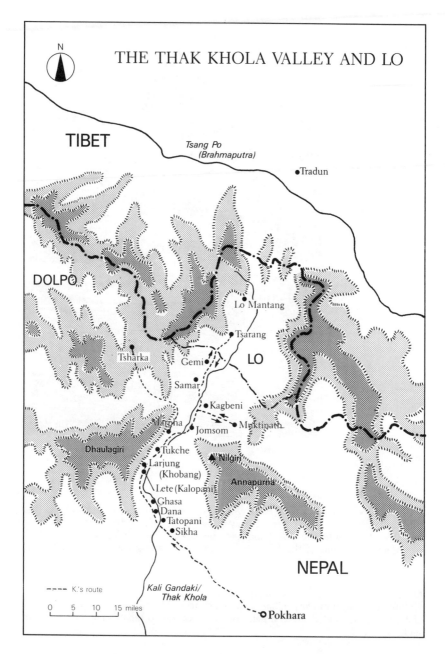

THE THAK KHOLA VALLEY AND LO

N

TIBET

Tsang Po
(Brahmaputra)

•Tradun

DOLPO

Lo Mantang

•Tsarang

Tsharka•

Gemi•

LO

Samar•

Kagbeni•

Marpha•

Jomsom•

•Muktinath

Dhaulagiri

•Tukche

Larjung•
(Khobang)

Nilgiri

Lete (Kalopani)•

Annapurna

Ghasa•
Dana•

•Tatopani
•Sikha

NEPAL

- - - - K.'s route

Kali Gandaki/
Thak Khola

0   5   10   15 miles

oPokhara

The Lands Between

The Kali Gandaki has never ranked particularly high on the list of the world's great rivers. It is not a cradle of civilization like the Nile or the Indus, and though—for Hindu pilgrims—the fossils of ancient sea creatures found in its bed do give it some claim to holiness, as a holy river it is just not in the same class as India's Ganga or even the Bagmati in the Kathmandu Valley. The Kali Gandaki seems to have escaped entirely the attentions of those men from the West who set out to find the sources of rivers from the Nile to the Brahmaputra, and it was not until 1963 that a European even claimed to have seen its source.

To confuse matters, the name changes as one proceeds north. Along most of its length, in the Hindu-inhabited lower foothills of Nepal, the river is called the Kali Gandaki, possibly due to the legend that the first man who attempted to cross it was swept away and drowned—a sacrifice to the bloodthirsty goddess Kali, who to this day has young male animals sacrificed to her on a massive scale throughout Nepal. And the waters of the river, carrying as they do a black silt, are indeed dark and forbidding. But while "Kali Gandaki" for the outsider serves well enough to identify the river along its entire extent, the people who live on its banks have their own terms for it. In the lands farther north which represent a typical Nepalese confusion of Hinduism and Buddhism, it becomes the Thak Khola and lends its name to the entire region as well as to the Thakali people who dwell on the rare patches of level ground between the river and the high, barren cliffs. Farther north still, in an area Tibetan in language as well as religion, the Thak Khola becomes the Tsang Po, a name borrowed from Tibet's largest river.

At this point, at an altitude of over ten thousand feet, the river is little more than a trickle during most of the year; it is easily forded on horseback and with no danger, if some inconvenience, even on foot. Even lower down, in the Thak Khola region, its course merely follows meandering and shifting streams in a bed of gray sand, gravel, and rock which is sometimes half a mile wide. Only in the lower hills south of Kalopani ("Black Water") where the gorge narrows and its walls become greener does the river, now again the Kali Gandaki, turn into a rushing torrent.

Since Thak Khola is tucked behind the massive shapes of Dhaulagiri and Annapurna, both over twenty-six thousand feet high, the summer monsoon which governs life in most of the rest of the country never reaches here, and the river only swells in the spring when the Himalayan snows melt. Yet even in full spate, its swift, frigid, shoulder-deep waters are forded by local farmers, holding hands to form a human chain. Indeed they have little choice. The bed is too wide here for a bridge, and the current at this time of year too fast-flowing for a boat. Yet so little flat and irrigable land exists here that both sides of the river must be farmed wherever possible.

To the outsider this would be just another minor river flowing through the Himalayas eventually to join the Ganga, except that it forms a gorge and a valley which for centuries have served as one of the most convenient routes between India and Tibet—between the hot, fetid plains of the Hindus and Muslims to the south, and those arid highlands of Buddhist Central Asia to the north. The river is older than the mountains. The valley is there by virtue of the river having prevented it from rising with the rest of the great Himalayan mass. So we have a gorge that was not cut through a range, but a range that grew up around a gorge. While this is true of all Himalayan river valleys, this one by some geographical accident remained that much more easily negotiable than most to allow men and pack animals to travel its entire length with a minimum of difficulty.

At one point the gorge has the distinction of being the deepest in the world, since its top is formed by the peaks of Dhaulagiri to the west and Annapurna to the east; yet this is a mere technicality to the traveler, who can never see both summits at the same time. Indeed one is so close to Dhaulagiri, and looks up its slopes at such an odd angle, that it appears lower and less imposing than the twenty-three-thousand-foot Nilgiri which dominates the east bank and, north of Kalopani, hides Annapurna from view. There is only a day or two of walking here when one feels enclosed at all, and even then there is none of the deep jungly gloom that one might expect from the world's deepest gorge, the gloomiest aspect of the scene being in fact the sinister, dark gray waters of the river itself.

By the time the Kali Gandaki becomes the Thak Khola, the valley has spread out into a wide and eerie moonscape. The Thakali villages maintain a precarious hold on life between the riverbed and the dry ocher cliffs, just high enough to avoid flooding, their meager fields of buckwheat, maize, and beans irrigated by the diverted watercourse. The squat stone houses are flat-roofed, and each house is built into its neighbor. The walls are thick and the courtyards deep, for we are now in a world where each day a howling wind springs up from the south with almost clockwork regularity. Reaching speeds of nearly forty miles per hour, this wind continues from about 10:30 every morning until well after dark, when it finally relents.

One might well expect this harsh terrain to be inhabited by a dull and backward people driven to an unfriendly corner of the world centuries ago by some war or invasion, finally taking refuge in a place where no one would care to look for them. Yet quite the contrary is true. Because of the valley's function as a kind of rough-and-ready highway between India and Tibet, a certain sophistication has grown up here. The Thakalis have from time immemorial been known as innkeepers, and their kitchens gleaming with polished brassware are perhaps the finest (and cleanest) in Nepal. As innkeepers on an international trade route they have more or less had to learn several languages other than their own, and have kept well abreast of the news of the outside world. Since their own land could provide so little in the way of subsistence, many other Thakalis became traders, another occupation in which one needs to keep informed and to communicate in a variety of languages. When in the nineteenth century certain members of the Serchan clan acquired a monopoly on the mule trains that traditionally exchanged Tibetan salt for grain from the south, they and their relatives became very wealthy indeed.

It has taken a certain ingenuity to prosper, and travelers have for centuries been surprised to find in this Himalayan hinterland a group of sophisticated people numbering a few thousand at most, often trilingual (in their own Thakali tongue, Nepali, and Tibetan), living between two worlds—a part of neither yet at home with both. If one excludes the village that became the winter headquarters of the Serchans—Dana, in the deepest part of the valley at about four thousand feet, with an ideal southern exposure and groves of sweet oranges—the Thak Khola heartland from Ghasa to Jomsom can be walked in a day and a half (or less by someone in a hurry); yet even within this small area the communities differ. At its southern end there is as much Hindu as Buddhist influence; in fact all the four traditional Thakali clans there, including the Serchans, tried to claim Hindu *thakuri* caste status by changing their names after the unification of Nepal when it became more advantageous to be Hindu than Buddhist.[1] But, though the names stuck, the Hindus never accepted this gesture, and most of the Thakalis themselves remained Buddhists. And as one proceeds north, their towns look more and more Tibetan, exhibiting all the trappings of a devout Himalayan Buddhist society: prayer wheels, prayer flags, mani walls, and temples.

Yet in the heart of Thakali country, it appears that business has always mattered more than religion. This is certainly true of Tukche, the regional capital. From a distance it has the wild look of a Gobi desert outpost—square, unadorned stone buildings, each standing like a miniature fortress with prayer flags flapping in the wind. Once inside the town, however, it is obvious that there is money here. The streets are laid out in straight lines. The houses are large and roomy, rivaled in rural Nepal only by those of the Sherpas. Their large courtyards were built for unloading and stabling caravans, and though there are several *gompas*, or Buddhist monasteries, and a very long mani wall, there is the definite feeling that religion has always taken second place to commerce. It is not until Marpha, several hours' march north, that one has a sense of dominating and pervasive Buddhism. These two towns, Tukche and Marpha, so similar and so different, were important stops for Kawaguchi, and it is worth looking at them, and their inhabitants, in a little more detail.

*　*　*

Just where the present inhabitants of the Thak Khola district originally came from has been the subject of much speculation and misunderstanding. They have been called both Indo-Aryan and Bhotia, and virtually all we know about them is contained in the four books of their myths and legends, the *Rhab*, which are read out at a great festival every twelve years in Tukche. These legends pick them up at Jumla, a once powerful kingdom to the west. No mention is made of why or when these people left Jumla, but they seem to have first passed through Thak Khola, then continued south as far as a village called Sikha, searching for Kathmandu before deciding that they liked neither the climate nor the bothersome nettles of the lowlands and turning back. At the spectacular falls of Rukse Chara they held a meeting and elected to head farther north, and at a spot not far from Larjung, which marks the real transition between the greener south and the more arid north (a point from which the traveler can actually see each succeeding ridge become drier and drier), they went through a ceremony of weighing earth, stone, and water. Determining that these elements

Tukche from the northwest.

were heavier here than anywhere else they had been, they decided to settle in this part of the valley. There seem to have been few other settlements at the time, and the only identifiable one is Thini, across the river from present-day Jomsom, which was then ruled by a raja into whose family the immigrants married.

At some stage, however, the valley appears to have been inhabited by troglodytes, for at certain places there are virtual cave cities. Though many of these caves were later used by hermits, they are far too numerous even for the most religious of communities. Whatever happened to these cave dwellers is as mysterious as everything else about them. Were they still in the valley when the wanderers from Jumla arrived, to be conquered or chased away by the travel-weary clans anxious for a place to settle? Yet there is no mention in the *Rhab* of glorious victories, though it is stated that the first villages were located on easily defended ridges, high above the sites of the present ones. It is of course possible that the wild cavemen had proved too much of a hindrance to the already flourishing salt-for-grain trade and had been driven away earlier by Tibetans and Bhotias from the north.

For, no matter what else may have occurred, trade in life's essentials continued. Salt from the salt flats of northern Tibet continued to find its way here to be bartered for grain from the south, and while the Tibetans and Bhotias may have been no mean businessmen, it was the Thakalis who found themselves sitting astride the most advantageous spot on the whole route. At an altitude of around 7800 feet, the cold winds here are just—but only just—bearable for the traders coming up from the foothills and the plains. Nor is it too hot for the Tibetans and Bhotias from colder climes. But that is not all. The best time for travel from the north—summer—is the monsoon season in the south, making movement all but impossible there; while winter, when the streams are low and the paths dry and secure in the south, finds the north bitterly cold and the passes blocked with snow. The Thakalis soon realized there was a natural need for middlemen right where they lived, people who could buy and store grain during the winter until the salt traders could journey southward in the summer. Tukche, with its spacious homes, its hostelries, and its storehouses, today stands on the spot where sometime in the past a market sprang up of its own accord, and the name is a combination of the words meaning "grain" and "flat place."

As mysterious in its own way as the fate of the cave dwellers is the question of why the people of Tukche and Marpha consider themselves so different. Did they come at different times in separate migrations, or did they all arrive together only to have some unrecorded event over the course of the years drive a wedge between them? The two towns are only a couple of hours' walk from one another, speak the same language, are both organized into four clans which changed their names at the same time, and adhere to the same religion. But the people of Tukche and the south (the region called Thaksatsae, comprising the villages of Larjung, Khobang, Sokung, Nakhung, and Ghasa) are quite adamant about it: those from Marpha and points north are "not Thakalis." They are instead Panchgaonlis, or the people of the "five villages" (Marpha, Thini, Syang, Chimang, and Chairo). The Panchgaonlis themselves, however, will tell you that anyone who lives along the Thak Khola is a Thakali. The only real difference seems to be economic. The inhabitants of Thaksatsae gradually grew wealthier, the Panchgaonlis got into debt to them, and while it became common practice for Panchgaonlis to work as servants for their southern cousins, the reverse was unthinkable.

Though the Thakalis of Thaksatsae have always been shrewd traders, it was not until 1862 that they got a real break—one that might well account for the disparity between Thaksatsae and Panchgaon; for it was then that they decided they were paying too much in taxes to the central government of the Ranas in Kathmandu, and managed to trade their annual land revenue of twelve thousand rupees for a salt customs contract. This—like the biblical role of tax collector—went to the highest bidder, and anything beyond the amount promised each year to the government (corresponding to his bid) was his to keep. To ensure that he received his due, the customs officer was given the title of *subbha* (district chief or magistrate) with an officially sanctioned monopoly on the salt trade. Thus, by law, anyone bringing Tibetan salt from the north had to sell it to the subbha, who could then resell it for any profit he could get. So lucrative was this arrangement that at one point the annual bid reached a hundred and fifty thousand rupees—most of which probably went toward the Ranas' ostentatious palaces in Kathmandu. The system was ideal not only for enriching a few families—and the most impressive houses in Tukche and Dana date from this period—but for producing generations of determined smugglers. It was at the home of the richest of the subbha families in Tukche that Kawaguchi was to stay as a guest in 1899.

* * *

The lands we now call Nepal and Tibet have for centuries been accustomed to rather fluid borders, and the idea of a definite line separating one from the other is a relatively recent innovation. The countries themselves have often been internally divided into an assortment of small, hostile principalities and kingdoms. Over the centuries Tibet united, expanded, contracted, and disintegrated time and time again as strong leaders rose and fell. Much the same thing happened in Nepal, which as we have seen only emerged in its present form in the late eighteenth century, and warlords in each land sometimes ruled large chunks of the other. Occupants of border areas were often not entirely sure whom they were supposed to belong to and thus remained a law unto themselves, at best owing a rough sort of allegiance to whichever of their neighbors was dominant, while they looked after their own well-being by taxing or robbing the travelers and traders who passed their way with anything worth taking.

Even the Thak Khola towns are walled in a halfhearted way, but north of Jomsom the villages assume the appearance of fortresses, reminding us that unsettled times are not far in the past. The last political remnant of the days of the feuding states is the kingdom of Lo, which by one of those quirks of history—though it juts right into Tibetan territory—wound up inside Nepal rather than Tibet. This was Kawaguchi's immediate goal, because the passes leading from Lo to Tibet were loosely guarded and easily traversed.

With Lo and its people, the Lobas, we are on slightly firmer ground than with the Thakalis, for here there is a written history that goes back to the fourteenth century when the first of its kings seems to have taken the throne. The most common interpretation of the dynasty's establishment is that Lo was for some time an outlying province of

72

the old western Tibetan kingdom of Purang and was administered by a provincial governor; eventually the position of governor became hereditary and evolved into the dynasty that still occupies the now largely ceremonial throne of Lo. Even so, the allegiance to Tibet was not shaken until about 1785 when Lo was forced to pay tribute to Jumla. Only a few years later Jumla itself was swallowed up by the Ghorkas under Prithvi Narayan Shah, and Lo was quite content with what it had heard of Ghorka military prowess not to wish to put it to the test and prudently switched its tribute from Jumla to Nepal without going through the bother of having to be defeated first. The symbolic submission made, Lo was allowed to go about its own business—which was a very profitable one until the Thakali subbhas monopolized the salt trade.

Between Lo, whose monarchy has made it a tight-knit little place, and Thak Khola, whose culture has made it equally tight-knit, lies a barren, steep, and narrow part of the valley known as Baragaon, or the "twelve villages" (though typically there are eighteen of them). The villages here have the same look about them as those of Tibet or Lo: tough, solid, square places reflecting the nature and appearance of the Bhotia inhabitants. But here there has never been any kind of central authority, and each fortified hamlet was once ruled by its own chieftain who squabbled and skirmished with his neighbors for the right to control and tax the caravans, or in lower Baragaon to supervise the pilgrim route. After the Thakalis began to dominate the salt trade in the nineteenth century, many of these villages found themselves in debt to their astute southern neighbors and were thus brought under some sort of control. All the same, it is likely that the merchant or traveler in these parts would have felt less secure than in well-governed Lo and Thak Khola; and though Kawaguchi lingers among the Lobas in Tukche, Marpha, and Tsarang, he has little to say about the eerie land of Baragaon.

Hand in hand with commerce, religion has provided a link with the outside world, at least as far up the valley as Muktinath in southern Baragaon, for soon after Jomsom a trail branches off east and climbs to this shrine, which is particularly holy to Hindus but also revered by Buddhists. The site is sacred to Vishnu, a shrine having existed here ap-

Looking north up the Thak Khola Valley through Baragaon toward Lo, from the climb to Muktinath.

parently for five thousand years. Nearby is a miraculous spring of burning water where the elements of earth, fire, air, and water all come together, and this is the spot holy to Buddhists. Suitably remote at thirteen thousand feet to make the pilgrimage difficult enough to be worthwhile, yet just accessible enough to have attracted large numbers of pilgrims for centuries, it is Muktinath, in a sense, that has kept one eye of the valley fixed spiritually on the south while its soul seems more properly to belong to Tibet and the north.

At certain times of the year, particularly during the great Dasain festival in the autumn, long lines of grim and silent Hindus from the plains of India can be seen making their way to and from the shrine. They are obviously not at home here, and they walk with a quick and purposeful step, their upper bodies and heads wrapped tightly as if to ward off not only the winds but the very strangeness of the place to which their faith has drawn them, nursing inside them a sense of virtue that is the only warmth they can feel. If they have been observant or lucky (or perhaps supplied by a Tibetan trader), they will also carry with them a saligram or two, yet another of the river's distinctions, and its chief claim to holiness. These smooth, round black rocks hold within them the fossils of ammonites, monovalve sea creatures up to a hundred million years old, for until about forty million years ago all of the Himalayas, as well as the plains of Tibet, lay on the ocean floor. Throughout India and Nepal these fossils are considered holy to Vishnu, in fact tiny incarnations of him. Vishnu, after all, is the preserver in the Hindu trinity (the others being Brahma the creator and Shiva the destroyer), and in these forms of life embedded in stone we have a startling example of preservation from an age scarcely imaginable, even for those brought up in the scientific tradition. Here in the valley even Buddhist temples might display a few saligrams, but the farther away one goes the more precious they become, and any pilgrim who has made the effort to come all this way would want to offer one to the Vishnu shrine or temple in his village in some other far-flung part of the continent.

No Hindu pilgrims, however, go beyond Muktinath, and even here they are aliens who have no influence beyond the confines of the shrine. Except for the wealthiest, they pass through carrying their own provisions and having little social or economic impact on the Bhotia villages. For Muktinath shares the valley with the Baragaon hamlets of Jarkot, Purang, and Dzong—places so Tibetan in appearance and religion that it is difficult to believe that Hindus have been trudging by them for centuries.

*   *   *

This is the valley that was to be home to Kawaguchi for the next fifteen months. A frontier and a meeting place of cultures. A highway where on any given day one was likely to meet burly Tibetan traders; colorful mule trains with their alternately surly and friendly drivers; pilgrims from India, Nepal, or Tibet; shorn monks spinning the prayer wheels set up on long mani walls; thin, long-haired, wild-eyed Hindu holy men; the rich and proud Thakalis in their mansions; the equally proud but notably poorer Lobas and Baragaonlis. It was a land of pilgrims, peddlers, priests, and saints; stern yet strangely welcoming. And it was fitting that here in this passage between one world and another Kawaguchi should put himself through his final training and begin his adventure.

1. Each clan, following *thakuri* practice, adopted a "chan" or "chand" ending to its name: thus Bhurki became Batachan, Salki became Tulachan, Chyoki became Gauchan, and Thimchin Serchan.

The Road North

Kawaguchi was now on his way. Yet soon after leaving Pokhara he did something so disturbingly typical that one is again left wondering how he ever got anywhere at all:

> On one occasion I was proceeding on horseback on a narrow path that ran along a very high precipice, when, deeply engrossed in thought as I was about the near future, I found myself all of a sudden thrown down to the ground, before I had time to free myself from a branch of a tree, which had caught me by the neck and caused the disaster, assisted by the horse's onward movement. Very fortunately my horse came to a halt just then, and as I never let go my hold on the bridle, I narrowly escaped from rolling a thousand fathoms down a craggy precipice, to reach the bottom a mangled carcass!

Since he does not enlighten us about the exact route he took from Pokhara, we can only guess where this disastrous bit of daydreaming took place; but as he was climbing toward a pass at the time it seems likely to have been around Ghorapani, or near the col that leads to Tatopani a day farther on. At any rate, he had hurt his hip so badly that he was unable to walk and had to be carried by his servants to the top of the pass, where he camped for several days and recovered with the aid of "diligent application of some camphor tincture." In no time he was back on his feet and writing his poetry, but he was lucky to have suffered this mishap in a populated lowland area where his servants did not yet feel at home and where there were probably frequent mule trains: for these men whom the Chiniya Lama had procured for him were scoundrels, and were only looking for their first opportunity to do away with him.

It was the old woman, who had become fond of him, who tipped him off. "She made a revelation to me, and it was not of a very reassuring kind; for according to her I was doomed to be killed." But nothing apparently would happen before they reached the lonely plains of western Tibet, so at least he had time to plan.

Just as Kawaguchi never addresses the question of whether his friend Chandra Das had hoped to bring his trip to an early end by sending him on a route that would lead to sure detection, he never even raises the possibility that the Chiniya Lama may have hoped to help him fulfill his expressed wish for martyrdom by deliberately sending him out with a gang of cutthroats. The mere fact that these servants were from Kham in eastern Tibet should have aroused his suspicions, since the Khampas have always been known as a lawless people. Haughty and headstrong, they affect a conscious disdain for those of the world not fortunate enough to have been born in Kham, and though it would of course be wrong to label them all as outlaws, the region has bred more than its share of brigands and rebels. Being so close to China, the Khampas have certainly never had much affection for the Chinese, and so, posing as a Chinese monk, Kawaguchi was fair game. All this must have been on his mind as they slowly worked their way up the Thak Khola Valley to Tukche.

With his usual restraint Kawaguchi mentions nothing of the thrill he must have felt on approaching Tukche, but one assumes he enjoyed the knowledge that at last he was getting somewhere. Earlier the same day or the day before he would have passed through Ghasa, and though the terrain there is still wooded and green the northern part of the village, inhabited by Panchgaonli immigrants, is the first place in Thak Khola to possess a fortified gate and prayer wheels. Next he would have traversed the alpine plain of Kalopani, still lush but dominated by the spectacular buttresses of Dhaulagiri and dotted with square, squat, whitewashed houses which have a distinctly northern look about them. At the twin villages of Larjung and Khobang—just north of the spot where the ancestors of the Thakalis weighed earth, water, and stone—

he would have noticed a clear transition. Vegetation is now sparser, the riverbed widens, and the wind begins to pick up. Roofs are now flat instead of slanted. It is only a couple of hours from here to Tukche, and he undoubtedly entered the town, as most travelers do, in the late afternoon when the wind is at its fiercest and the solid stone walls of the houses look at once forbidding and reassuring.

Kawaguchi had, again from the Chiniya Lama, an introduction to the subbha of the day, Harkaman Serchan. Harkaman had been involved in a long rivalry with his brother and an outsider for control of the customs contract during its most lucrative period. His house was the largest in a town known for its fine mansions, and the centerpiece in a street that boasted an impressive mani wall at least a hundred yards long, with a substantial chapel-like gateway at its northern end. These mani walls would become more and more familiar to the traveler as he moved onward. They are free-standing walls, or sometimes simply irregular piles of flat stones, but each stone is carved either with the figure of a Buddhist deity or a mantra, the most popular of these being the compassionate Bodhisattva Chenrisig's *Om mani padme hum*. The house itself (which still stands and is in the process of being restored) is three stories high and arranged around a courtyard. Over the entrance is a large chapel where Kawaguchi stayed.

It must have been an exciting establishment in those days, as every caravan had to stop there. The northern trading season was just beginning and the monsoon had not yet cut off the southern trails, so it would have been one of the busiest times of the year, with Gurung mule drivers from the foothills and perhaps an occasional Newari trader up from Pokhara; while from the north would come the Baragaonlis, Lobas, and Tibetans, all unwashed and wrapped in bulky *chubas* with their feet encased in colorful felt boots, their long, greasy hair and turquoise earrings poking out below jauntily cocked fur hats. There would have been a constant exchange of news and greetings, interspersed with haggling—much of it in Tibetan and therefore intelligible to Kawaguchi, so the explorer had no end of worthwhile eavesdropping to do as he sat above the courtyard pretending to read or meditate. And it was from the talk of the traders that he learned the very unwelcome news that the passes he had hoped to use from Lo into Tibet had been recently reinforced to the point where it would now be foolish for him to stick to his plans.

More encouraging, however, was that he managed to get rid of his two murderous servants here, and the way in which he did so is instructive, for while Kawaguchi—as we know—could be at his most unpleasantly holier-than-thou when moralizing about alcohol and tobacco, it seems that he was never above using alcohol for furthering his own purposes. One night the servants got drunk (with perhaps a little encouragement from the abstemious monk) and began to quarrel. "In brief, each accused the other of the somewhat cheerless intention of making short work of me when the opportunity should arrive." Since neither was anxious to share the booty, each then came to Kawaguchi self-righteously demanding the other's dismissal. "I could not have had a better opportunity, and I there and then dismissed them both, after having paid them off rather liberally." This put a neat end to the threat they posed.

In Tukche he was also to acquire another in that colorful series of companions who were to so enliven his trip. We have already had our first look at Chandra Das and the Chiniya Lama. Now we can add to the list a Mongolian called Serab Gyaltsen, a learned lama who had put in twenty years of hard study at Sera, near Lhasa, but had "yielded to feminine temptation" and been "compelled to pass his life in obscure seclusion." He now resided in Tsarang, the second largest town in Lo, several days' march to the north. Serab Gyaltsen was also a guest at Harkaman Serchan's—it being common for priests to be housed and fed for the spiritual benefit their presence would bring to the household— and though the two would undoubtedly have met and hit it off in any case, it was only due to the bad news Kawaguchi had just heard about the passes that in the end the two were to spend more than a year in each other's company.

For poor Kawaguchi was in a quandary. The road he had planned to take had become too dangerous, and it was imperative that he find another if his journey was to maintain its momentum. At the same time, presumably, he shrank from the idea of staying too long among the sophisticated and widely traveled Thakalis, who were bound to find him out sooner or later. (In fact, according to his nephew Akira, he was so worried about this that he moved out of Harkaman Serchan's house and stayed for a while in a gompa at the northern end of the town.) Serab Gyaltsen, however, offered him just the solution he needed. Anyone who had spent twenty years in one of Lhasa's leading universities studying for his *geshe* degree (which can only be inadequately translated as "Doctor of Divinity") must have missed cultured conversation in a backwater like Tsarang, and Kawaguchi for his part found the Mongolian to be a man "possessed of profound knowledge" from whom much undoubtedly could be learned. So it was decided that they should go together to Serab Gyaltsen's home in Tsarang, where they

One of Tukche's Buddhist temples.

would exchange lessons on Chinese and Tibetan Buddhism, and share the task of treating the sick.

In due course the two set off one morning by way of Muktinath. Now it is another of the odd facets of Kawaguchi's personality that, though his mission as a whole put him firmly out of step with his times, there was a side to him that was overbearingly contemporary, and proud of it. In one of the most spectacular settings in the Himalayas, a sheltered glen hemmed in on three sides by snow peaks and high passes, sprinkled with Buddhist villages, and surprisingly fertile amidst desert surroundings due to the springs that pilgrims venerate, Kawaguchi chose to ignore the scenery, which usually moved him deeply, in order to deliver a silly attack on the folk beliefs held sacred for centuries in both India and Tibet. As if he had never heard of similar beliefs which abound in Japan, he describes the holy springs of Muktinath in the tones of a self-conscious colonial delivering judgment on heathen rites:

> A spot of particular fame there was called Sala Mebar, Chula Mebar, Dola Mebar, which means burning in earth, burning in water, burning in rock. On seeing this spot I found this mystery to be nothing more than the fancy of the ignorant natives, who saw a burning jet of natural gas escaping from a crevice in a slab of rock, that formed a lid, so to say, over and close to the surface of a beautiful crystal-like fountain, which was about one by two feet in size, so that its prolonged flame looked, at first glance, as if it were crawling over the water.

Though Kawaguchi can often be quite good company, there are times when one wants to take the complacent little monk by the scruff of the neck and give him a good shaking (Serab Gyaltsen was later to do just this). After all, this was the same man who subsequently based all his own major decisions on revelations received while meditating, who heard mystic voices in the debating garden of Sera, and believed that his miraculous escapes from death were a reward for having saved the lives of fish and chickens. It seems, then, a little harsh of him not to allow "ignorant natives" (how that phrase grates on the ear today) their own innocent beliefs.

It took them another three days of travel through Baragaon to reach

Tsarang. On their first night out of Muktinath, they returned to the river and camped on its banks, not far from Kagbeni. Foreshadowing the many problems he was to have in Tibet with river crossings, Kawaguchi here almost lost his horse when crossing a tributary, and only saved its life by hurling rocks into the current to help it gain a foothold.

Two more nights were spent in the local villages of Samar and Gemi. Curiously, he makes no mention of Gemi's famous mani wall, which is over three hundred yards long and is said to be made of the intestines of a demon slain hereabouts by Padmasambhava while on his way to Tibet. The walls of the surrounding cliffs are stained red, supposedly with the demon's blood and lungs. Here was a good opportunity to heap more scorn on both superstition and Padmasambhava, but mercifully he let the opportunity pass.

* * *

Tsarang, their destination, must have looked inviting after three days among bare hillsides: at 11,700 feet the narrow valley opens into a fertile oasis dominated by snowcapped mountains to the east and west. It is a small place of only fifty or sixty houses, but there are two large monasteries and a palace where the raja of Lo sometimes stays. Colors look different at this altitude, and though the principal tones here are all pastels—blue, red, green, and white, set against the brownish gray of the barren hills—they have a peculiar intensity. The village's two stupa gates, meant to guard against demons rather than human invaders, are of an aged white with the red and blue stripes characteristic of the Sakyapa sect (of which more later), as are the smaller stupas and chortens of the mani walls; the only colors that are not somewhat muted are the bright blue of the sky and the brilliant green of the barley fields in summer. These are the colors of Tibet, and in many ways Tsarang was so like Tibet that Kawaguchi was to include the year he spent there in the title of the English version of his book when in fact he only stayed two years in Tibet itself.

He seems to have thoroughly enjoyed his spell in Tsarang—indeed he came uncomfortably close to never getting away. In this tiny village, which most visitors would find dull and confining after a few days, he was to follow a typically rigorous schedule that left him with few idle moments.

> My work with Serab Gyaltsen consisted in this: a lecture on Buddhism for three solid hours in the morning, which required much preparation, and exercises in Tibetan rhetoric and penmanship for another three hours in the afternoon, which was, however, of a very easy nature, and gave me occasion to engage in discussions with my teacher. . . . So time passed on, I spending seven to nine hours a day in preparation, besides the six hours of the regular daily lessons. Out of the twenty-four hours, thirteen to fifteen were thus taken up for purposes of study every day.

Here we have Kawaguchi at his best, just as we saw him at his worst in Muktinath. Of course his life depended on his knowledge of things Tibetan and on his linguistic ability, but, beyond that, he had brought with him from Japan an intellectual curiosity that enabled him to drive himself well beyond the limits of ordinary human beings where study was concerned, and to derive real pleasure from it.

But he could also drive himself beyond normal physical limits when he had to, and having some idea of what awaited him if he actually reached Tibet, he devoted one day a week to physical training:

> Sundays I invariably spent in mountaineering of a somewhat unusual character. I had an idea that I should never be able to compass the arduous journey before me, toiling on in a rare atmosphere through trackless wilderness at great heights while burdened with heavy luggage on my back, unless I had a thorough training beforehand for the purpose. Guided by these thoughts, I made a point of carrying on my back a heavy load of stones when making my Sunday climb, and of making the ascents with all possible speed. I was in excellent health then, and I felt that the mountaineering made it still better, especially with regard to my lungs.

He was able to engage in this strange activity without exciting suspicion simply by turning it into a ritual, for this is a part of the world where one can get away with virtually anything by making it seem pious, and when the villagers mistook his physical training for a religious exercise he was not inclined to disillusion them.

Kawaguchi's year in Tsarang was in many ways the best time of his entire trip. Though there was the excitement of being well into his journey, near his goal, and in disguise, he was in nothing like the sort of danger he would be exposed to in Tibet itself. Here he could relax. In this village environment where everyone knew everyone else he became a celebrity, and he seems to have reveled in the isolated beauty of the place. But it was also in Tsarang that Kawaguchi first began to voice objections to the Tibetan way of life. The Tsarangese, he tells us, were "creatures of animal instincts." When there was no agricultural work to be done, as was inevitable during much of the year in such a harsh climate, they thought of "nothing but eating, drinking, and sleeping, their minds being otherwise filled with thoughts pertaining to sensual love. . . . Their ruling passion is that of carnal love, and that applies to all ages from the very young to the very old."

This is another case where Kawaguchi's moralizing made him a very poor anthropologist indeed. Later and more objective observers have told us of the triple life led by the Lobas: spring was the agricultural season, when everyone worked at plowing and sowing; summer was largely spent in tents near the high grazing grounds for the benefit of their animals; and winter—when it was far too cold for any of these activities—was the trading season, when much of the population would head south.

But Kawaguchi found it difficult to be objective simply because he was involved (Chandra Das would later describe him as "a truthful narrator, but . . . not a scientific discoverer"). Serab Gyaltsen had arranged for him to stay with the headman of Tsarang, who had two pretty daughters aged eighteen and twenty-three; and both girls used to interrupt his studies with tea, sweets, and gossip, leaving one to wonder how much of his precious study time was actually spent defending his virtue. After all, with the womanizing Mongolian as an example, the ladies of Tsarang would probably have had no precedent for a monk who took the vow of celibacy seriously.

Simple licentiousness, however, was by no means all that he found to object to. A daily bath is nearly as important to the Japanese as eating: to someone like Kawaguchi who looked upon meals as a time-consuming necessity rather than a pleasure, it was probably even more important. Imagine, then, his discomfort in a place where people who washed even their faces were considered uncouth:

> The days I spent in Tsarang were, in a sense, the days of my tutelage in the art of living amidst filth and filthy habits. In point of uncleanliness, Tibetans stand very high among the inhabitants of the earth, but I think the natives of Tsarang go still higher in this respect. . . . To say that they think nothing of making a cup of tea for you with the same fingers with which they have just blown their nose, is to give only a very mild instance of their filthiness; and I have no courage to dwell here on their many other doings, which are altogether beyond imagination for those who have not seen them done, and are too loathsome, even unto sickening, to recall to mind. As it was, my life among these slovenly people did one good thing for me, in that it thoroughly prepared me for what I had to endure in Tibet.

This is a theme to which he returns again and again, for it seems to have disturbed him deeply. Later he dwells at some length on how a Tibetan "does not even wash or wipe himself after the calls of nature, but behaves like the lower animals in this respect," and how in order to keep up his disguise he was compelled to do likewise in a land where everything is done openly. He also informs us that it is necessary at a betrothal to show how black with grime a girl is in order to make a good impression, and his chapter on Lhasa he calls "A Metropolis of Filth." And yet, though other explorers and travelers have echoed his sentiments, one does feel that Kawaguchi carries it a bit too far to be convincing, that he is writing too much with his audience in mind. In *Three Years in Tibet* he seems very conscious of being a Japanese who considers himself the equal of his European readers, though wary of their attitudes of racial superiority. He is thus anxious to appear a gentleman in his standards and not to give the impression of anything primitive or backward about Japan or the Japanese. To his readers at home (and his material was first published as a series of newspaper articles in Japan) he wanted to make it quite clear that his eccentricities went only so far: that while he may have had to make use of such "filthy habits" to gain his ends, he was certainly never attracted by them. Still less could women living in such circumstances prove any temptation to his precious chastity.

But it was largely thanks to Serab Gyaltsen that his squeamishness was not allowed to spoil an interesting year. In fact one longs to have met this jovial Mongolian face to face. Kawaguchi tells us that he had a quick temper, in common with other Mongolians, but that he was also quick to be reconciled, which set the pattern for their religious discussions. He was a "profound and widely read scholar who could have risen in life but for his carnal weakness" (and again one is struck by the sort of people Kawaguchi chose to befriend).

Something about the atmosphere of Tsarang and the influence of his companion seems to have led Kawaguchi himself to indulge in some uncharacteristically violent fits of temper, and he had frequent disputes with Serab Gyaltsen over our old friend Padmasambhava. One must remember that Padmasambhava is revered in Tibet as a second Buddha, particularly by the older sects, a fact of which Kawaguchi was aware but which he could never really accept or fully appreciate. "His teaching is a sort of parody on Buddhism proper," we find him saying, "and an attempt to sanctify the sexual relations of humankind, explaining and interpreting all the important passages and tenets in the sacred Text from a sensual standpoint." Another typical comment describes his life as "simply his teachings translated into actual practice, for he lived with eight women whom he called his wives, drank intoxicants to his heart's content, and fed freely on animal food"—an oversimplification that would have appealed hugely to the free and easy villagers of Tsarang, who were far less interested in the finer points of doctrine than in having a good time; and if they could do so with the blessing of their religion, so much the better.

On at least one occasion Kawaguchi and Serab Gyaltsen came to blows in the course of a religious debate. "Thereupon, flying into a terrible rage, he caught hold of my clothes near the throat with one hand, and, with the other picking up a bar belonging to a table that stood between us, was about to visit me with a blow." It is refreshing here to see the usually taciturn monk coming out of his shell and wrestling around the headman's chapel with his Mongolian tutor (whom he engagingly refers to as "my Serab"), teacups and ceremonial implements clattering to the floor.

Apparently the villagers thought so too, as he tells us they took a great deal of interest in these quarrels, and it is easy to picture the scene: on a day in the slack season, or perhaps after the day's work, the grubby but dignified Tsarangese gather under the chapel window, waiting for events to transpire. The men are wrapped in long woolen chubas; the women have on gaily striped aprons, in front and behind. Both men and women wear turquoise earrings, though in addition the women have elaborate necklaces of turquoise and pink coral, and sometimes head ornaments of the same stones. Perhaps someone has contributed a pot of chang, or a fire has been made and some salty buttered tea is being brewed to add to the cheer. It is a time for gossip and sexual innuendo but by no means one of idleness, for all hands are employed at something. Some people are mending boots or farm tools; others are spinning wool with hand spindles. Those with nothing else to do twirl hand-held prayer wheels and chant mantras even as they converse. Suddenly voices raised in anger are heard from within the chapel, there is the sound of scuffling, and two shaven heads appear at the window. One monk holds the other by the throat while brandishing a cudgel—and the villagers loudly express their appreciation at the sight. But soon the angry voices are replaced by laughter, and the two are friends again as they go about cleaning up the mess inside.

These quarrels apparently were sometimes misunderstood by the villagers, for another activity shared by the two monks was that of treating the sick, and there was thought by some to be professional jealousy between them. It may be remembered that Kawaguchi's maternal grandfather had been a doctor. His medical books had come into the family, and the inquisitive young bucket maker had undoubtedly had a look at them; later, during those years of erratic study and wandering in Japan, he had also taught himself the rudiments of both traditional Japanese and Western medicine. Before Kawaguchi's arrival Serab Gyaltsen had been the sole doctor of Tsarang ("Every Mongolian poses for a physician in Tibet," according to Chandra Das), and while this must have given him some interesting opportunities for intimate conversation with the women of the village, he seems to have been willing enough to share his practice (one imagines Kawaguchi wound up with all the men and old hags). But while Serab Gyaltsen naturally enough charged a nominal fee for his services, Kawaguchi practiced for nothing.

Well, not exactly for nothing. Instead of payment he exacted promises of abstention from alcohol and chewing tobacco (reminiscent of all those earlier "farewell presents"). This probably had a lot to do with the success of his cures, as many complaints were no doubt the result of simple overindulgence coupled with an inadequate diet. And though the majority might have preferred to pay for these services, rumor had it that the quarrels between the two monks were because the "Chinese lama" had ruined the Mongolian's lucrative little side business.

Yet such could hardly have been the case, for when a plot developed that had as its object trapping Kawaguchi in Tsarang forever, it was Serab Gyaltsen who was at its center. The worthy Serab, however, seems to have seriously misjudged his friend, because the plot was to ease him into marriage with the younger of his host's pretty daughters, and a more counterproductive plan can hardly be imagined. In several schools of Tibetan Buddhism there is no objection to monks marrying (with the exception of the *gelongs*, or those who have taken full vows)—indeed the head of the Sakya sect, which is popular in Thak Khola and Lo, is duty-bound to marry and produce an heir. It was therefore probably considered priggish of the "Chinese lama" to hang on to his celibacy—just as it was thought eccentric of him to run up and down mountains with a load of stones on his back or to wash his face occasionally. The conspirators, however, had no way of judging the horror they had awakened in his heart, and it is not long after discovering this scheme that we find him making somewhat hasty plans for escaping southward.

It was, of course, as much from himself as from anything else that he was escaping. After all, he had been quite content in Tsarang, and while never really forgetting what he had originally come to do (he was quite as busy collecting information on clandestine routes as he had been at Boudha), he certainly appears to have been in no hurry to leave before then. This is partly explained by the climate, for if he was to travel by secret high passes it would have to be during those few brief months of summer when they would be clear of snow and the traveler would "be secure as a rule from being frozen to death." Yet had he not uncovered the plot when he did, would he have overcome his pleasant inertia of that year? And had he stayed another year, would he have ever got away? A good deal, surely, lay behind the offhand comment with which he dismissed the prospect of a local bride, where he says "fortunately my faith proved stronger than temptations, and enabled me to remain true to the teachings of the Blessed One." The same, too, can be said of his memorable line congratulating himself on emerging unscathed from the jaws of marriage: "Had I yielded then, Tsarang would have to-day one more dirt-covered and grease-shining priest among its apathetic inhabitants, and that would be all."

In any case, Kawaguchi had by this time decided on a route so perilous that even the hardy Tsarangese thought no one in his right mind would bother to take it, and he had arrived at this decision in a characteristic way. At Boudha the previous year he had come up with the route through Lo by talking to beggars; now he took up with smugglers. Yet in this part of the world smuggling has always been an honorable enough occupation, and almost everyone in Tsarang (including the monks) probably engaged in it now and again.

> The Tibetan government had begun to levy customs duties even on personal valuables. It was a most outrageous act; supposing one wanted to do trade with the inhabitants of the north-west plain of Tibet, and to take thither a stock of coral ornaments, or some useful knick-knacks imported from Europe, how could one avoid being unjustly set upon and robbed of the best part of one's would-be profit, on first setting foot upon Tibetan soil? Ah! there must be ways and bye-ways by which to accomplish this, and be absolutely safe from guards and sentinels!

And so again the prude and moralizer is brushed aside by the adventurer (who is never very far from the surface), and once more we have Kawaguchi sitting with his informants in the afternoon sun or by a warm fire, perhaps plying them with drink. ("Having once got the villagers into the right humor . . . it was not necessarily a very hazardous job to keep tapping them for information.")

*   *   *

In the end, three things converged to induce Kawaguchi to leave
Tsarang when he did. First was the practical consideration that once he
had chosen his route—through Dolpo—he had only the three months
of summer to attempt his crossing. Second, and probably most important, was the scheme to get him married. And third was a chance acquaintance he had struck up with one Adam Naring, the *mukiya*, or
headman, of the chief Panchgaonli village of Marpha.

Marpha was the jumping-off place for Dolpo—a barren district
tucked behind Dhaulagiri, and said to be—at an average altitude of sixteen thousand feet—the highest inhabited spot in the world. An open invitation from Adam Naring gave Kawaguchi just the excuse he needed
to backtrack there without arousing suspicion. Like most of the inhabitants of Thak Khola, Adam Naring spent much of his time on the
road. He owned a yak ranch in Tibet just north of Lo and passed that
way occasionally, while at other times he would head south to Pokhara
or as far afield as Kathmandu or India. It was on one of his trips
through Lo that he met Kawaguchi and invited him to stay at his house
sometime to read, for the benefit of his family, the scriptures he had
brought back with him from Tibet. While Kawaguchi had no very high
opinion of this sort of thing ("I may remark that these people generally
keep a good store of the texts, not because they make use of them
themselves, but more as a matter of form, the form showing a deep
reverence for their religion"), he was no more averse to using their
simpleminded piety for his own purposes than he was to getting people
drunk and pumping them for information.

Kawaguchi left Tsarang on March 10, 1899, and his send-off was
typical of the warmhearted hospitality of the people of the high Himalayas:

> Nearly a year's stay in Tsarang had made me acquainted practical-
> ly with its entire population, and, on my departure, all these peo-
> ple favored me with farewell presents of buckwheat flour, bread,
> maru, butter, fried peaches [presumably a misprint: dried peaches
> are still a staple for travelers here]—all in various quantities—while
> some gave me kata [ceremonial white scarves] and silver coins. . . .

The broad-mindedness of these merry villagers is evinced by the fact that he received this impressive send-off in spite of running away from an impending marriage, and in spite of the "results" he achieved there:

> My stay in Tsarang was not entirely devoid of results; for while there I succeeded in persuading about fifteen persons to give up the use of intoxicants, and some thirty others to abandon the habit of chewing tobacco. These were all persons who had at one time or another received medical treatment from me, and whom I persuaded to give pledges of abstinence as the price they were to pay for my medicine.

If the farewell was tearful on the part of the villagers, there was also a certain sense of insecurity on the monk's side. Though relieved to have escaped the traps they had set for him, Kawaguchi was now leaving a place that in the midst of uncertainty had represented, however tenuously, home and security. As every traveler to remote places knows, such temporary homes can exert a far stronger emotional pull than one's real home, and in fact it was not long after his departure that things began to go seriously wrong.

He was, however, pleased with a bit of judicious trading he had done before leaving: he had managed to tempt a monk from the largest monastery there into buying his white horse in exchange for a set of the scriptures, "mostly in manuscript and penned by a Sakya Pandit," which it took two horses to carry. He tells us it was worth six hundred rupees (about $200), showing that Tibetan commercial instincts had begun to rub off on him, and we can only speculate as to who got the better deal. Probably both parties thought they had.

So it was to the pleasant little town of Marpha that he retreated, with its winding alleys, its orchards, its neat, whitewashed houses, its swift watercourse running down the main street, and a gompa perched under the cliffs. On arrival, he found that his friend was absent in India, but he was installed anyway in the chapel of the headman's fine house on the main street, marked by its huge wooden pillars and overlooking a peach orchard. Though it can get very cold and windy in Marpha, which is nearly nine thousand feet up, it must have seemed

Marpha street scene. The balconied house on the left
is where Kawaguchi stayed.

positively tropical after Tsarang, and here Kawaguchi happily read the
sacred texts for two weeks until this peaceful interlude collapsed.

The cause was his reckless habit of corresponding with friends back
in Japan and even with the notorious Chandra Das, since obviously this
activity increased immeasurably the chances of his being exposed. Apparently while in Tsarang he had entrusted a packet of letters to a
"trader of Tukche" who was on his way to Calcutta and who on his
return brought a reply from Das. Das's letter was anything but encouraging. He continued his unabating efforts to convince the obstinate young Japanese not to go to Tibet and even enclosed a recent
issue of the Mahabodhi Society's *Journal* containing an article about
the unsuccessful attempt by another Japanese to enter Tibet from the
Chinese side (this could have been Nomi Kan, who later died in a second attempt; or Teramoto Enga, another monk who eventually succeeded in meeting the Dalai Lama during his exile in Mongolia; or
possibly even Narita Yasuteru, the spy who visited Lhasa for a short
time while Kawaguchi was there).

But of more immediate importance were the rumors being spread around Marpha by the messenger from Tukche, and again one can only wonder whether Das himself had a hand in persuading the messenger to circulate them. They were simple enough, but to the Marphalis frightening. First there was the undeniable news that the monk staying in Adam Naring's chapel was corresponding with an official employed by the British in India—an official who earned six hundred rupees a month, no less. But from this it was only a short step to the conclusion that the stranger himself must be a British agent.

Now the last thing that anyone in Thak Khola wanted was trouble with the government in distant Kathmandu over harboring a British spy. One of the few real achievements of the Rana period was to keep Nepal independent, and this had been accomplished by a huge and highly efficient standing army; yet even during the unification of Nepal the famous Ghorkha soldiers had never marched up this valley. The cozy arrangement with the Ranas concerning the salt tax had worked well enough for over thirty years, the subbha being almost invariably a local man, which ensured that all quarrels remained within the family. And since a little smuggling was a common local means of supplementing one's income, the kind of incident that would bring in outside officials and soldiers would be a disaster for the entire area.

So public opinion in the tidy little town divided. Most thought the stranger was just too dangerous to keep around. His piety was no guarantee that he was not a spy: best to play it safe by kicking him out and asking questions later. A minority, however—his host, who had meanwhile returned from India, among them—felt that Kawaguchi was as sincere as his behavior suggested and that it would be an offense to their own religion to treat him inhospitably.

It was under these circumstances that a very nervous Adam Naring ("with indescribable fear written on his face") held a secret interview with his guest. In Kawaguchi's account of this interview he cannot quite hide his pride in the way he manipulated the unfortunate headman. The simple Buddhist scholar was in fact turning into quite a schemer.

Poor honest soul! What he said to me, when by ourselves, was of course to the effect that if there were any truth in the rumor, he and his folks would be visited with what punishment heaven only knew. I had expected this for some time past, and had made up my mind how to act as soon as Naring approached me on the subject. I turned around and, looking him squarely in the face, said: "If you promise me, under oath, that you will not divulge for three full years to come what I may tell you, I will let you in on my secret; but if you do not care to do so, we can only let the rumor take care of itself, and wait for the Nepal Government to take any steps it may deem fit to take." I knew Adam Naring was a man of conscience, who could be trusted with a secret: he signified his willingness to take an oath, and I placed before him a copy of the sacred Scripture. . . .

It was still a desperate gamble. Here, before he had even arrived in Tibet, he was forced to reveal his secret—for the second time, in fact, if it was true that he had taken the Chiniya Lama into his confidence too. At this rate there would be a trail of people all over Asia who knew who he was. He showed Adam Naring his Japanese passport and told him the full story of why he had undertaken the journey. Finding his host greatly relieved, he further upped his standing with him by releasing him from his promise.

Adam Naring was in practice to prove a very good friend. Feeling that he was taxing his hospitality too far, Kawaguchi moved from his house to the temple that overlooks the village, yet the headman continued to provide for him and, to help him on his way, donated about seventy-five pounds of luggage and provisions—as well as a guide and porter to get him through most of Dolpo.

The course of preparation he had begun in Darjeeling was now over. There now lay before Kawaguchi a hazardous and grueling march: first through Dolpo, then west to Kailash, and all the way back across to Lhasa. Even going as quickly and directly as possible, this is a long trip, but Kawaguchi never went anywhere in a straight line. There were too many holy places to visit, too many interesting things to see—and, besides, he would seldom have the slightest idea where he was or in which direction he was heading.

Snow for My Bed and Rock for My Pillow

Dolpo is a land of poor and scattered villages separated from one another by lofty passes, of meager fields where only the hardiest of crops survive to feed the hardiest of people. This is the stronghold of Tibet's oldest religions—the Bon and Padmasambhava's Nyingmapa Buddhism—and some villages have a temple devoted to each. No trade routes pass through here as they do along the river, and there are few opportunities to earn much beyond the bare minimum. Nor is the sophistication of the river valley found here. The houses are dark, cramped, and mean; and standards of hygiene are low even compared to the poorest parts of rural Tibet.

That Kawaguchi actually made his way through this uninviting region was more a matter of persistence than prowess, for in spite of his "mountaineering" in Lo he had a struggle to cope with everything from the thin atmosphere to keeping his footing. Not that the experience was without its comic side, however. There is something very familiar to present-day trekkers and would-be climbers in the way he compares his own progress with that of his surefooted Nepali porter from Marpha:

> As for my guide-carrier, he hopped, and skipped, and balanced, and leaped, with the agility and sureness of a monkey, his staff playing for him the part of a boat-hook in a most skillful hand, and, in spite of his seventy-five pounds' burden, he was so much at home on the difficult ascent, that he was ever and anon at my side to help me out of dangerous plights into which I would frequently fall, with my staff stuck fast between two rocks, or while I involuntarily acted the *rôle* of a ball dancer on a loosened boulder.

Overcome with altitude sickness and exhaustion, he was forced several times to stop for an entire day to recuperate, and without the other to push him on he might never have survived, as he insisted on resting at heights where the guide knew full well that "poisonous gases" (in fact the lack of oxygen) could kill anyone who fell asleep. But eventually they reached the wild and lonely hilltop outpost of Tsharka, a village that looks like a citadel from below, though it can hardly have held much attraction for invaders. Even so, with about forty multistory houses, it is the chief settlement in this part of Dolpo. Kawaguchi took little interest in it, remarking only that its inhabitants were followers of the Bon.

Then, several days farther on, he surprised his guide—who had been instructed to lead him on a pilgrimage of the holy places of Dolpo, then back to Marpha—by informing him that he intended to continue alone. Despite the Nepali's efforts to dissuade this mad monk, whose performance so far had hardly been one to inspire confidence, "I was not to be moved, and the man went back with hot tears of farewell, thinking no doubt that he had seen the last of me."

Four days later, on July 4, 1900, he reached the pass that he judged to be the border with Tibet. It was just over three years since he had left Japan.

The history of exploration is full of mystifying little ceremonies performed by men far from home who have reached a goal after a long struggle. The British were fond of throwing their hats in the air and giving three cheers. The Scotsman James Bruce on finding the source of the Blue Nile drank a toast in the water of the spring to his fiancée (who had in fact married someone else in his absence). We might now have expected Kawaguchi to perform a short Buddhist service, to pray for the well-being of the Japanese imperial family, or at least to compose a poem. Yet he chose this moment for the mundane. "How could I prevent myself from being transported with mingled feelings of joy, gratitude, and hope? But I was tired and hungry." And so he took out some *tsampa*, or roasted barley flour, the Tibetan staple; mixed it with snow, butter, pepper, and salt; and ate two bowlfuls. Then, admitting that he had no idea of the proper direction, he decided to make as quickly as possible for Lake Manasarovar, "following impulse and instinct more than anything else." That very day he sighted his first black yak-hair tents and made his first contact with Tibetan people on Tibetan soil.

Here again one notices a great difference between Kawaguchi and virtually all other explorers in Tibet (with the exception of the Pundits), and it is this even more than its ultimate success that makes his trip unique. For there is a sameness to almost all earlier attempts to reach Lhasa, whether they were carried out with an armed expedition or by more surreptitious means. Once the explorers had arrived at the border regions of Tibet, there would be a wholesale rush for the capital, involving as little contact with the local inhabitants as possible. The theory was that if one could somehow get into Lhasa without anyone knowing, or get near enough to run out of provisions and throw oneself on the mercy of the government, the Tibetans would somehow regard it all as a "good show," pat the intrepid adventurer on the back, and congratulate him on his success. But though Tibet is vast and its population small, it generally proved impossible to meet no one at all, and invariably word of the intruders preceded them. Sometimes the party would find itself surrounded by silent Tibetans who remained almost out of sight and never attempted to communicate. Then they would be stopped frustratingly close to Lhasa, sometimes within only a day or two, by a group of officials under armed escort and politely but firmly asked to return by the way they had come. Negotiations continued for varying lengths of time, the Tibetan side showing a marked reluctance to resort to violence, and a willingness to compromise on the route to be taken out of the country, but also an implacable firmness born of the conviction that their own lives hung in the balance. Once it was clear, however, that the unwanted guests were in fact going to leave, the Tibetans would become friendly and supply fresh horses, armed guards, and food; and it is striking just how well some of these arrogant intruders were treated, for the Tibetans were proving, not to be a hard people, but one that simply wished to be left alone. By the 1890s it was like an often played game with distinct rules—or perhaps a well-rehearsed gambit with variations, since the Tibetans always won.

Kawaguchi was to turn all this around. Not only did he set out determinedly in the opposite direction to his goal (he would not reach Lhasa for another nine months), but he constantly sought out people. Indeed he had little choice, as he was often on the point of death from starvation or exposure and in need of their assistance. Besides, whenever he was not in the company of Tibetans he tended almost immediately to get hopelessly lost. Still, he is the only explorer of Tibet we have up to this point who actually shared the daily life of ordinary local people. It is a pity perhaps that his observations were not more "scientific" and detailed (just what did the inside of a nomad's tent look like, or what were people wearing?), but the picture he gives us of life on the western plains among pilgrims and residents alike, enlivened as it is with tales of domestic quarrels and human interest, is unsurpassed. Of course he was helped in this by his Oriental features, and the dirtier and more weatherbeaten he became, the more he must have fitted into the local scene; yet it is worth noting that he was still suspected sometimes of being not only a British agent but even an Englishman by people who had no idea what one looked like.

Nevertheless, he did not approach this first tent without misgivings, as the last thing he wanted was to arouse suspicions during his first few hours in Tibet. There was a choice of two paths: one would take him out of sight of the tents, the other right by them.

> With nothing else to help me arrive at a decision, I then entered on what is termed "Danjikwan sanmai" in Japanese-Buddhist terminology, a meditative process of making up one's mind, when neither logic nor accurate knowledge is present to draw upon for arriving at a conclusion. The process is, in short, one of abnegating self and then forming a judgment, a method which borders on divination, or an assertion of instinctive powers.

It was a method he would employ quite often, and for more important decisions than this one. On this occasion he got the answer he wanted and proceeded toward the tents.

His initial greeting was one he would soon become accustomed to—in fact he must have already experienced it in Tsarang and Dolpo: the hostility of a pack of Tibetan mastiffs. These huge creatures are high-altitude dwellers and, unless born in a lower region, have difficulty surviving at less than about twelve thousand feet. But on their home ground they are some of the world's best watchdogs, and the stranger stands little chance of getting near a Tibetan house or tent without an invitation. Kawaguchi had fortunately learned the accepted way of dealing with these savage animals, which was not to get violent but simply to wave one's walking stick in front of their muzzles. This put the traveler and the dogs in a state of armed truce. The traveler would get no farther, but at least avoided being eaten alive while he waited for events to develop.

When an old lady appeared and called the dogs off, he had his story ready. He did not of course reveal that he had only just crossed into Tibet, but let on that he was a pilgrim searching for the cave of a holy recluse named Gelong Rimpoche. A well-known figure in western Tibet who was visited not only by local nomads but by pilgrims from far and wide, Gelong Rimpoche (whose reputation had reached Kawaguchi in Tsarang) provided a perfectly plausible excuse for a solitary pilgrim to be wandering around here. This pilgrim was welcomed and offered the hospitality of the tent.

Tibetan hospitality invariably means tea: a unique concoction of salt, rancid yak butter, natural soda, and strong tea, all boiled together for a long time and stirred up in what looks like a butter churn. It takes some getting used to but is nourishing and invigorating, and along with tsampa is the staple diet of most Tibetans. Like the locals themselves, Kawaguchi carried inside his robes a wooden teacup which was never washed, and during his time in Tibet he was to live off little else besides tea and tsampa. Tibetans are all great tea drinkers, and some are known to consume as many as fifty or sixty cups a day. Since it was afternoon when he arrived at the tent, Kawaguchi turned down any food and accepted only this drink, an act of renunciation that greatly impressed the old lady.

On the difficult trek from Marpha he had worn out his Tibetan boots, and he asked if he could stay long enough to repair them—a time-consuming process that involves soaking yak hide in water for at least two days until it is soft enough to be worked. This was not possible, since the lady and her son were moving on the next day, but the son went out of his way to take him to his professed destination— Gelong Rimpoche's cave. Here he would have an opportunity both to mend his boots and meet a genuine Tibetan holy man.

Though Kawaguchi was by no means always impressed by these pious figures, some of whom he found ·to be blatant fakes or rogues, this initial experience was a happy one. He makes no mention of the sect to which the lama belonged, but while cave dwelling is not limited to any one sect, it tends to be particularly popular among the Kargyupa. His followers came from a radius of about a hundred miles, and on most mornings he would receive about twenty of them outside his cave, where he delivered a brief sermon, then bestowed a personal blessing on each one. Each of the devotees would leave an offering— usually food, such as dried peaches, raisins, tea, butter, or tsampa. The lama collected rather more than he could use himself, and as he does not appear to have been interested in material wealth, his cave was probably a kind of regional storehouse, to fall back on in hard times. He was certainly to prove more than generous with Kawaguchi on his two visits. Except for the brief time every day when he addressed his vis- itors, he spent most of his life in meditation and religious practices.

Kawaguchi stayed for several days, largely in the company of the lama's attendant, who helped him repair his boots ("I was more suc- cessful at sticking the needle into my finger than in getting on with the job"). At prescribed times he also sought out Gelong Rimpoche, whose first, shrewd words to Kawaguchi were that he was not a man to be wandering alone in the wilderness (indeed, some months later when Kawaguchi called on him again after his pilgrimage to Kailash, it became fairly obvious that his disguise had not taken in the lama at all). Their meetings were congenial: they indulged in at least one vigorous debate, they bandied Buddhist riddles between them, and they parted friends. Kawaguchi's assessment of him as "a man of true charity, dear- ly loving his fellow creatures" was praise as high as any he ever gave.

With his stores generous replenished, he then set off again, only to plunge almost immediately into the sort of difficulties that seemed always to beset him when alone. A glance at the map will show that the route he now had to follow was bound to cause problems. Though this whole area is referred to as the "western plains," here along the southern bank of Tibet's greatest river—the Tsang Po, or Brah- maputra—the terrain consists of a series of river valleys, each river (and there were at least five to be crossed in addition to the Tsang Po itself) being a large tributary. Crossings on foot in such a wild and remote region are particularly hazardous. There are, of course, no bridges, and the current is remarkably wide and swift at that time of year when the mountain snow melts rapidly. Despite the heat of the sun, which in midsummer is intense, the water to be forded can be very near the freezing point.

His first experience of crossing a river described as 180 yards wide, only a few hours after leaving Gelong Rimpoche's cave, was anything but encouraging. After taking his daily meal on the bank he took off his boots and trousers, plunged in, and was immediately forced to retreat.

> Oh! that plunge! it nearly killed me; the water was bitingly cold, and I saw at once that I could never survive the crossing of it. I at once turned round and crawled up the bank, but the contact with the water had already chilled me, and produced in me a sort of convulsion. What was to be done?

What indeed? He could hardly retreat in disgrace to the lama's cave, so there was nothing for it but to try somehow to get across. One of the medicines he always carried with him was a bottle of clove oil, and, hoping that a layer of this would help protect him a little from the cold, he smeared himself all over with it. His next attempt was more successful, and though his legs went numb before he was halfway across he managed to struggle to the far side, where he found himself "almost a frigid body, stiff and numb in every part."

It took two more hours of lying in the sun on the riverbank and trying to massage himself with his stiff hands for his circulation to recover to the point where he could walk. But even then "my legs were so flabby I felt as if they were going to drop off." His luggage, with all the supplies he had received from Gelong Rimpoche, now proved too heavy. He tried dividing it into two bundles, tying them to his walking stick, and slinging the whole affair across his back like a coolie. This only produced chafed and aching shoulders. In the next two hours he scarcely traveled a mile and a half, and when he reached the bank of another river he gave up for the day, exhausted. Clearly it was going to be a long trip to Kailash.

His vows, of course, made it impossible to eat again that day, but drinking was permissible and it is fortunate that the prevailing beverage was so nourishing. But if he was going to drink tea, he had first to make it, and this meant forcing himself to gather dried yak dung for fuel. And then at this altitude water boils at such a low temperature that it took at least two hours for the tea to be ready. That night he found it too cold to sleep; instead, he composed a poem to the moon and sat up for the rest of the night in meditation.

When rising slow among the mountain heights,
　The moon I see in those Tibetan wilds,
My fancy views that orb as Sovereign Lord
　Of the Celestial Land, my country dear,
Those islands smiling in the far-off east.

The homesick/patriotic flavor of this, and some of his other poems, is, like his private New Year ceremonies, a little strange. Did he in fact allow himself a moment of homesickness here alone in the wilds; or, as seems more likely, did he simply allow his romanticism to run away with him? In practice, there is ample evidence to suggest that he was never in any hurry to return to the country he had left without regret— and to which he never really learned to relate.

At any rate, his musings seem to have induced a sort of amnesia as regards the more practical aspects of the journey, for by morning he had forgotten the directions he had been given by the lama's attendant. Taking off in precisely the wrong direction, he soon found himself faced with another difficult river crossing, and he was on the point of despair when he sighted another solitary monk. This wayfarer was a pilgrim from Kham on his way to visit Gelong Rimpoche, and without his help—he carried the luggage and led Kawaguchi by the hand—he might well have been unequal to this crossing. The surprised Khampa was rewarded with a large supply of tsampa and dried peaches which poor Kawaguchi was only too happy to get off his back. According to the Khampa, there were some nomads only two days' journey away, and our traveler now headed in their direction. But his troubles were only beginning.

Soon there was shortness of breath and acute nausea, forcing him to resort to a traditional Japanese medicine whose virtues he constantly extols but which almost always seemed to provoke the most violent reactions in him. Called Hotan, its recipe was originally given to an Edo pharmacist by a Dutch doctor during one of those visits by the Dutch of Nagasaki to the Japanese capital in the days when this was the only contact the Japanese had with the outside world. As such it is akin to other early imports from the West like *tempura*, *kasutera*, and *tabako*; but it certainly has the smell of an Oriental medicine, and the Dutch

Hotan label.

may have picked it up in Indonesia—or the Japanese may have modified it. The main ingredients are calcium and menthol, but there are any number of others such as "dragon's brains" which effectively mask whatever the more active ingredients may be. Very popular during Kawaguchi's time, it was judged such an effective deterrent to contagious diseases that soldiers of the Imperial Japanese Army carried it during the first Sino-Japanese War and the Russo-Japanese War. It is also supposed to be good for pets (from rabbits to goldfish), and even today the label advises that a full dose given to a horse before a long journey will ward off fatigue.

This "soothing restorative" was now to produce in Kawaguchi instant and alarming results in the form of a mouthful of blood, which finished off his journey for the day. His account is necessarily vague at this point, but it indicates that he passed out on the spot and was woken by a shower of hailstones sometime in the night. His body "cracked and ached all over," and it was only with great effort that he got himself into a sitting position, worked his racing pulse and breathing back to normal, and decided that he was "not yet to die." He must have been at around fifteen thousand feet and suffering from acute altitude sickness as well as exhaustion and exposure, and it is certainly fortunate that this was midsummer. He was also lucky to have been so rudely awakened by a hailstorm, for it can be extremely dangerous to sleep when one is too high and unacclimatized, and in sitting out the night in meditation and controlling his breathing he undoubtedly saved his own life.

Soon this exercise of "spiritual conquest over bodily ailment" had brought him round to the point where he became a little irritated at his own weakness: "both the scene and the situation would have furnished me with enough matter for my soul's musings, but, alas! for my bodily pains." In a state verging on euphoria he spent the last hours of the night composing poetry:

O Mind! By Dharma's genial light and warmth
    The pain-inflicting snows are melted fast,
And flow in rushing streams that sweep away
    Delusive Ego and Non-Ego both.

Thus he discovered for himself what many monks in Tibet practice as a matter of course: meditating away the cold. Certain Kargyupa monks even do an exercise where wet towels are placed on their bare shoulders in sub-freezing weather and they must raise their body heat to the point where they can dry them. Though this practice, known as *thumo reskiang*, was actually performed by a Frenchwoman (Alexandra David-Neel) early in this century, most skeptical Westerners continued to believe that it was impossible until it was observed and confirmed scientifically after the dispersal of Tibetan culture in 1959.

In the morning he felt well enough to eat some raisins for breakfast and continue, and before noon he came to a small stream where he brewed his tea and had his main meal of Tibetan tea and tsampa. Soon afterward he was relieved to sight tents in the distance, and he knew that after two nights in the open he had to reach them and obtain shelter for a few days. Reach them he did—only to be greeted by six mastiffs: "and it was a right hot reception, to appreciate which I had to put all my remaining energy into the gentle warning of my staff." Thus he survived the first, and in retrospect the mildest, of four narrow escapes from death in western Tibet; and he calls it merely "a foretaste of distressing experiences." He had been in the country only a week.

Yet what happened next was possibly even harder to bear, for from the tent emerged a woman of such striking beauty that the celibate could not refrain from mentioning it repeatedly. Fortunately for all concerned she was safely, if stormily, married to a man who would become one of Kawaguchi's closest friends.

His name was Alchu Tulku. "Tulku" is a title given to incarnate lamas, those who are discovered to be Bodhisattvas in human form (we shall have occasion to look a little more closely at this uniquely Tibetan institution later). Any tulku would be a man of some standing, respected for his birth and often quite wealthy as well (Alchu Tulku owned sixty yaks and two hundred sheep). But Kawaguchi's respect for him—and he was rescued by him twice in due course—was tempered by the fact that part of the time he spent in his company was devoted to mediating the quarrels between the lama and his wife; indeed, he helped patch up a marriage that in his eyes at least was unholy, since he learned to his horror that, as a monk of the reformed Gelupa sect, Alchu Tulku should have been celibate. Yet he could hardly choose his rescuers, and, as he said, "it was enough for me that after my distressing experiences, he received me with open arms, treated me with the utmost kindness, and behaved in a manner bespeaking a large heart and a deeply charitable mind." Torn between his beliefs and the ragged reality of everyday life, Kawaguchi often had to give those who did not live up to his own strict standards the benefit of the doubt.

On the evening before his departure, however, things came to a head. Returning from lunch and a long religious discussion in the neighboring tent of a Ladakhi trader with whom he would leave the next day, he found himself in the midst of a domestic quarrel of major proportions.

I saw that a wonderful metamorphosis had come over the erstwhile beauty. Her face was burning red and undergoing the most disagreeable contortions I had ever seen, as she went on calling her husband names and otherwise insulting him in the vilest language imaginable.

And what do couples find to quarrel about on the plains of western Tibet? Nothing very original, it would seem. "It was all about 'another woman' and also about the husband's partiality for his own relatives." The scene quickly deteriorated.

A man of quiet disposition as the lama was, he heroically maintained his self-composure and silence until she dared call him "beast," when he rose and feigned to beat her. He probably did so because he was irritated by my appearance on the scene just at that juncture. But that was a blundering move on his part, for the moment he raised his fist, the now thoroughly maddened termagant threw herself at his feet, and, with eyes shut, shouted, shrieked, and howled, daring him to kill and eat her!

Showing more resourcefulness than he generally did when it came to finding his way, Kawaguchi now played the peacemaker. He got the hysterical woman to bed, then led his friend away to another tent nearby. If he had ever had any doubts about his independent way of life and strict adherence to his vows, these were now dispelled.

And so the last night I spent with my kind host brought me a rude awakening, which caused me to shed tears of deep sympathy, not necessarily for Alchu Tulku only, but for all my brethren of the Order, whose moral weakness had betrayed them into breaking their vows of celibacy, and who in consequence were forced to go through such scenes as I have described.

* * *

The next few days were fairly easy, as he was accompanied by the Ladakhi with whom he had lunched and his six servants. Though they were on foot the baggage was taken care of, and they crossed the Kyang Chu with no difficulty, even though the water reached a depth of three or four feet and they had to be careful of floating chunks of ice. After parting from the trader, Kawaguchi spent several days with a prosperous nomad—a friend of Alchu Tulku's—and acquired what would become a faithful traveling companion: a sheep, which he could use as a beast of burden.

But at first this creature, like Gelong Rimpoche, seemed to have sized up Kawaguchi, decided he was heading for trouble, and wanted nothing to do with him:

> ... There ensued a tug of war between the sheep and its master, and a very lively one it was. I argued with the animal, adducing various proofs of my determination, among which I may mention a rather free use of one of my staves. But the sheep showed that it had a stronger determination than mine, and I began to be dragged backward. My severe exertions even threatened to cause me some serious injury. . . .

Perhaps it was ordained that the meek should inherit Tibet, for while other explorers have regaled us with tales of fighting off carnivorous beasts or shooting something for the pot, few would care to tell us in such detail of ignominious defeat at the hands of a humble sheep. In the end a compromise was reached: the sheep agreed to go along with its new master, but only on condition that one of its old friends was purchased as a companion. The two would prove good beasts of burden, and though fording rivers became occasionally an even tougher proposition, at least once they saved their master from freezing to death.

Reasonably good luck kept him in company for another few days, including a night as the guest of the district chief—a further test of his disguise. His medical skills ("a sickly old woman came to me . . . and begged me to examine her and tell her when she would die; a pleasant request indeed!") gained him guides for the difficult crossing of the upper Tsang Po, or the Tamchak Khanbab, so that even though he describes the river as being a mile wide here, the task was accomplished with comparative ease. On the far side, however, he was to leave inhabited districts behind and begin a trek tailor-made for disaster, given his propensity for getting lost at the best of times: before him stretched ten to fifteen days of walking with no prospect of seeing other human beings. His guides, on taking their leave, cheerfully advised him to recite the sacred texts from time to time to avoid being eaten by snow leopards.

But it was a slower if more persistent enemy that first had its way with him, as Tibet once again reminded the solitary wanderer that its secrets were not to be given up easily, nor to the faint of heart. For after the first day there was no water to be found, and soon his thirst was so great that he would have been only too happy to be confronted with one of those rivers which until now had proved his most trying obstacle. On the third day he began to be plagued by mirages, the air of the plains being extremely dry. "I could not help imagining myself to be a mere shadow, wandering in mad quest of a soothing draught in the hot region of the nether world, where all water turned to fire when brought to the mouth." All he had for comfort was the occasional pinch of Hotan, which this time at least did not make him cough up blood.

When finally he did come to a small hidden pool, it was stagnant: "vermilion red, thick, and (what was worse) alive with myriads of little creatures!" Health considerations aside, a Buddhist vegetarian could hardly drink these things, so, thirsty as he was, he remembered an old Buddhist precept and carefully strained them out through a piece of cotton cloth. The water afterward was still red, but at least there was nothing squirming in it. One can only marvel at the constitution he must have had to survive such a drink at all. "That quenching draught, how delicious it was! I imagine God's nectar could not be sweeter. But a second bowlful—no, I could not take it." Instead he made a fire to brew some tea and prepare lunch. But noon was upon him before the water boiled, and so he had to have his tsampa with a brick-colored lukewarm liquid—yet he still describes this meal as one of the most enjoyable he had in Tibet.

And now when things were looking up a little he was overtaken by a sandstorm. He emerged little the worse for wear (he and his sheep had sensibly kept moving to avoid being buried alive), only to face, in the morning, the worst of all his river crossings: that of the last large tributary of the Tsang Po, known as the Chema-yungdung-gi-chu. The day before, he had nearly died of thirst; now he would find himself in rather more water than he could handle—indeed he came close to drowning.

When he arrived at the river at around 9:00 A.M. there was still treacherous ice along its banks. While he waited for it to melt he built a fire and got his meal out of the way. Then he rubbed himself down with clove oil and prepared for the plunge, but his sheep—with more instinctive knowledge about rivers than Kawaguchi possessed—had the good sense to refuse to move with the luggage on their backs, thus condemning the poor monk to three trips: one with the sheep, a return to get the baggage, and finally back again carrying all his gear.

Even though he had been expecting the worst, the first crossing proved a shock, as the water was shoulder-deep and his clothes got soaked through. He was exasperated enough to betray a little irritation with his sheep: ". . . of course they might have been washed down and drowned but for the assistance I gave them by means of the ropes." (They might also have been happily browsing near a nomad's tents had they not made his acquaintance.) He started on the return journey immediately without his clothes (at least he got a bath) and, unencumbered, found it comparatively easy. Even so, it took him half an hour and a rubdown with clove oil to recover sufficiently to feel ready for the last stage of the operation. It was still July, which meant the sun's rays would have been fierce and the air temperature around 68° F.

With all his baggage, and still stark-naked, he began his final passage, and got halfway across before losing his footing and being swept away by the current. Realizing that to lose his baggage, which contained all his food, clothing, and medicine, would be to lose his life, he clung desperately to the bundle, but it was an unequal struggle: the brute force of a near-freezing torrent against a frail, naked creature clinging to his means of survival. He had in fact given up hope and uttered a final prayer (for another life, in which to fulfill his obligations) when he struck bottom with one of his sticks, and he had just enough energy to drag himself, freezing, numb, and naked, to the shore. Luckily he was on the right side of the river, but 250 yards downstream from his sheep ("leisurely grazing, perfectly unconscious of their master's sad plight"). Recovery, this time, required an hour of massaging his heart and lungs in the warm sunlight; only then did he feel strong enough to be able to

Swept away.

open up his baggage, which was wrapped tightly in animal skins and almost waterproof, and find his Hotan ("... Hotan, my life-saving Hotan, which Mrs. Ichibei Watanabe of Osaka gave me when bidding me farewell"). A good dose of it sent him into convulsions for nearly three hours. By the time he came round it was getting cold, and the two trips it took him to haul his belongings toward the sheep reminded him of some ancient Japanese torture. When he had finished he had "neither the courage nor the energy" to go about collecting dung and making a fire, and he spent the night wrapped in a clammy cloak.

Luckily the next morning dawned fine and he was able to get a fire going and dry his clothes. Even more important, he dried the set of scriptures he had with him, presumably the set for which he had traded his horse in Tsarang and which was to survive his entire adventure. He set off at about 1:00 P.M., but having cut his foot badly in the river, and with his damp luggage heavier than it had been, he found the going very slow indeed. That night he camped by a small pond, where a violent snowstorm accompanied by thunder and lightning made a fire impossible, so there was no tea. In the morning he was again unable to make a fire and had to be content with only a few raisins for breakfast.

A high pass now blocked his way, but before he could reach the top another blizzard forced him to turn back and descend. By nightfall the snow was a foot deep, he had found no shelter of any kind, and finally his sheep just gave up and refused to move. There was less possibility than ever of a fire, so, snuggling between the two wretched animals and wrapped in everything he had, he hoped to pass the long night in meditation. But after midnight even meditation seemed to fail him.

> . . . I began to feel that my power of sensation was gradually deserting me. I seemed to be in a trance, and vaguely thought that that must be the feeling of a man on the point of death. . . . I was now wandering in a dream-land. . . . Regret, resignation, and the hope of rebirth took turns in my mind, and then all became a blank.

In the morning, though, he was surprised to find himself awake. His timepiece told him it was 10:30, and the skies were still cloudy and threatening. He was not even sure if he had been unconscious for only one night or more, but rather than waste time worrying about it he forced some tsampa and snow down his throat, and fed some to the sheep as well. Then his only thought was to descend as fast as possible in order to find a sheltered camping place in which to rest and lick his wounds.

He had spent three hellish nights in succession since the disastrous river crossing, and he was now due for a bit of luck—which he found in the form of some yak herders' tents in the middle of this supposedly uninhabited region. Just imagine his despair, however, when the suspicious occupants of the first two tents refused him admission. But at the third and last one he was invited in and allowed to recuperate for a day and two nights.

To have survived acute thirst, a near drowning, and almost freezing to death, all within weeks of entering Tibet, is a tribute, if not to his judgment, at least to his courage. But to have been able to find enough strength to go on after only a day and a half in a stranger's tent argues an incredible resilience; yet at five o'clock on the second morning he was again ready for the road. Admittedly, he had little choice in the matter: the journey ahead could scarcely be worse than what came before. And at least this time the problems he invariably encountered were of the comic variety—for his ordeals were punctuated with some of the most ridiculous scenes that any explorer could conjure up. We have already seen him being swept off his horse by a low branch while he was daydreaming, then brawling with his teacher in the headman's chapel in Tsarang, getting caught in the middle of a violent marital quarrel, and fighting a losing battle with a sheep. He now ran into a herd of kyang, or Tibetan wild asses, an animal whose antics are funny enough in themselves.

It has a curious habit of turning round and round, when it comes within seeing distance of a man. Even a mile and a quarter away, it will commence this turning round at every short stage of its approach, and after each turn it will stop for a while, to look at the man over its own back, like a fox. Ultimately it comes up quite close. When quite near it will look scared, and at the slightest thing will wheel around and dash away, but only to stop and look back. When one thinks that it has run away, it will be found that it has circled back quite near, to take, as it were, a silent survey of the stranger from behind. Altogether it is an animal of very queer habits.

An animal with which, perhaps, Kawaguchi might have felt at home.

But his sheep did not like them at all and made a run for it. Giving chase, the poor monk eventually ran out of breath and collapsed from the effort of the race. "While it lasted the horses seemed thoroughly to enjoy it, and getting into the spirit of the thing they galloped with me, but only to chase my sheep further away from me." How long it went on before he finally fell helpless to the ground he does not say, but as soon as he did so the sheep, too, came to a halt ("the horses also stopped and seemed quite astonished at the whole performance"). It then occurred to him to change tactics, with the result that he recaptured his frightened crew simply by walking quietly over to them.

During the chase one of the sheep had taken the opportunity to divest itself of part of the luggage—including fifty rupees, the pocket watch, and the compass—and as they were on a plain covered with deep grass it proved quite impossible to find anything. But he refused to let it get him down, telling himself that he did not really need the money, and the watch and compass might only excite suspicion among the Tibetans; perhaps it was even providential. The compass, after all, had done him little good, and he might also have remembered that meal of lukewarm water and tsampa: without the watch it would be impossible to tell exactly when noon occurred.

Somewhere during this dreadful journey, in fact, Kawaguchi seems to have lost all track of time. When he had left his guides after crossing the upper Tsang Po he had before him the prospect of a ten- to fifteen-day journey through uninhabited lands. Yet according to his account he spent only about five days alone—much of the time in a weakened and confused state when he could have made little headway—before resting for two nights in the herders' tent. On the very next day, which began with the wild kyang chase, he came across the pilgrim route he had hoped to find, and soon after chanced upon the tent that was to harbor him for the following two months. That comes to a week in all; but, though he is sometimes vague about dates, we are also told that he crossed the Tsang Po on July 23, and reached the pilgrims' road on August 2—a total of eleven days. The reader is offered no explanation for this discrepancy.

Though he did not immediately realize it, when he reached this tent his troubles—at least his physical troubles—were temporarily at an end. He was at first, however, more than a little apprehensive, for though he was cheerfully offered hospitality at the first tent he approached, he soon discovered that it was occupied by pilgrims from a region bordering Kham called Dam Gya-sho. It will be recalled that the two Khampas who had accompanied him from Boudha to Tukche had planned to rob and murder him, and apparently their neighbors from Dam Gya-sho enjoyed a similar reputation. He had even heard a slogan attributed to them that went: "No murder, no food; no pilgrimage, no absolution. On! onward on your pilgrimage, killing men and visiting temples!" These people were a long way from home and so in the past few months must have had ample opportunity to do both.

Nonetheless he accepted their hospitality, survived the night with no problems, and moved on with his new companions until they were within sight of Mt. Kailash. On first laying eyes on the holy mountain Kawaguchi was quite overcome. He confessed his sins, prostrated himself 108 times, repledged himself to the accomplishment of his mysterious "26 desires" (he never tells us exactly what they are, though he refers to them frequently), and composed an impromptu poem—all to the astonishment of his rough-and-ready friends, who promptly asked him to preach to them. They were, after all, on a pilgrimage.

For all his protestations and snide remarks about "ignorant natives," Kawaguchi seems to have possessed a gift not only for getting on with almost anyone if he cared to, but for expressing himself in terms effective with common people or scholars as the situation demanded, and here his sermon provoked deep emotion. Though we have no real reason to suspect that he was anything but sincere in wishing to teach the Dharma, it must be admitted that on this and other occasions his preaching won him very welcome material results. This time he was invited to join the party for the duration of the pilgrimage. So impressed was he with the power of Buddhism to soften the hearts of these inveterate brigands—and just possibly elated at the prospect of two months of tents, fires, and companionship—that he himself broke down and wept. Like Japanese Olympic athletes and professional boxers of today, our traveler was never averse to shedding tears of joy.

But if his physical problems were over for a while, other ones were just beginning, since Tibet for Kawaguchi would be a constant confrontation. What he never seemed to realize was that the Buddhist faith itself had gone through much the same confrontation over a period of seven or eight hundred years. But while late Indian Buddhism had proved itself flexible and receptive, so that eventually it reached an accommodation with Tibet that produced one of the world's most religiously oriented nations, Kawaguchi himself refused to bend.

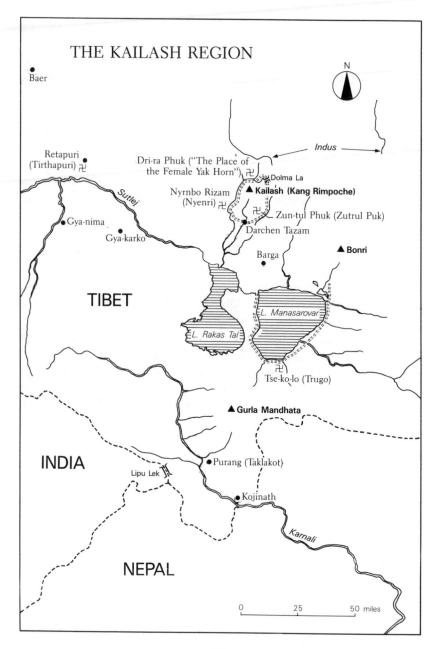

THE KAILASH REGION

Baer

Retapuri (Tirthapuri) 卍

Dri-ra Phuk ("The Place of the Female Yak Horn") 卍

Indus

Dolma La

Nyrnbo Rizam (Nyenri) 卍

▲ Kailash (Kang Rimpoche)

Sutlej

Zun-tul Phuk (Zutrul Puk)

Gya-nima

Darchen Tazam

Gya-karko

Barga

▲ Bonri

TIBET

L. Manasarovar

L. Rakas Tal

Tse-ko-lo (Trugo) 卍

▲ Gurla Mandhata

INDIA

Lipu Lek

● Purang (Taklakot)

● Kojinath

Karnali

NEPAL

0   25   50 miles

Confrontation with Tibet

Two days later they came within sight of Lake Manasarovar, with Mt. Kailash looming over its northwest corner. This was the first of the goals Kawaguchi had set himself when he crossed the border, trusting to "impulse and instinct"; and reaching it—by whatever route—was no mean achievement. The lake, which lies on an empty plain where nothing grows, is sacred to Hindus and Buddhists alike, for whom it represents the source of four great rivers: the Tsang Po, the Indus, the Sutlej, and the holy Ganga itself. In reality it is the source of none of them, but all rise within sixty miles of it, and the faithful are not in the least put off by any visible contradiction of an accepted truth. They simply contend that all these rivers are linked by underground channels to "the fountainhead."

Kawaguchi, in sharp contrast to his condescending attitude at Muktinath more than a year before, seemed equally receptive to the power of hallowed lore, saying that "the things mentioned in the scriptures cannot be seen with our mortal eyes," and that one felt a "holy elevation" there. Perhaps the experiences of the past few months had humbled him, making him respond more easily to the forces that moved the Tibetans themselves:

> Mount Kailasa itself towers so majestically above the peaks around, that I fancied I saw in it the image of our mighty Lord Buddha, calmly addressing his five hundred disciples. Verily, verily, it was a natural mandala. The hunger and thirst, the perils of dashing stream and freezing blizzard, the pain of writhing under heavy burdens, the anxiety of wandering over trackless wilds, the exhaus-

tion and the lacerations, all the troubles and sufferings I had just come through, seemed like dust, which was washed away and purified by the spiritual waters of the lake. . . .

Yet it was sitting on the shores of these "spiritual waters" that Kawaguchi heard a story that must have intruded rather on the sanctity of his surroundings. The superior of a temple there told it in passing to illustrate his disapproval of the behavior of many of his fellow monks; and it concerned Alchu Tulku. It seems that Kawaguchi's friend, while in charge of another well-known and well-endowed temple, had fallen in love with a beautiful woman and, after transferring most of the temple's wealth to her father, had absconded—taking with him as much as he could carry of any remaining valuables. Kawaguchi was shocked and upset—he liked his former host and was sincerely grateful for his hospitality—and in his disappointment told himself "it was at least a comfort to think that things in Japan were better than this"; an odd remark, considering the circumstances that had helped drive him from his own country.

* * *

In penetrating the Kailash region Kawaguchi had entered an area where many others had been before him: pilgrims from India, but also Europeans—missionaries, explorers, and big-game hunters—who in the last two hundred years had at some time stood beside the lake. With the exception of the first of them, that determined Jesuit Ippolito Desideri, who passed this way in 1715, they were rather a dry and colorless lot, interested in either winning the Royal Geographical Society's coveted gold medal or in bagging trophies. Their incursions did sometimes yield solid scientific results: it was discovered quite early on, for instance, that there was not one lake but two, connected periodically by a channel flowing through a high bank of shingle. Yet, in keeping with the times, they displayed no sensitivity toward deeply held local beliefs, and thus for all their surveying, map making, and mountain measuring managed to miss the true character of the region. One traveler showed his disrespect by trying (unsuccessfully) to fish in this sacred stretch of water, while another so upset local feelings by launching a rubber boat on it that the provincial governor was later executed.

Though not a pioneer in this sense, Kawaguchi was about to become the first foreign traveler to do the holy circuit of Mt. Kailash and offer some insight into the religious life he encountered on the way (the second was Sven Hedin in 1907, who despite his faults at least approached the region with a measure of respect). Even so, as a product of the Meiji era, he felt obliged, alas, to make some "scientific" observation from time to time. He comments at some length, for example, on the channel between the lakes, discusses water levels and seasonal rainfall, and reaches precisely the opposite conclusions to those formed by more competent geographers on the direction in which the hidden channel flowed. He even takes Western map makers to task for not noticing that the larger lake is shaped like a lotus flower. And it is a positive relief when he returns to less mundane matters.

*   *   *

Moving around Manasarovar toward the sacred mountain, the party came to the temporary market centers of Gya-nima and Gya-karko, where they called a halt. Deserted for most of the year, these two sites become lively bazaars from mid-July to mid-September, when Tibetan nomads barter wool, butter, and yak tails for grain, sugar, and cotton cloth with merchants from the Indian Himalayas. Kawaguchi saw more than five hundred people at each when he was there. Among the throng at Gya-karko, however, he met an Indian trader from the mountains just west of Nepal—the area where most of the Pundits were recruited—who took him for one of these British-trained spies. The trader, assuming that he had some influence with his British masters, promised not to give him away in return for a little help with his export business when they both went back to India. Kawaguchi, in turn, insisted he was Chinese, and, following an almost inevitable pattern, a Chinese speaker was then produced by the resourceful Indian. But, compared with his experience with the Chiniya Lama, this was a walkover, since the man spoke the language poorly and had no real reading skills at all. So confident did Kawaguchi feel, in fact, that he entrusted the trader not only with letters to Japan but one to Chandra

Das himself, telling him how far he had progressed. One would dearly like to know how they were addressed. It seems incredibly foolhardy of him to write again to the most notorious and widely hated man in Tibet, when this correspondence had only recently brought him to the very brink of disaster.

Anyway, he had little time to brood about its consequences: he had other problems much closer to home. Among the pilgrims in his group was a girl of about nineteen called Dawa—"not beautiful and not ugly: a comely little thing she was"—who had set her sights on him. Tibetans are affectionate, and, though unwashed, their women seem to have exercised a certain fascination over this bearded bachelor; his escape from the headman's daughter in Tsarang had perhaps been narrower than he admits, and he had clearly been impressed by the beauty of Alchu Tulku's wife. Indeed, it is at this point that we are told: "But I, though not old, had had my own experiences in these matters in my younger days."

With some justice probably, Kawaguchi felt that Dawa was more in love with the idea of marrying a respected "lama" than with his actual person. Our traveler did not of course qualify for that title, but it is unlikely that Dawa's family had ever been in such close contact with a priest of Kawaguchi's learning and piety. In Tibet, not only are lamas treated with uncommon respect but, among the ignorant, they are often feared for their knowledge of esoteric matters. They are regarded, in other words, as useful people to have in the family, even if their vows need bending to get them there.

By emphasizing in his daily sermons "the horrors of hell that sinners create for themselves even in this world, and which follow them into eternity as the price they pay for momentary pleasures," Kawaguchi hoped to erect a barrier between himself and Dawa, but the determined young lady refused to take the hint. She followed him around the camp, plying him with stories of her family's wealth, of all that would be his if he returned home with her; she stressed the joys of living with a wife. She must also have tried giving him a foretaste of what these were, as "the wiles of temptation now came thick and fast upon me." In self-defense, the monk tried calling to mind the Buddha's temptation at Bodh Gaya, when after his enlightenment he was confronted by the three daughters of the King of the Underworld who took on beautiful and voluptuous forms. This is a favorite theme of Buddhist art, and paintings of the Buddha seated in calm meditation under the bodhi tree, oblivious to the seductive delights surrounding him, are found in most Tibetan temples.

In her frustration with the obstinate monk's behavior, Dawa resorted to insulting him—which inspired this poem in reply:

> You call me stupid; that am I, I grant;
>   But yet in love-affairs being wiser grown,
>   'Tis safe for me to be more stupid still.

Mere words, however, had little effect, for women "know a language unspoken, which is far more telling, appealing, and enticing, than that which mere sound and articulation can convey." The worst moment for "this common mortal struggling on" came at Gya-karko, when Dawa's father and brothers were all out at the market and their guest sat alone in a tent clumsily mending his boots. Suddenly, Dawa

> . . . almost frightened me with her boldness. I am neither a piece of wood nor a block of stone, and I should have been supernatural if I had not felt the power of temptation. But to yield to such a folly would be against my own profession. Moreover, I remembered with awe the omnipresence of the Lord Buddha, and was thus enabled to keep my heart under control.

Poor Kawaguchi. All he wanted was to investigate places of pilgrimage, study, and collect books. Hunger and loneliness he could bear —indeed he seemed to almost relish them—but this was the sorest trial of all.

Desperate for a way to distract the girl, he asked her—apparently under conditions of some duress—if for all her bragging about her happy home in eastern Tibet she even knew if her mother was still alive or not. This simple question had a more striking effect than he had bargained for, since her mother had in fact been ill when the pilgrimage began, and Dawa was indeed concerned about her. It was now the girl's turn to be frightened: her "Chinese lama" was perhaps more of a sorcerer than she had thought, and if he had some sort of second sight, then perhaps he could cast spells on people, too. . . .

At least it put an abrupt, if temporary, stop to her advances, and, virtue intact, Kawaguchi continued with the family on their pilgrimage around "nature's mandala." Their next destination was Retapuri (Tirthapuri on most maps). Approaching it, four of them—Dawa, her father, and another woman, with Kawaguchi in tow—decided they wanted to visit the temple there, which meant fording a small river along the way. Dawa, tough as any young Tibetan, simply hitched up her clothes and crossed the hip-deep freezing stream without a second thought; but the foreign pilgrim reached the far bank too numb to walk, and, after telling the others to go on, he sat for an hour treating himself with moxibustion. It was a trifling incident, but it makes one wonder what sort of marriage they would have had if Kawaguchi had given in; and it probably contributed to his grumpiness when he did catch up with them. For, whereas the sights of the previous few days had raised him to spiritual heights, the temple's mani walls reminded him only of railway cars, while the cry of a strange bird sounded like the whistle of a steam engine.

Retapuri is a Sanskrit word meaning "Town of the Hungry Devils," and it was given to the spot by Paldan Atisha, Tibet's first great Buddhist reformer. Since Kawaguchi was now at the outer limit of his journey in western Tibet and from here on would be traveling more or less toward Lhasa, this seems as good a moment as any to stop again for a while and take up the story of Tibetan Buddhism where we left off.

* * *

The influx of imported knowledge that followed in the wake of Padmasambhava's exorcising of Tibet did not last, and only a generation after his departure a Bon reaction set in under an unsavory king named Lang Dharma, remembered by Buddhist historians as a figure conspicuous for his cruelty even in an age of prevailing violence. He took the throne around the year 900 after murdering his brother, and in a bloodthirsty reign of only three years managed to undo most of what Padmasambhava and Santarakshita had accomplished. Indeed he might well have succeeded in his aim of eliminating Buddhism entirely if his sacking of the monasteries and slaughter of their communities had not been put to an end by one of the surviving monks, who took pity on the man and killed him to prevent his acquiring any more bad karma. (This act of compassionate manslaughter is still reproduced in ritual dances in Tibetan monasteries.) But the damage had been done and the Dharma had lost its impetus. The Buddhism that emerged from the carnage retained many of the Tartric and sexual rites without the discipline necessary to give them spiritual value. Practiced in small monastic enclaves with no central guidance, it remained fragile and eclectic.

Now, whenever the Dharma is in need of assistance, the Tibetans believe that an incarnation of Manjusri, the Bodhisattva who created the Kathmandu Valley, comes into the world wielding his Sword of Wisdom and his Book of Knowledge to save the day. King Trison Detson, host to Buddhist precursors in Tibet, was one; it was now time for another. He came in the form of a Bengali teacher from another distinguished Indian university—Vikramashila—and he can be seen as one of a dying breed of Indian Buddhist sages. For by his time, in the mid-eleventh century, the doctrines of his faith had been largely preempted by the Hindus, who now regarded the Buddha as one of Vishnu's ten incarnations; the universities were for all practical purposes Hindu institutions; and within a hundred years the wavering flame of Buddhism in India would be extinguished, the monasteries and centers of learning fallen victim to the Muslim invader, their monks dispersed or killed and their libraries burned. His own university was so thoroughly obliterated that even its site is not known.

Thus Paldan Atisha's arrival in Tibet was significant for the Dharma as a whole. The religious revival he inspired there was responsible for preserving a threatened heritage in almost its entirety; as the British scholars Richardson and Snellgrove put it: "By the twelfth century a skilled minority of Tibetans had transferred to Tibetan soil not only the texts, but the whole way of life of Indian Buddhist monks and yogins." On a regional level, moreover, the Tibetan investment in him (Atisha's votaries in India had been unwilling to release him, and a good deal of gold was used as an incentive) was repaid by widespread reforms. Atisha himself established a new and tightly disciplined sect called the Kadampa, which in turn led to the founding of two branches, the Sakyapa and Kargyupa, both instituted by followers who felt he might have gone too far in eliminating Tantric and mystical practices. Padmasambhava's older, unreformed sect remained but was known henceforward as the Nyingmapa, or "those of the ancient teachings." Given the vitality of these new sects, and with the ensuing wave of cultural importation, Buddhism was assured a firm footing in Tibet; and the question was no longer whether it would survive, but which of its forms would predominate.

Only a crude outline of the advance and decline of these various branches of the faith can be given here. The Sakyapa, or "blue earth people"—whose name derives from the clay lining the valley in central Tibet where their main monastery is found—rose to early political prominence with the help of Kublai Khan. A Sakya monk named Phagspa was among assorted missionaries invited to his court to proselytize, and Kublai, liking what he heard of the Sakya interpretation of Buddhism, had himself initiated into it; his support thus marked the beginning of Mongolian and Chinese interference in Tibetan affairs. In contrast, the other ascendant sect, the Kargyupa, remained influential largely because of the moral examples set by its charismatic founders, Marpa (who under Atisha's influence made repeated trips to India to study and bring back books) and Milarepa, the finest of Tibet's poets. An ascetic who lived in caves clad only in a thin cotton garment and subsisting on a diet of raw nettles, Milarepa appealed greatly to Kawaguchi, and the latter was to write about him in his *Himaraya no Hikari* ("The Light of the Himalayas").

Growing wealth and power, rather than doctrinal differences, were the cause of increased rivalry between the sects, and the monasteries began to arm themselves and fortify their buildings; outbreaks of violence, particularly between the dominant Sakyapa and members of the Kargyupa faction, gave vent to a traditional hot-bloodedness that Buddhism had only partly tamed. But in time Sakyapa rule, dependent as it was on the military backing of the Mongols, disintegrated as Mongolian power waned, leaving Tibet again without a central administration. Monastic discipline slackened; the more degenerate Tantric practices revived at the expense of scholarship.

It was at this low ebb that another reformer—another incarnation of

Manjusri—took the situation in hand. Tsong Khapa was born at the end of the fourteenth century in a country tired of internecine warfare, and his new Gelupa or "Virtuous Order," which was grafted onto Atisha's original sect and to a large extent replaced it, had immediate appeal. (The ceremonial hats worn by its monks earned it the name "Yellow Hat Sect," while the Nyingmapa, Sakyapa, and Kargyupa have become known collectively, if not entirely accurately, as the "Red Hat Sects.") Characterized by celibacy, hard study, and abstention from alcohol, the "Yellow Hats" also maintained a strict avoidance of political involvement, at least in the early stages of their rapid development; and when eventually, over two centuries later, the sheer size and organization of this order did bring it power, its popularity helped it to acquire a lasting authority.

One of the early problems the sect faced was that of unifying its leadership. Unlike the Sakyapa, whose abbots were obliged to marry and produce heirs, the Gelupa's vows seemed to preclude the possibility of a dynasty. The problem, however, was solved by an interesting adaptation of the doctrines of reincarnation. Since all beings die and are reborn, and since Bodhisattvas specifically choose not to enter nirvana in order to assist the living, it was judged that such spiritually advanced beings should be able to predict and, to some extent, control where their rebirth will occur. They would thus be available in a next life to take up the burdens that an aging body forced them to leave behind in this one. This was the origin of Tibet's tulkus, or incarnate Bodhisattvas; and the most important figure in the Gelupa sect came to be thought of, not merely as a man, but as the earthly manifestation of Chenrisig, or Avalokiteshvara in Sanskrit—the Bodhisattva of Compassion.

Not that the idea of a line of incarnations was new in Tibet: the heads of the Karmapa, a subsect of the Kargyupa, which was to have a long rivalry with the Gelupa (and has gained numerous Western followers in recent years), form the oldest line of tulkus. But the one established to preside over the "Yellow Hats," and ultimately the entire nation, became the most famous—and a source of intense curiosity for early explorers. Outside Tibet, those who inherit this position are generally known by the Mongolian title of Dalai Lama (meaning "Great

Chenrisig, the Bodhisattva of Compassion.

Ocean," with "of Wisdom" implied), though the Tibetans themselves invariably refer to them as the Gywalya Rimpoche, or "Precious King."

Shortly before an incumbent dies he is expected to leave some indication of where to look for him in his next incarnation. After an interval of several years a search is then begun for a male child of the right age with thirty-two bodily signs indicating his supernatural nature. Since there is likely to be more than one child who fits all the requirements, and because different factions at court may for their own reasons support one or the other, as a final test the boy—around two or three years old at the time—is asked to pick out articles that belonged to the previous Dalai Lama from among similar but slightly different ones.

After passing these various tests, he then has to be confirmed by the State Oracle. The child's education begins immediately if he is recognized as authentic, though he usually remains at home in the care of his parents until the age of about five, when he is taken to Lhasa to be raised in the monastic tradition.

All important monasteries are headed by tulkus, and several thousand of these incarnations are to be found among the Mongolians and Tibetans (as well as the Himalayan Buddhists of Nepal and India). The most eminent of them are chosen in much the same way as the Dalai Lama; lesser ones (like the wayward Alchu Tulku) through a simpler process subject to the approval of the Dalai Lama and sometimes the State Oracle.

The present Dalai Lama is the fourteenth to inherit the title. Obviously a system of this sort, in the hands of the unscrupulous and ambitious, is open to abuse and manipulation. One or two of the line have been suspect, some have spent most of their lives in exile, others never emerged from the shadow of the regent who wielded power when they were young, for the very nature of the system ensures that there are periods when the ruler is a child.

The first two Dalai Lamas were not known as such during their lifetimes, but were simply the leaders of Tsong Khapa's new sect (the first was his nephew). The title was bestowed on them posthumously by the third, who received it from his Mongolian allies. The fourth, logically enough, was a Mongolian prince. But it was not until the time of the fifth, remembered as the greatest of them all, that the Dalai Lamas established themselves as leaders of all Tibetan Buddhists. It was unfortunate, perhaps, that Mongolian military aid had to be called in to deal with secular and religious rivals, and that this also dealt a final blow to any independent secular power; nevertheless, he was able to establish a governmental system which, until it was violently overtaken by the twentieth century, worked remarkably well and to which— whatever its faults—the Tibetan people have shown a singular attachment.

The famous Potala palace, just outside old Lhasa, was also his creation. Though he died long before its completion, his chief minister (believed by many—vows notwithstanding—to have been the Fifth

Dalai Lama's natural son) was afraid that his death, if revealed, would reverse the progress they had made; so, using the plausible explanation—plausible in Tibet, at least—that the Dalai Lama was meditating in seclusion, he concealed the fact for nine years. Thus, when the building *was* finished and the lama's death announced, the government was faced with a search for a successor a good deal older than the usual toddler.

This led to one of the most attractive, yet tragic, episodes in Tibetan history. For the Sixth Dalai Lama was a profligate, inordinately fond of wine, women, archery, and verse—but popular with his people all the same. The problem was that he had been recognized when he was already twelve, and that he came from a Nyingmapa family, had never experienced monastic life, and was far more interested in sport than in religion. What the Gelupa hierarchy got, then, was an independent personality, unshaped by any early tutelage; and though he was scarcely the most capable, spiritual, or powerful of the lineage, he was certainly the most interesting, remembered chiefly for his nocturnal exploits and his love poems. The latter are almost as well known in Tibet as the very different poetry of Milarepa, and his favorite taverns and brothels have forever after been painted yellow in memory of his patronage. Unfortunately he came, not at a time of peace when the country could fully appreciate him, but of almost continuous struggle, both domestic and external, involving China and Mongolia. Reluctantly caught up in this, he was spirited away and probably murdered in 1704—though a persistent and hopeful legend has it that he escaped and lived out his life as a goatherd in Mongolia.

Not knowing when the Sixth Dalai Lama had died made the selection of his successor somewhat suspect. The most unfortunate result of the love poet's tenure, however, was that from then on the Chinese began to meddle actively in Tibetan politics, trying, among other things, to influence the choice of incarnations. The Dalai Lama's position consequently became a very risky one indeed. Few lived long past the age at which real responsibility was given them, and almost each time one died there were rival claimants supported respectively by the Chinese and Tibetans. It was not until the end of the nineteenth century, when the thirteenth incumbent—whom Kawaguchi was to meet in Lhasa—began his reign, that any of the line managed again not only to survive their teens but to grasp the reins of power.

The Thirteenth Dalai Lama's accession came at a critical moment in his country's history. Much to their indignation, the Tibetans had been treated for some time as a colony by China, and two Chinese envoys, called Ambans, had been stationed in Lhasa along with a number of troops. It was Chinese policy that had originally closed Tibet, but now—with the British encroaching on the Indian side, and the Russians eyeing this territory as an ideal base from which to harass the British—the Tibetans themselves decided that seclusion was their safest course.

This was the age of the Pundits, tramping the length and breadth of the country in disguise (counting paces on rosaries with a hundred beads, not a hundred and eight, and measuring altitude with special boiling-point thermometers concealed in walking sticks). But there was a further, less immediate reason for Tibetan paranoia, one symptomatic of a system stagnating after being too long in power. The Gelupa hierarchy had now enjoyed an almost absolute authority for roughly two hundred years, and the senior monks of the huge monasteries of Sera, Drepung, and Ganden were so accustomed to leadership that these institutions had come to be known as "the three pillars of the state." Power had not only corrupted but turned inward and bred a strong conservatism in place of the openness with which Father Desideri had been greeted in the Seventh Dalai Lama's time. These administrators, in the sincere belief that they were acting for the good of the country, were bitterly opposed to any change or influence from the outside world. And these were the "fanatical lamas" referred to in travelers' tales—an image as unrecognizable to Desideri's readers as to Westerners today who have found Tibetan monks in exile to be some of the friendliest and most accessible people in Asia.

It was into this lingering atmosphere of suspicion, both justified and imagined, that Kawaguchi headed on his way to Lhasa; and over the next year and a half there were only intermittent moments when he felt safe at all.

Across Western Tibet

Kawaguchi had a way of swinging between extremes. On the one hand he rather liked Tibetans, and he certainly had a knack for getting on with them when he wanted to; but certain places and events provoked inexplicably harsh invective: "The Tibetans," for example, "may indeed be regarded as devils that live on dung, being the most filthy race of all the people I have ever seen or heard of"—a tasteless remark he inserted in his description of Retapuri, where he wholeheartedly agreed with Atisha's name for the place ("Town of the Hungry Devils"). Yet what set him off had nothing to do with local customs—it was what he saw inside the temple: images of Padmasambhava and the Buddha set beside one another as equals, a sight so common in Tibet and northern Nepal that it is hard to believe he was being exposed to it for the first time.

> When I noticed the two images being worshiped side by side, a sensation of nausea came over me ... for Lobon[1] was in practice a devil in the disguise of a priest, and behaved as if he had been born for the very purpose of corrupting and preventing the spread of the holy doctrines of Buddha.

Here again Kawaguchi has simply let his emotions get the better of him. Of course he was being put through severe trials by little Dawa, who in her country-girl simplicity possibly looked to Padmasambhava for inspiration, or at least justification. But to be such a poor historian as to claim acquaintance with Padmasambhava's life and yet not recognize how instrumental he had been in establishing Buddhism in Tibet when all else had failed is inexcusable.

There was one other Padmasambhava image at Retapuri, one that had supposedly appeared spontaneously in the rock. Though natural images of this sort are not uncommon hereabouts, pilgrims and worshipers were afraid to look this one in the face, for fear of going blind. Kawaguchi, however, was of course careful to give it a good stare—and perhaps the battle-scarred old demon chaser stared back, amused by this irate little monk, since Kawaguchi seemed a bit subdued by the experience. Not subdued enough to put in a good word for his nemesis, but enough to make the surprising comment that "such frauds are not unknown in Japan"—a rare criticism in English of his homeland.

Almost as though ashamed of himself for his outburst in the temple (where he stayed two nights), Kawaguchi was lavish in his praise of the natural wonders he found on a tour of the neighborhhood, including some hot springs nearby which must have sorely tempted him. But since the real object of his visit—the holy circuit of Mt. Kailash—still lay ahead, he soon returned to his companions' tents (a short walk which, owing to his defective homing instinct, took him almost all day and sent him to bed on an empty stomach). These circuits, or *khora* (*parikarma* in Sanskrit), are one of the chief pastimes in Tibet. They are always done in a clockwise direction—the way the earth turns and prayer wheels spin—except by followers of the Bon, who observe similar rituals but move in the opposite direction.[2] The circular tour of the stupa at Boudha, where Kawaguchi had made his plans in the company of beggar pilgrims, is one of the most famous of these khora, as are the two holy circuits known as the Barkhor and Lingkhor in Lhasa. Kawaguchi was now about to embark on the most celebrated and arduous of them all.

The party of pilgrims split up temporarily so that each, according to his or her strength, could do as many circuits as possible. The outer route which they were all to take, and which was indeed the only one tackled by ordinary mortals, was estimated by Kawaguchi to be fifty miles in circumference (Sven Hedin was later to put it at twenty-eight), and it rises at the Dolma La to well over eighteen thousand feet. It would take the Japanese four days to complete, and even so he had to do the most difficult parts by yak. In the same amount of time, and on foot, the Tibetan men of his party hoped to complete three circuits, and the women two.

There were two other khora inside, and though shorter they were much higher—on the face of the mountain itself—and much more challenging. Only pilgrims who had done the outer route twenty-one times could get permission from the chief priests of the temples along the way to do the middle circuit. Those who went to all this trouble were devout enough to be careless of their lives, as the middle course was so dangerous that many died in the undertaking. The innermost and highest route was considered fit only for supernatural beings.

At the north, east, south, and west points of the outer route were the Four Temples of Kang Rimpoche (the Tibetan name for the holy mountain). These had at one time all belonged to the Drukpa sect, a subsect of the Kargyupa which has survived only in Bhutan. Though by Kawaguchi's time they had been absorbed by other sects, their revenue was still channeled to the court of Bhutan. The temple with the largest income (about $5000 during the three months of the summer pilgrimage season), located to the west of the mountain, was dedicated to the Buddha Amitabha and was the first that Kawaguchi visited. Surprised to find a parallel with his own country, where temples devoted to Amitabha were equally well endowed, he was also impressed by the Tibetan workmanship of the central image, which awoke in him "pious thoughts."

The scenery in the "Golden Valley" beyond was overwhelming (he tells us there were at least seven waterfalls over a thousand feet high), and for once Kawaguchi found himself unable to record it to his satisfaction in verse. The second night he spent in the northern temple—"the Place of the Female Yak Horn"—where he got on so well with the chief priest that he thought they had an affinity from a previous life (the affinity was helped by "a cup of tea with plenty of butter in it, for I had told him that I made it a rule to dispense with the evening meal"). The priest also lent him his own room with a southern view toward Kailash, bathed in moonlight, and here Kawaguchi's earlier pre-Retapuri mood returned as he passed the night in one of his mystical transports. So taken was he with the place and with his new friend that he spent the whole of the next day there.

The most taxing part of the journey lay directly ahead—the climb to the 18,600-foot Dolma La (which Kawaguchi calls "the Hill of Salvation")—and his kind host lent him a yak for this purpose. Even so, by the time he reached the crest he was suffering from severe symptoms of altitude sickness. Yet even on this pass he observed sturdy pilgrims prostrating their way around the mountain. This is an extreme form of religious penance practiced in Tibet. It is often called by Western writers (happily with more accuracy than "Red Hat Sects" or "living Buddhas") "measuring one's length upon the ground," and it can be seen on all the holy circuits. There is a kind of standard uniform for those prostrating themselves, consisting of a long apron and a pair of wooden hand sandals—the latter because their hands spend as much time on the ground as their feet. The action involves lying at full length, arms stretched out before one's head, and touching the earth with one's forehead. As this is done, the wooden sandals make a distinctive clacking and scraping noise in sliding forward. Some people do so much of this that they can be recognized by the large calluses on their foreheads. The most devout undertake long journeys in this manner: trips from remote areas to Lhasa, or across western Tibet to Kailash. And others spend years of their lives working their painful way around holy circuits like the Barkhor or the Lingkhor in Lhasa.

But the most interesting pilgrim Kawaguchi ran across was a Khampa who was asking forgiveness not only for the sins he had already committed but for those he would undoubtedly commit in the future. His prayer was something Kawaguchi thought worth translating:

> "O Saint Kang Rimpoche! O great Shakyamuni! O all Buddhas and Bodhisattvas in the ten quarters of the world and in the time past, present and future! I have been wicked in the past. I have murdered a number of men. I have taken a great deal that did not belong to me. I have robbed husbands of their wives. I have quarreled ever so many times, and I have also thrashed people. Of all those great sins I repent, and so I solemnly perform my penance here on this hill for them. I believe that by this act of confession and repentance, I have been absolved from these sins. I also perform here penance for my prospective sins, for I may in future repeat them, may rob people of their goods and wives, or thrash and beat them."

This original form of atonement, however, was more than just a curiosity, as it served to remind the traveler that his own companions were very likely to be of the same stamp ("These were . . . people who took other men's lives with the same equanimity with which they cut their vegetables" is how he put it), and that in a few days, when they were no longer on holy ground, their attitude toward him could be expected to change.

At the highest point on the pass he found a natural stone image of Tara (Dolma in Tibetan—hence the name of the pass: the Dolma La), whom he calls rather oddly "the mother of the Savior." "Mother of Salvation," which he uses later, is a little better, but perhaps "Redemptrix" would be better still. She is a female deity who in her twenty-one manifestations symbolizes different aspects of compassion, and other rock formations visible from the pass were meant to represent all twenty-one forms. Tara was born from the tears of the same Bodhisattva of Compassion, Chenrisig, as is found so frequently in Tibetan mythology, and who is incarnated as the Dalai Lama. Chenrisig once vowed to release all sentient beings from suffering, and wept when after working at it for some time he found that their numbers were in no way reduced. Though he never succeeded in his aim, Tara sprang from his tears to help him. By far her most popular manifestations are the Green and White Taras, personifying the active and motherly features of compassion respectively, and we have already noted that the Nepalese and Chinese queens of King Srontsan Gampo were regarded as their incarnations.

After descending from the pass, Kawaguchi arrived at the third temple—to the east of the mountain—called Zun-tul Phuk, or "the Cave of Miracles," one of the many caves in Tibet and northern Nepal associated with Milarepa. Rather surprisingly he devotes far less space to this temple and Milarepa, for whom he had unreserved admiration (". . . he did much to diffuse the true tenets of Buddhism. He was also a great poet. . . . His biography . . . reads like a romance or great epic, full of sublime conceptions"), than he does to Retapuri and Padmasambhava.

He says nothing at all about the last temple, Gyang-tak Gompa, which he visited briefly before arriving at the post station of Darchen Tazam, a sizable town for that part of the country, consisting of about thirty stone houses located just to the north of and between lakes Manasarovar and Rakas Tal. Here he rejoined his companions, and together they began the long easterly trek toward Lhasa.

Two days later, deciding they were no longer on hallowed ground, the men of the party announced that it was time for them to resume their worldly affairs—which they celebrated by shooting some deer. Obviously it was also time for Kawaguchi to think about separating himself from the family. The next day, when his hosts shot a wolf "merely for pleasure, not with the object of eating its flesh or using its skin," his shaky resolve was strengthened. Yet for some reason he held on for a while longer. He says he did not want to arouse suspicion, but he was even told bluntly by his hosts that as their pilgrimage was over he should take his leave. Did he, quite rightly, feel that taking his chances with a family of brigands was at least as safe as striking out on his own? Or was the affection lavished on him by little Dawa perhaps more of an attraction than he was willing to admit?

For it had now become a game in which both seemed to understand a set of unwritten rules. Dawa raised the bidding by fabricating a story to the effect that if the reluctant monk refused to marry her he would be killed by her uncle—and by making sure that the object of her affections overheard her discussing this with an aunt. Kawaguchi never makes it clear whether he actually believed the tale or not, but as he muses over this unexpected opportunity for martyrdom he seems more than merely eccentric: "I thought that if I should suffer death through having resisted a temptation, my death would be highly approved by the holy Founder. He would be displeased if I should disobey my conscience for the mere fear of death."

At any rate, a few days later it was again arranged that the two should find themselves alone in the encampment. "I saw that a conspiracy was developing and that matters were growing quite critical." Dawa now confronted him directly with the yarn about a plot to force him into marrying her. He had already prepared his answer, though, saying that threats were of no real concern to him, now that his pilgrimage was over.

I would not harbor any ill-will, even if I should be killed now by her

135

father and uncles. I should rather thank them for hastening my departure to the plane of the Bodhisattvas. . . . I would therefore ask to be killed that very evening.

Dawa, whose entire family apparently had been eavesdropping outside the tent, had probably been given one last chance to wrap up the affair one way or the other, and one can't help feeling sorry for her. Anyway, everyone now rushed into the tent at once. One of her uncles began abusing her for flirting; her father came to her defense; and this was the beginning of a brawl that ended, not with the death of the reluctant suitor, but with Dawa and her aunt in tears, the brothers pummeling one another with stones and fists, and poor Kawaguchi (who had made an ill-advised attempt to break the whole thing up) a "passive spectator . . . for I had to lie prostrate from the pain" after a good roundhouse punch to the jaw. Eventually the quarrel wound down without serious injury or death, but not before the brothers had confirmed Kawaguchi's worst fears by accusing one another of multiple robberies and murders.

This was to be the last night Kawaguchi spent in the tents of these robber pilgrims, and it was probably the only time since the first night that he was seriously worried for his safety, even though after the fight everyone was too drained emotionally and physically to do much harm. In the morning the group broke up, each brother going a different way, and Kawaguchi was again on his own with two new sheep. Selling him these almost worthless beasts for an exorbitant price was the only villainous thing this family did to the strange priest they had supported for six weeks, from August 2 to September 16 or 17. When he next met one of them it would be under very different circumstances indeed.

* * *

His first night alone was spent in the snow, and he discovered at once that even the rough comfort of the tents had softened him up. So, on the following day, when he happened upon a small monastery inhabited only by a couple of monks, he stopped for two days to rest. It now became obvious how bad his deal on the sheep had been, for one of them died here, and at a loss as to what else to do he read a service for it before giving the meat to four traders who were passing by. He also sold the survivor to them, though he could only get half what he had paid for it.

The traders were good enough to allow him to accompany them, and even to ride their yaks when he was tired; this made it possible to cross the Chema-yangdung-gi-chu, where he had nearly drowned, as well as the upper Tsang Po with no difficulty. It was getting cooler now, however, and the days were much shorter than they had been in July when he had passed this way before. The sun had lost much of its power, which meant that while there was less snow melting and the rivers were lower, it would be harder than ever to recover from a plunge in the water. The nights were a trial, as the traders had no tents.

After a few days he had to part with them since they were going in a different direction, and though he had formed no close personal bonds this time, the prospect of traveling alone again plainly frightened him. The next three chapters of his book reflect this feeling: "An Ominous Outlook," "A Cheerless Prospect," and "At Death's Door."

> . . . I was again thrown on my own wits and my own legs for continuing my journey. After having travelled for so many days with the help of other people, I had now to travel alone with nothing but my back on which to carry my effects, and my journey on the following day was a cheerless and fatiguing one. The load weighed heavily upon my back, and the time I occupied in taking rest was perhaps longer than that spent in actual progress. At last I was so much exhausted that I could hardly move my limbs.

But he was not in an entirely uninhabited region, and before quite succumbing to the rigors of the journey he saw a man with a yak coming his way and begged a lift for his luggage.

Soon afterward, however, he had his first experience of highwaymen (except, of course, as one of them). His newfound companion fled and hid at the sight of them, but Kawaguchi thought it would be safer to confront them head-on—or perhaps just felt too weak to run away. Seeing that he was a poor priest who probably had little worth stealing, they asked him instead for a divination that would direct them to some wealthy traders. Apparently unscrupulous monks often made a good living out of this sort of activity, so Kawaguchi cooked up some bogus ceremony, and sent them in the direction he thought least likely to be rewarding. It was a fair enough exchange, since he was not paid for his services.

That night and the next he slept in the tent belonging to the man with the yak, then set off on his own again after buying a goat from him. Since leaving Dawa and her family he had spent only two days by himself, and each had taken him two days to recover from. At this rate it would be a very long road to Lhasa.

With his usual luck he was now overtaken by a snowstorm. Soaked to the skin and unable to see, he staggered on until a horseman came to his rescue and kindly led him to a cluster of four or five tents, where he spent the night. But here the pattern of things changed. Usually, as a priest, he was made welcome and allowed to repay any hospitality he received by preaching and reading the scriptures aloud, and though his rescuer left early in the morning, Kawaguchi naturally assumed that he would spend the next night with the same people. For some reason, perhaps feeling in a meditative mood, he spoke to no one else in the party for the rest of the day but followed them after they struck camp and moved on—only to discover that in the evening no one would allow him inside. At the last tent an old woman even chased him out with a pair of fire tongs.

Despairing, he sat in the cold wind near the tents and in a typical gesture began to chant the scriptures, praying for the souls of these unfriendly people. Luck, or karma (or perhaps a little more cunning than he is willing to admit), now came to his aid, for his chanting was misinterpreted as an attempt to conjure up evil spirits to punish them, and so alarmed were the occupants of the last tent that in the end they invited him in just to keep an eye on him. "A Buddhist service was held that evening," he remarks dryly.

Though he was probably happy to get away from his unobliging hostess the next morning, his departure let him in for what soon became the most harrowing adventure of his entire journey—one that made his earlier ordeals seem like mere rehearsals. It began with his getting robbed, and a very odd robbery it was, for the whole episode seems to have passed off in a casual, almost friendly manner. When the two thieves had gone through his belongings, taken his money and food, and returned his holy books and bedding, for some reason he mentioned the silver pagoda he was carrying on his person as a present to the Dalai Lama. He warned them that as laymen they would not know how to handle it and could only expect bad luck if they took it. This unnerved the superstitious bandits and they refused to even touch it, though they accepted its blessing willingly enough. Now there was a custom that Kawaguchi had heard about for Tibetan robbers to leave their victims with three days' worth of provisions—provided the victim had the presence of mind to ask for them, and to "read the Texts." Having softened them up by blessing them with the pagoda, however, he was just about to ask for the traditional allowance of food when horsemen appeared in the distance, causing the robbers to panic and flee. But no help was at hand, as the horsemen approached no nearer, and the only consolation he was left with was that his much lighter luggage could all be carried by the goat. On the other hand, he had not yet taken his meal that day and his supplies were gone. When evening came he spent the night huddled between two rocks.

There was supposed to be a post town not far to the northeast, and this now became Kawaguchi's goal, but since he somehow turned due south it is hardly surprising that he never reached it. Snow began to fall at around 3:00 P.M.. Cold and very hungry, he survived the night with the help of breathing exercises. The next day, arriving at the Kyang Chu River, he recognized an area through which he had previously passed and where he remembered spending some time with herdsmen, which raised his spirits. But there was no one to be seen, and nothing to eat except snow. All the same, he still hoped that, after fording the river, he might find his old friend Alchu Tulku somewhere thereabouts.

The river was frozen, though not thickly enough to support him, so he had to break the ice and wade. He divided the luggage for the crossing, and the goat managed to lose its portion, leaving only the bedding and the holy texts. On the far bank of the river came snow blindness accompanied by a terrible pain in the eyes. Snow began to fall again in the late afternoon. That night, bundled in his blanket and attempting to meditate, he was racked by chills, until gradually his body turned completely numb. At this of all times he was inspired to write a poem. It was not one of his best:

> Upon these plains of snow, my bed is snow,
>   My pillow snow; my food also the same;
> And this my snowy journey, full of pain.

But it did help sustain him through that dreadful night, "and I felt more than ever thankful for the beauty of the Japanese language."

The third day after the robbery dawned sunny, bringing little enough warmth but fresh torture for his eyes. He could not see at all and he was so weak (it was now his fourth day without food) that he kept tripping and falling on tiny pebbles. At last, when all seemed lost, salvation appeared in the form of a lone horseman.

It would seem obvious that anyone clawing his way through the snow would be in need of help, yet the rescue was effected in as strange a way as the robbery had been four days earlier. Though apparently concerned and full of sympathy, instead of mounting Kawaguchi on his horse the man simply threw him some sweets made of milk and brown sugar, directed him to his tent about two miles off, then rode on ahead to prepare a proper welcome. It took poor Kawaguchi three hours to cover those two miles, and he staggered into camp to a festive meal of rice with butter and raisins.

If, as seems probable, he in fact broke his rule of not eating after midday, he can certainly be forgiven, for another night of fasting would undoubtedly have killed him; anyway, he had long since lost his watch. He tells us that he arrived at about eleven o'clock, but he had already been crawling along for some time before the horseman found him, and it then took him several more hours to reach the tents. In any event, he found himself unable to swallow much of the rich food; sleep was also impossible because of the pain in his eyes.

Nor had fortune quite had its fill of him yet. It was almost as if Kawaguchi himself were going over a checklist: robbery, exposure, starvation, snow blindness; now what else could possibly go wrong? Well, he had not yet been attacked by guard dogs.

His hosts, being pilgrims, had arranged to move on again the next day, and in the morning, still weak and blind, as he waited for them to strike camp he tottered about among the four or five other tents. There he was set upon by the usual pack of ferocious mastiffs. Too feeble to defend himself, he went down under their onslaught. Luckily the people in this camp were much friendlier than the ones who had only reluctantly taken him in five days before. Men drove off the dogs with stones, and as he lay there bleeding heavily an old lady brought him some medicine "which she said was a marvellous cure for such wounds."

Now, as countless travelers have pointed out, there is something perversely comforting about hitting rock bottom. If Kawaguchi was not to die then and there, things simply had to get better.

> It was impossible for me to stand up. But as it was equally impossible that I should lie down there forever, I asked the people what they would advise me to do, and if they did not know the whereabouts of Alchu Lama, whom I thought to be in that vicinity.

This occasioned some excitement, since the lama was well known as a physician and was supposed to be not far off. Someone volunteered to take him on a horse.

He was first taken to the wrong encampment—that of Alchu Tulku's father-in-law—and here, to his surprise, he was greeted by the "beautiful rescuer" of several months past.

> "Where is your Lama?" I asked.
> "He lives about two miles east of this place."
> "I wish to find him. Have you no one to take me to him?"
> "I have nothing to do with the Lama any more, nor can I take you. But if you want to go there, I will direct the man who has brought you here to accompany you."
> "But why do you not yourself return to your own home?"
> "Oh, there is no man so wicked as he; I intend to leave him."
> "That is not good," said I.

Apparently relations between husband and wife had not improved since Kawaguchi had left them quarreling bitterly.

Over lunch, which was the first substantial meal he had had for five days, they had a good long talk, and then he was conveyed to his friend's tents. There—though Kawaguchi would later be quite disparaging about traditional Tibetan medicine—Alchu Tulku's treatment was fully successful in curing both his eyes and a mauled leg. It is interesting that he was given purgatives (though there can have been little enough to purge after a period of near starvation) "in order to prevent the diffusion throughout my system of poison which some of the dogs injected by their bites." This sounds like a rough-and-ready—but plausible—precaution against rabies.

As soon as he felt up to it he asked about the lama's domestic problems. Unfortunately we are not told all the details, but Kawaguchi seems to have thought that once the vows had been broken in the first place, it would only be a further mockery of them for the couple to part. And so instead of trying to reimpose celibacy on his friend, who at this juncture might well have seen the point of it, he set about repairing their relationship. He began by convincing the lama that a husband should be "charitable" to his wife, and made him so ashamed of himself that he sent two servants to bring her back. She returned "after making some fuss."

Kawaguchi was definitely recovering, as he now proposed to preach to the couple from the "Discourses on the Five Vices." This is a Japanese text of the Jodo Pure Land sect and unknown in Tibet, but it was obviously one that recommended itself to Alchu Tulku and his wife, treating as it did "all imaginable sins and vices conceived by mankind." As always he knew just how to suit his sermon to his listeners. Soon, of course, there were tears, a great many of them: tears of gratitude, joy, and remorse.

Our Japanese wanderer stayed with his friends for ten days, and was pleased to be able to repay the lama's kindness by reconciling him with his wife. Once again he had bounced back from the brink of death and regained both his health and his spirits. Things were looking up. He had made it all the way to Kailash and back to near his starting point in Tibet. Now all he had to do was get to Lhasa.

* * *

When the time came for Kawaguchi to take his leave of the couple, the three decided to go together as far as the cave of another old friend, Gelong Rimpoche. Here, after saying goodbye, Kawaguchi had a private chat with the recluse—and a very disturbing chat it was, for it seemed that Gelong Rimpoche had seen right through him.

There was obviously something wrong with Kawaguchi's disguise. He could get away with it for short periods, but after a while suspicions always arose. This seems to have had less to do with any deficiencies in his Tibetan than with the attitudes he expressed, since he was no more capable of keeping silent here than he had been in Japan, and, as we have seen, he was unable to conceal his disgust with Padmasambhava and some of the practices of Tibetan Buddhists. The two talked in riddles, a system they had developed during their first meeting, but the gist was that there were rumors all over the western plains about the "Chinese lama" who had just made a pilgrimage to Mt. Kailash; and these rumors made him out to be, not Chinese at all, but English.

Now, the recluse seemed quite fond of his visitor and had no intention of turning him in, but he did hint at the dangers ahead and advised him strongly to return to Nepal through Lo; and indeed if Kawaguchi had returned at this point, it would have involved no loss of honor. His pilgrimage had certainly been arduous enough. He had done a complete circuit of Mt. Kailash, had seen the summer markets of Gya-nima and Gya-karko, and had spent three and a half months in disguise and on intimate terms with nomads and pilgrims—not to mention his fifteen months in forbidden Nepal. But all his suffering in the end had only whetted his appetite for more adventure. There was too much he had not seen to turn back now. Ahead lay the ancient capital and fortified monastery of Sakya; the huge monastery of Tashi Lhumpo, home of the Panchen Lama, and Shigatse, Tibet's second city; the mysterious Yamdruk Tso, or Turquoise Lake, one of the highest lakes in the world; and of course the wonders of Lhasa itself. Nothing was going to stop him now but physical coercion or death.

The two priests talked until well into the evening, and by then Kawaguchi was convinced he had got rid of Gelong Rimpoche's suspicions, for the lama loaded him down with provisions and even gave him twenty *tankas* (about $2.50) in Tibetan silver. More important still, he performed a mysterious initiation ceremony for Kawaguchi's benefit—

the sort of thing we would expect him to disapprove of, but for which he seemed genuinely grateful.

In fact it seems most likely that the shrewd old hermit was convinced not so much of the traveler's identity as of his sincerity. Kawaguchi may not have been entirely credible as the person he claimed to be, but he was even less so as a spy. A devout Tibetan Buddhist like Gelong Rimpoche (particularly one far removed from any conservative monastic center) could probably see little reason to keep a devout foreign Buddhist out of Tibet. Besides, it was obvious that the pilgrim would not be dissuaded, so why not help rather than hinder this dedicated believer?

There were two ways from here to Lhasa: the highroad, which was easier but more roundabout, and the mountain road, which was shorter. Gelong Rimpoche recommended the mountain road because many of his followers lived along it, and when they saw the provisions carried in a bag of his they would be only too happy to help the pilgrim on his way. Much as this might have eased the journey physically, Kawaguchi felt it was better to go by the more anonymous highroad, in view of all the rumors about him.

The good luck that had for so long deserted him while on the march now returned, and he always found tents to lodge in. In fact his first night out found him again in the company of Alchu Tulku, who had been so impressed with the sermon on the Five Vices that he was going around telling his friends about it. Alchu happened that night to be staying with a friend in a tent right in Kawaguchi's path, so he was detained to preach.

And now suddenly his spirits are as high as they ever have been, and his health so improved that a breast-deep river crossing, where the sandy bottom kept sucking his feet down, is barely rated a mention. But he became overconfident, made the mistake of not following directions, and as a result very nearly landed himself again in serious difficulties. The episode—his last comic scene before finding the highroad to Lhasa—ranks among his best.

Rather than listening to the wisdom of the local inhabitants, he tried what looked like a shortcut and soon found himself in the middle of a stretch of mud flats, narrow streams, and bogs. In attempting to cross one bog about four yards wide which did not appear very deep, he became mired in quicksand. He rapidly got rid of all his baggage, which he was just able to throw to higher ground. Then throwing dignity to the winds as well he wriggled out of all his clothes, so that he was floundering about stark-naked—and by this time almost flat on his face. Slowly, with the help of his sticks, he managed to work himself erect. Then, standing on one stick which he had laid flat, he used the other to maneuver himself to the bank . . . and he was home—not dry, but safe. After wringing out his clothes, the bog acrobat went cheerfully, and rather proudly, on his way—only to find that he had been in sight of a tent all along. From the tent the highroad itself was visible, but so, presumably, had been his naked antics.

By the standards of most of the world he was still in the wild, for until the Chinese occupation in the 1950s roads in Tibet were nothing more than beaten tracks (indeed most are little better even today); but being on the main route allowed him to relax a bit. Even Kawaguchi was unlikely to get lost, there were frequent travelers, and post towns appeared every four or five days. It may not exactly have been the old Tokaido, but it was security to cling to.

There were pleasant surprises as well. One day he came across a tent set up as a chang shop seemingly in the middle of nowhere. The little tavern, which served the ubiquitous beer of Tibet, had been installed to cater to a salt, wool, and cattle fair, and the proprietress happened to be an old friend from Tsarang. (As he traveled eastward Kawaguchi would be moving nearer and nearer Lo, and this temporary market was a link in the famous salt trade that had enriched the Thak Khola Valley and especially the Thakalis of Tukche.)

It was through her that he was introduced to one of the most important people in the district, an old man called Gyal Bum, who offered him lodging. And it was while staying as his guest that the monk again suffered from internal hemorrhaging and began coughing blood (the altitude, he reckoned, was over fifteen thousand feet). Luckily this was known as an affliction that often beset Chinese pilgrims, thus doing his disguise no harm. His host, moreover, had a traditional remedy that soon put him back in shape, marking the third time in the last couple of weeks that his life may have been saved by Tibetan medicine.

In spite of their wealth (they owned two thousand yaks and five hundred sheep, yet lived in tents), both Gyal Bum and his elderly wife were more interested in the next world than in this, and they invited their newfound "Chinese lama" to spend the winter preaching and reading the texts. But Kawaguchi, besides worrying about his health and the persistent rumors that followed him, feared that a winter in this high place would be more than he could bear at the best of times, so he did not stay.

Here on the highroad he was almost never short of company. Opportunities for more heroic exploits also came his way:

> It was a sandy swampy country, and after some four *ri* (ten miles) we came to a plain of soft white sand which was very tiring to the feet, so that I thankfully accepted [the] offer of a bare-backed horse. I am not a good horseman, but I trotted on bravely for a while, till the pain in my hip-bone became unbearable. Then I changed my position and rode sideways, like a lady, but then my legs began to hurt me, so I jumped off at last and resumed my journey on foot.

Another river crossing—again through a half-frozen current, as it was now the end of October—brought him to the largest settlement he had seen since leaving Marpha: the trading, administrative, and monastic center of Tradun. Though there are only about twenty permanent buildings in the town, and only a dozen monks in the impressive monastery said to contain the hair of seven Buddhas, Tradun must have seemed quite a metropolis after the past five months. This is the way he would have come from Lo had he stuck to his original plan, and he had now returned to a point just sixty miles north of Tsarang where he could expect to meet any number of acquaintances. Yet, oddly enough, though the shapes of Annapurna and Dhaulagiri were quite recognizable from here, and even after meeting his old friend at the chang shop, he did not seem to realize just where he was.

Thus he was caught unawares when, after looking over the gompa, he ran smack into one of the men he probably least wished to see: a notorious drunkard and gambler from Tsarang who had often accused him of being a British spy during his stay there. But Kawaguchi was now becoming quick-witted. This was no longer the innocent monk who had left Japan almost four years before. Composing himself, he greeted the man with a smile, and surprised him further by suggesting they celebrate their reunion with a little drink. Not that he himself would have anything, of course, but he would happily treat an old friend.

> Ordering my landlord to bring a large quantity of the best liquor I plied him with drink until four in the morning. I did not take anything myself, but made believe to be drunk. After many glasses I got him dead drunk, and he fell asleep. I also pretended to sleep. But as soon as the landlord awoke at about half past five, I also rose and told him that the man lying there was a dear friend of mine, and that I would have him treated with the best liquor whenever he awoke, and that he was never to let him go out of the house. If he should ask for my whereabouts, he was to be told that I had gone towards Tsarang. With these orders I paid my bills, tipped the landlord liberally, and set out on my journey at six o'clock.

He knew that he had to move fast, for he was not quite sure how thoroughly his drunken "friend" would fall for the bait. If he awoke sober enough to think of the reward that might be his for turning in a spy, then Kawaguchi could well be in trouble. But his luck held and he was overtaken by a large caravan—eighty or ninety horses and sixteen men—led by two trader monks. That evening he spoke with the leaders, asking for permission to accompany them, and was confronted by yet another Chinese speaker. He tried fobbing him off with his usual "Foshee dialect" ruse, and it was perhaps fortunate that this time the man was literate as well as articulate in Chinese, since Kawaguchi's story was not believed until he had read and explained a number of characters—and of course at this he excelled.

There followed a grilling on Tibetan Buddhism and grammar, the latter being of absorbing interest to one of the caravan leaders. Again Kawaguchi had occasion to be grateful for the excellent, if violent, tuition he had received from Serab Gyaltsen in Tsarang, because he so impressed the wealthy monks with his answers that they offered to hire him as a grammar instructor. Though the caravan got off to a hurried start every morning, it stopped each day at two in the afternoon to allow the animals to graze. With a crowd of servants to take care of practical matters there was plenty of time for cultured debate and study, so finding a lone scholar here in the back of beyond was probably an ideal diversion. The caravan had already come all the way from the border areas near Ladakh with dried pears, silk, raisins, and woolen goods, which they hoped to trade for tea, scroll paintings, and Buddhist images in Lhasa—provided they could avoid being plundered by highwaymen between here and Lhatse, about three weeks away. Time undoubtedly hung heavy for the more educated during the long afternoons.

It was on November 2 or 3 that Kawaguchi took up with the caravan, and he would remain with it until the twenty-fourth when they successfully reached Lhatse. As a member of a large and fairly swift-moving group which covered between twenty and twenty-five miles a day, kept away from towns for the sake of grazing, and contained no women, everything would have been perfect for Kawaguchi had it not been for the jealousy and suspicion of one unpleasant companion. He was in the company of this "pedantic monk" quite a lot, because they were the only two in the whole caravan who were on foot, and they would set out together early in the morning to be overtaken by the main body later. Like Kawaguchi, he was only a hanger-on: a poor scholar monk on his way to Lhasa to pursue his studies. Having a high opinion of himself, he was unhappy about this new companion's superior knowledge, particularly of grammar—a subject of which he himself was totally ignorant. In the evening around the dung fire in the tent he would bait the newcomer, for he was also ignorant enough to suspect him of being an Englishman.

The story of Chandra Das's escapades over two decades before was, of course, well known to all Tibetans and lost nothing in the retelling. It now became a favorite theme of Kawaguchi's rival, and we can imagine it awakening fresh horror in the warmth of a yak-hair tent on the steppes of central Tibet: the assembled monks, heads none too newly shaven and bundled in grubby fur-lined robes, craning forward to listen or to throw in opinions between loud sips of tea. Like children with a frightening fairy tale, they would thoroughly enjoy hearing again how twenty-three years ago the "vile Hindu" had "robbed Tibet of her Buddhism," which he had taken away with him to India. This would then involve an account of how Tibet's greatest scholar of the day, Senchen Dorjechan, tutor to the Panchen Lama, had been executed by drowning for having unknowingly assisted the traveler, and how he had bravely met his death, urging his nervous executioners to carry out their duty. And, as an ending, they would hear about the orgy of reprisals ordered by the conservative authorities, who deprived many of their property and imprisoned others for life. The whole episode had passed so far into legend as to become a tale recited by parents to frighten wayward offspring, with Das as the chief bogeyman, capable of the blackest of black magic.

Once the "pedantic monk" had baited Kawaguchi a few times, others began to join in, trying to make him admit that when in India he had made the acquaintance of the notorious Das. This, of course, was precisely what he had done, and one night he was nearly in despair, feeling "besieged by . . . the enemy," when help came almost miraculously from a very unexpected quarter. For Kawaguchi managed to think of interjecting into the discussion the question of who was greater: the Buddha or Padmasambhava. This being a topic Tibetans never tired of debating, attention was shifted from him to this more important matter. And here again one can't resist the idea of an amused Padmasambhava playing innocent games with Kawaguchi: he starves him, leads him in the wrong direction, nearly freezes him to death, puts temptations in his way, and almost exposes his secret—but never lets the final blow fall, and at times like this even comes to his aid. Like Gelong Rimpoche, he seems to feel that the game is too much fun to put an end to.

Kawaguchi's conceited adversary actually commanded little respect in the company, and once it became obvious that the newcomer's learning had found favor with the majority of the trader monks, even this would-be scholar saw there was little to be gained by remaining his enemy. Now left in peace, all Kawaguchi had to do was keep on his feet until around 2:00 P.M. every day, then give a lesson on Tibetan grammar, which was his favorite subject anyway. For river crossings there were horses to ride, and at nights there was a tent with a warm fire and plenty of bedding. If the fleas and lice that made sleep difficult for every traveler from Desideri to Heinrich Harrer were a problem, it was a problem too minor to be mentioned. They were still in wild country where bandits were a constant danger, but in the end they reached Lhatse and the more settled lands of Tsang without any mishaps.

Three incidents stood out on this three-week journey between Tradun and Lhatse. The first was seeing a rare wild yak, or *dongyak*. It was hardly surprising that later in Japan respectable academics who had never been any nearer Tibet than their university libraries found his description outrageous:

> Its size was twice or three times that of the domesticated animal, and it stood about seven feet high. It was smaller than the elephant, but its eyes looked dangerous. . . . Once I saw the dried and very large tongue of a young dongyak, which was being used as a brush for horses.

Yet this observation was to be fully vindicated. The dongyak does indeed exist,[3] and photographs taken by Sven Hedin a few years later showed it to be just this big.

Another incident was minor: Kawaguchi's first sight of cultivated fields in Tibet. This was on November 20, only a few days from Lhatse. He had now been in Tibet, and more or less constantly on the move, for five months, and though it was far too late in the year for anything to be growing, he must have experienced a feeling akin to sighting land after a long sea voyage.

It was near the same place that the third incident occurred, something that both deeply distressed him and so fascinated him that he has left us a detailed description. This was a visit to a collective slaughterhouse. Late autumn is the best time for butchering animals, not only because they are fattest then, but because the meat can be conveniently dried and frozen over the winter. Preserved meat is one of Tibet's staples, and the smaller animals like sheep and goats are kept whole (a practical, if grotesque, way of carrying them is to fit the abdominal cavity over one's forehead, and people wearing carcasses like hats are a common sight in and around Tibetan marketplaces).

Tibetans eat meat less for reasons of taste than out of sheer necessity; as Kawaguchi's experience so far confirms, there are not nearly enough fertile valleys to feed the population. Since the average Tibetan, moreover, will go to great lengths to avoid killing even an insect or a worm, we can hardly expect them to butcher sheep, goats, and yaks without some feeling of unease. One indication of this is that animals are not slaughtered in villages or near tents, but in common abattoirs that serve a large area and are removed from where people actually live. This explains why something like two hundred and fifty sheep and thirty-five yaks were being dispatched on the day Kawaguchi happened by.

While removing the scene of the slaughter from population centers might be dismissed as hypocritical, in other ways the operation Kawaguchi witnessed was carried out rather more humanely than in most other societies. Each animal had a prayer read to it and was blessed with a book and a rosary—to enable it to achieve a better incarnation—and was then swiftly beheaded with a single blow. Even so, the monk was overcome with pity. "What cruelty! how could I bear to see it? Desirous, however, of knowing something about the operations, I stood and watched the spectacle." His eyes filled with tears, and he fancied that he saw tears also in the eyes of a yak waiting to die in a pool of blood shed by its fellows. In the end, fascinated as he was, he had to turn away.

Arrival at Lhatse in Tsang province marked the transition from the wilds to what Kawaguchi calls the interior, for power and culture have always been centered in the two neighboring provinces of U and Tsang. At first he mistakenly called Lhatse the third metropolis in Tibet (he later corrected himself after visiting Gyantse), and by Tibetan standards it is a fairly large town. The Tsang Po Valley here is quite rich and contains some of the best-looking farmland on the Tibetan plateau, supplying the inhabitants with barley, wheat, beans, and butter at a lower price—we are told—than anywhere else in the country. It is also here that two important trade routes join: one from the west, which the caravan had been following, and the other from Solu Khumbu and Kathmandu in Nepal to the southwest.

Our traveler could well congratulate himself, as he was now within five days' journey of Shigatse. Yet here in the more inhabited regions, with larger and more famous monasteries, he could also expect to meet more sophisticated Tibetans than he had come across so far. Already he had noted a refinement in the speech of the four hundred inhabitants of a post town several days back. If he were not to give himself away—and he was always his own worst enemy—he would have to be more careful than ever.

1. Kawaguchi invariably used this name for Padmasambhava.

2. Ignorant tourists in Tibet, following ill-mannered Chinese guides, also make themselves conspicuous by doing everything in the wrong direction.

3. They have, however, been hunted to near extinction by the Chinese since 1959.

The Treasures of Tsang

Just what "Tibet" is and where it is located is not as simple a question as it might seem. Even the origin and meaning of the name (which, like "Japan," is used only by foreigners—the Tibetan word is *Bod*) is obscure. About the only thing on which everyone has always seemed to agree is that the provinces of U and Tsang lie at the heart of it all.

Perhaps the closest one can come to a traditional view of the country is to imagine a great invisible net encircling the scattered speakers of Tibetan dialects and the followers of Tibet's dominant religion—a net not physically but culturally confining, and held at the center by U-Tsang. The northern and western plains, inhabited primarily by nomads and pilgrims, though always very loosely administered, have remained under the nominal control of Lhasa (and subject to the fickle influence of small autonomous kingdoms). The more settled but politically distant border areas, from Amdo and Kham in the east, south through India's Arunachal Pradesh, west through Sikkim and northern Nepal to Spiti, Lahol, and Ladakh in northwestern India, might be called "emotionally Tibetan." None of the Tibetan-speaking Buddhists in this vast arc have ever objected very strongly to being outside Lhasa's jurisdiction (though the people of Kham and Amdo have always disliked the Chinese), but all feel the strong spiritual pull of Lhasa and the other great centers of their faith.[1]

These two outlying blocs combine with the focal area of U-Tsang to form "three Tibets"—a concept that at least provides a convenient way of looking at a complex political, geographical, and religious situation. It also may help explain why Kawaguchi was so loath to abandon his travels, as Gelong Rimpoche had suggested, on the western plains.

For he had now been to two Tibets: a year in the settled, semi-independent region of Lo, and six months in the nomadic west. And he now stood on the threshold of the third and most important: what the Jesuits referred to as "the country of Utsang," what the Chinese called "Weitsang," and what to Waddell was "Tibet proper."

But while to outsiders the provinces of U and Tsang may appear a single entity, they have always enjoyed a vigorous rivalry. U—with the capital, Lhasa; the three great monasteries of Drepung, Sera, and Ganden; the haunting Yamdruk Tso, or "Turquoise Lake"; and the Yarlung Valley, where the ancient kings dwelt and where Padmasambhava built the Samye monastery—has more often exercised the greater political power. Yet Tsang is the home of Shigatse and Gyantse, Tibet's second and third largest cities, the Tashi Lhumpo monastery, the fertile and properous Lhatse region, and the once powerful Sakya monastery.

Tsang has often taken advantage of weak regencies in Lhasa to assert itself, leading foreign observers to believe in a rivalry between Tibet's two greatest tulkus: the Dalai Lama of Lhasa, and the Panchen Lama of Shigatse. Their relationship is in fact a far more subtle one and has been sadly misunderstood by everyone from British and Chinese imperialists to Chinese Communists, who have tried to throw their weight behind one or the other in a power struggle usually irrelevant to most Tibetans, and even to the two lamas themselves.

Reaching Lhatse unscathed was a cause for general celebration among the members of the caravan. From here on they could feel relatively secure from brigands. Kawaguchi himself would probably have been happy with a thanksgiving prayer or two, and perhaps a recital of his "26 Desires," but the trader monks had a more lively form of celebration in mind: they stayed up all night at a party "enlivened by the presence of several girls." Beyond that simple description there is, refreshingly, no condemnation of the conduct of his companions.

Having come this far, Kawaguchi was anxious not to miss Sakya, so while the main body of the caravan continued on the direct route to Shigatse he made a detour, along with the caravan leader and one or two others. About fifteen miles south of the main trail, Sakya was just far enough out of the way to remain a mystery to the outside world.

One of the Pundits—No. 9—had passed through in 1872 but left no detailed description, and Das had had surprisingly little to say of his 1881 visit except that the town was a den of thieves and the cattle all had to be locked up at night; indeed, even as late as 1894, Waddell could still call it "undescribed." Kawaguchi was thus in a position to add a great deal to our knowledge of this secluded monastery, founded in 1071. If, however, he realized this, he gave no indication of it. Or perhaps in the light of the strange and hurried end to his stay there, he thought it better not to dwell on the opportunity he had missed.

The southern monastery (Kawaguchi does not even mention the 108 chapels of the northern part, across the river) is outranked in size only by the Potala in Lhasa. In contrast to most Tibetan temples, which are painted a cheerful white and trimmed with dark blue and red, its looming walls are a forbidding blue-gray, the dominant color of all the valley's dwellings; this is a wash produced from the local clay, the "blue earth" from which Sakya derives its name. It requires no great imagination to see this stronghold as the headquarters of a church militant that converted Kublai Khan and skirmished with the rival Kargyupa for several centuries.

Centuries of Mongol endowments, however, made Sakya the repository of enormous wealth, and it remained ostentatiously wealthy even after its political decline. The temple's main chamber (which survived the Cultural Revolution) is huge—a long rectangle, unlike the usual squarish format. The chanting of the monks, more varied and melodic than that of other sects, adds to its grandeur. Almost lost in the profusion of treasure is a thirty-five-foot image of Sakyamuni, coated in gold; and at first the Japanese pilgrim was overwhelmed: "Once inside we were lost in a sea of dazzling gold; the splendor was simply beyond description."

But soon his old Zen sense of discipline began to assert itself:

> The disorderly manner in which the images are arranged, however, greatly detracts from the impression produced by their intrinsic merits. The spectacle is a grand exhibition of Buddhist fine arts . . . but its effect is greatly impaired by the tasteless and excessive decorations.

Not everyone would agree with Kawaguchi's assessment, for there is a certain charm and fascination in the homely jumble of a Tibetan temple that is missing in the standardization and rather sterile orderliness of temples in Japan.

But once he was off there was no stopping him. This was the first big monastery he had visited, and he was promptly offended by a smell that is common to them. It is a compound of the burning butter in the lamps and the butter tea drunk by the monks, who throw the dregs on the floor, where they soon go rancid. This is one reason why shoes are not removed on entering a Tibetan temple: the floors are usually sticky with this residue (the other is that is often far too cold). The odor is powerful and all-pervading: "Strangely enough the Tibetans regard this smell as a sweet one, but I declare myself emphatically to the contrary."

These, however, are quibbles, and under normal circumstances Kawaguchi would have spend a good deal of time exploring the greatest of Sakya's treasures: its library, famed throughout Tibet. One of the sect's original tenets was that too much reliance on meditation at the expense of learning could lead to self-delusion rather than enlightenment—an attitude that coincided with Kawaguchi's own complaints about Zen. The result was an accumulation of works, apparently in both Tibetan and Sanskrit, some of them unique. All of Sakya's manuscripts were handwritten rather than printed, and most prized of all were those penned in gold and silver on huge, dark blue pages, six feet or more long, and said to have been prepared under the orders of Kublai Khan for Phagspa, the Sakya monk who converted him. (It may also be recalled that the scriptures Kawaguchi had obtained in exchange for his white horse were "penned by a Sakya Pandit.") But our hero's talent for behaving tactlessly precluded any study in this fabulous place. His first offense was committed in the presence of the sect's leader, to whose mansion he and his companions were invited— an honor by no means accorded to every visitor, and an indication of the respect in which the caravan leader must have been held.

In the eleventh century, when the sect was founded, theories of reincarnation had not progressed sufficiently for the head of the Sakyapa to be an incarnate lama, so that one of his duties was to marry and produce an heir. In theory, once the heir had been successfully provided, the lama was supposed to live separately from his wife; but, needless to say, theory and practice sometimes diverged. On the rare occasions when there was no heir the title had gone to the eldest nephew, ensuring that the Sakya Pandit—as he was called—remained a descendant of the founder. At one time a priest-king whose status was comparable to that achieved later by the Dalai Lamas, he was still treated with considerable respect by the Nyingmapa as well as his own adherents. Thus there were well-established rules on how he should be greeted: ". . . not only the public at large, but also priests salute him with the rite of 'three bows' [full prostrations on the floor] which as laid down by Buddha is a mark of reverence due only to high priests and not laymen." Kawaguchi, however, was not going to kowtow to anyone he considered undeserving, and the fact that his host was "married, takes meat for dinner, and even drinks wine, as do all secular people," meant that he received from this righteous monk "only such respect as would be due to a person of his [secular] rank." This deeply embarrassed Kawaguchi's companions, who were beginning to lose patience with their grammar teacher anyway. But worse, if possible, was to come.

The next day he went to call on the order's spiritual superior, responsible for the instruction of his five hundred charges, and head of the celibate branch of the Sakya hierarchy. Kawaguchi found him roughhousing with a little boy. To the ever-suspicious bachelor it appeared that the two were behaving like father and son. Though he was unable to confirm this suspicion until much later in Lhasa, he now threw one of his priggish tantrums and, instead of staying to study in what was probably Tibet's most comprehensive library, he was suddenly "loath to remain with such a degenerate priest." He left town the following day.

If we find ourselves a little irritated by this conduct, we are not alone, and a fascinating Tibetan reaction to the incident has been handed down by Alexandra David-Neel. Her story seems slightly garbled, but as she is known to have actually met Kawaguchi in Japan in 1915 or thereabouts, at the start of her own long quest for Lhasa, he may have told her a different version from the one given in his book. At any rate, the essentials are the same.

One day I related to a Lama the story of the Reverend Ekai Kawaguchi who, desirous of learning Tibetan grammar, had applied to a famous master. The latter belonged to the religious Order and gave himself out to be a *gelong*. After staying with him a few days the pupil discovered that his professor had transgressed against the law of celibacy and was the father of a little boy. This fact filled him with such profound abhorrence that he packed up his books and belongings and took his departure.

"What a booby!" exclaimed the Lama on hearing the anecdote. "Was the grammarian less skilled in grammar for having given way to the temptations of the flesh? What relation is there between these things and in what way did the moral purity of his professor concern the student? The intelligent man gleans knowledge wherever it is to be found. Is not that man a fool who refuses to pick up a jewel lying in a dirty vessel because of the filth adhering to the vessel?"[2]

It was still three or four days' walk to Shigatse, and as he had left Sakya in haste and without his companions, he was now on his own again. Fortunately in this well-inhabited country he soon fell in with

A prayer flag and stupa.

more traders who let him stow his bags aboard their pack animals. There were also a lot more interesting things to see here than on the barren western plains. One day, for example, he noticed five placid and well-fed vultures sitting contemplatively on a hillside. Asking about them, he was told that the most common way of disposing of the dead in Tibet was to cut up the corpse and feed it to vultures—an act of both practical and religious significance in a country short of firewood where the ground is frozen solid for most of the year, and where the body is thought of as nothing more than an insignificant repository for the spirit. But these birds were a little different, since not enough people died here to keep them fed—so they were allotted a meat ration from Shigatse's Tashi Lhumpo monastery. It is hard to think of another single act that so well sums up the character and the contradictions of the Tibetan people.

Within a day's march of Shigatse stood another of the treasures of Tsang: the monastery of Narthang, Tibet's main publishing house. Here in two buildings each measuring about sixty by a hundred and eighty feet were stored wooden printing blocks of all the Buddhist books in the country, both those translated from Pali and Sanskrit, and original Tibetan works. Kawaguchi makes no mention of where the blocks were carved, but tells us that the three hundred monks there were all printers, constantly engaged in filling orders. Printer monks, who wash no more than anyone else in Tibet, soon tend to become impregnated with the soot-based ink they use. Their robes are almost black, and their arms and faces become deeply stained, making them look like coal miners (Tibetan cooks have much the same appearance). The printing is all done by hand, a page at a time, by first spreading ink on the block, then smoothing the paper over it. The long rectangular sheets are then gathered between wooden covers—not bound but merely tied together, the loose pages being flipped over onto a separate pile when read (though, often enough, these handmade volumes remain objects of veneration, seldom opened). For Kawaguchi it must have been tempting simply to order one of everything, but of course he could never have carried them all; anyway, he was short of money after the robbery, and he would have risked being accused of "stealing Tibet's Buddhism." His manners here, in any case, seem to have improved, either because his mood at Sakya had passed, or because he was genuinely impressed by the priest in charge, who treated him hospitably and gave him "valuable information on Buddhism."

Another eight miles across a plain would bring him to Shigatse and the giant monastery of Tashi Lhumpo; but, before his arrival, it might be as well to take a look at the history of the Panchen Lamas, whose seat this monastery is, and about whom there have been so many misunderstandings.

* * *

There have only been about half as many Panchen Lamas as Dalai Lamas, the most recent being the seventh.[3] There are two reasons for this. One is that the title only dates from the time of the Fifth Dalai Lama, who conferred it on his tutor, declaring that he was the incarnation of Opame (Amithaba); and successive Panchen Lamas have often fulfilled the same tutorial function, though occasionally the role of teacher has been reversed. The second reason is that they have tended to live longer than the Dalai Lamas: despite Chinese efforts—as in recent years—to play the two hierarchs off against each other, the abbots of Tashi Lhumpo have usually been far less involved politically, and thus far less susceptible to poisoning.

It has been argued—again, by foreigners rather than by the Tibetans themselves—that, as the incarnation of Opame, the Panchen Lama outranks the incarnation of Chenrisig, since in the Mahayana pantheon the two traditionally have a teacher-student relationship. This is of course to ignore the obvious: that the very institution was created by a shrewd Dalai Lama who already had rivals enough without creating an office that transcended his own. And the question of who, in practice, was tutor to whom was largely an accident of age. It is safest to say that to the Tibetans both incarnations represent very holy figures: the Panchen Lama a more purely spiritual one, the Dalai Lama a fusion of the spiritual and political.

Being closer to India, and farther from the court in Lhasa, however, has meant that the Panchen Lamas have until recently been slightly more exposed to the outside world. While no Dalai Lama until the thirteenth had any significant contact with a Westerner (the ninth, who died as an adolescent, granted a brief audience to Thomas Manning), the Third Panchen Lama developed a close friendship with the Scotsman George Bogle, the first British Representative in India to visit Tibet. It was in fact at the Panchen Lama's invitation that he came to Shigatse in 1774, for the lama was mediating a dispute between the East India Company and Bhutan. This in itself must have confused most foreign powers as to the Panchen Lama's true status, but in addition this particular incarnation was well versed in foreign languages (his mother was from Ladakh and had taught him Hindustani; he was also fluent in Persian, the diplomatic language of central and south Asia in those days), and one of the ways he kept abreast of events outside Tibet was by offering meals to wandering Hindu ascetics and questioning them, in Hindustani, through a window.

The Dalai Lama was an infant at the time of Bogle's visit, and the regency in Lhasa would not grant him permission to proceed to the capital. So instead he stayed on in Shigatse, studying Tibetan, carrying out both official and unofficial instructions from Warren Hastings— and finding time as well to become the first Briton to marry a Tibetan. The close personal relations between Warren Hastings's Representative and the Panchen Lama, who during this weak regency was in practice the most important figure in the country, lulled the British into expecting good trade relations between the two nations. The Chinese also felt they could make some advantageous arrangement, and some time after Bogle's departure they invited the Panchen Lama to Peking (as a mark of respect the emperor met him at a point several weeks' march from the capital and even walked forty paces from his throne to greet him). But there, while still in his forties, the lama tragically died of smallpox. Bogle himself died at about the same time in India, and, with the two principals deceased, the hoped-for diplomatic and trade relationship came to nothing.

There is an interesting epilogue, for in 1783 Samuel Turner, the next British Representative sent by Hastings to Tibet, was received by the new Panchen Lama, who was then only eighteen months old, and the child made such a deep impression on him that the worldly and practical envoy very nearly believed he was in fact an incarnation, born with his previous intelligence intact. Like his predecessor, this Fourth Panchen Lama was well liked by the people, and he was seen much later, as a vigorous old man of around sixty, by another Westerner—the Frenchman Abbé Huc: Chandra Das in due course also joined the list of visitors, being present in Shigatse at the next incumbent's death (he was asked to treat the ailing lama, and had occasion to be grateful that he had declined: after failing to cure him, his doctors were flogged—in some cases to death). The sixth, who is supposed to have been the son of a madman and a mute, was first seen by Kawaguchi in Shigatse in 1900 at the age of eighteen; five years later they would meet in Bodh Gaya, to the consternation of the British, and after another nine years Kawaguchi, at the Panchen Lama's bidding, would make his second journey to Tibet.

*　*　*

The town of Shigatse itself lies on a plain, nestled at the foot of a large and barren outcropping. Standing free of this is another hill composed of a single rock on which, until it was destroyed in the 1960s, stood a fortress resembling a miniature Potala. In Kawaguchi's day the town housed some thirty thousand people—at a rough local estimate—while the monastery of Tashi Lhumpo contained up to five thousand monks, depending on the season, which made it ten times the size of Sakya. Because it is so closely associated with the Panchen Lamas it is often forgotten that this monastery was actually founded by the First Dalai Lama, Ganden Tub, in the fifteenth century as part of an ultimately successful campaign to spread the influence of the new Gelupa sect beyond Lhasa.

Kawaguchi's visit was at least more successful than his stay at Sakya, and he remained in the community from the fifth to the fifteenth of December—for the first time claiming not to be Chinese but Tibetan. "I asked for the dormitory called Peetuk Khamtsen, which is allotted to Lamaist monks from the northeastern plateau, since I had feigned to be one of these." The Panchen Lama was away at the time, and this perhaps made it easier; Tashi Lhumpo would be far more relaxed without its abbot and his attendants. But unfortunately he makes no comment on his reasons for the change. He may just have wanted to see if he could get away with it, or perhaps he was worried that since

Chinese influence had always been strong at Shigatse there might be too many Chinese about.

Nor, characteristically, does Kawaguchi treat us to any detailed description of the place, providing only brief anecdotes and observations on the lives of the people he encountered. He does not even mention, for example, the grand palace of the Panchen Lama, noticing instead that while for the most part the monks were exemplary in their conduct, they did have a weakness for alcohol. For this reason it was the custom for every monk returning to the monastery to have his breath tested by the guard at the gate, and so the not-very-subtle habit of chewing garlic was a common expedient.

But if his account of Tashi Lhumpo is sketchy, we have Kawaguchi's impatience principally to blame, and its cause was one that followed a certain pattern. One day he called on the Panchen Lama's tutor, hoping to increase his already substantial knowledge of Tibetan grammar in one of the principal seats of learning. Though he did not find this scholar playing with a young offspring, he did find the venerable old gentleman unable to answer even the simplest questions, and the inquisitive visitor was referred instead to a learned physician living in a monastery called Engon along the road to Lhasa.

Kawaguchi was puzzled and disappointed, and he delayed his departure only long enough to be able to witness the return of the young Panchen Lama. The procession was the sort of spectacle that may now have disappeared from the world forever, for he entered Shigatse carried on a palanquin decorated with silk and gold brocades, and escorted by about three hundred mounted attendants who, instead of arms, bore Buddhist ritual implements. All along the route, loyal followers prostrated themselves in the thick dust of Shigatse, as they still do today in front of Tashi Lhumpo.

On his final night at the monastery he preached to the monks in his dormitory, and apparently made a hit:

> They confessed to me that, priests as they were, they found no interest in the theoretical and dry expositions of Buddha's teachings to which they had been used to listen, but that my delivery was so easy and pleasing that it roused in them a real zest for Buddhism.

This fact is a sad commentary on the ignorance of the average Tibetan priest.

Given his usual geographical vagueness, Kawaguchi's directions regarding his route onward are impossible to follow, but he has left us some interesting little sketches of the life he found along the way. On the road to Engon, for example, he spent the night in a peasant's house and was surprised to find a boy of twelve sitting by the turf fire practicing his writing. In a country where paper and ink are precious commodities, he was using the traditional method of scratching out his letters with a bamboo pen on a board sprinkled with white powder, the same practice followed by novice *thanka* painters. Surprised, Kawaguchi made inquiries and discovered that all the poor tenants hereabouts made an effort to learn writing and elementary mathematics, since otherwise they were likely to be cheated by their landlords. Literacy was therefore much higher here than among the poor of Lhasa itself.

The next day he reached Engon, which was actually two separate establishments: a monastery and a convent spectacularly located on the twin summits of a mountain involving a two-hour climb from the valley floor. But the interview with the "celebrated grammarian" to which he had so looked forward again proved a failure. He had expected an authority, but he found instead a bumpkin who was stumped by even the most straightforward problems, and who seemed scarcely to know the difference between Sanskrit and Tibetan grammar.

Just what are we to make of all this? After all, the Tibetans had transferred virtually the entire body of Indian Mahayana and Vajrayana thought to Tibet between the eighth and twelfth centuries, and had made translations so painstakingly accurate that Kawaguchi, for one, had come all this way to find them. He himself had studied under a solid but by no means renowned scholar in Tsarang who had a degree from Sera. But why should his learning, picked up in only a year from the lusty Mongolian, prove superior to that of both the tutor to the Panchen Lama (one of the country's foremost scholars) and the man to whom that tutor had referred him for further knowledge?

There are in fact two possible explanations. One is that Tibetan scholarship may indeed have become moribund, as had so much else about the Gelupa since the time of the Fifth Dalai Lama. Even sympathetic observers like David Snellgrove and Hugh Richardson comment on a lack of originality and spontaneity:

> In the major Gelupa establishments . . . the main emphasis was on learning by rote to such an extent that writing and note-taking were discouraged when not actually forbidden. Learning to write and compose good Tibetan was regarded as the work of clerks and officials and so positively harmful to the acquisition of true religious knowledge. . . . But at the end of their training some of these highly expert 'scholars' might be unable even to write their own name properly, however well they might read.

At one remove from these large institutions, however, there were places where composition was actively taught, and though degrees from Sera, Drepung, Ganden, or Tashi Lhumpo were essential to advancement, it was often men who had first completed their studies at more thoroughgoing, if less prestigious, monasteries who in the end proved to be most knowledgeable.

This may partially explain Kawaguchi's disappointments, but one suspects there must be more to it. These, after all, were not run-of-the-mill graduates who were falling so short of the mark, and one is forced to wonder about the impression this rather overbearing monk was making.

For more enlightenment we might look back to one of Tibet's favorite stories: that of the poet Milarepa and his teacher Marpa. When the young Milarepa, eager for knowledge, sought out the well-known Marpa he found, not a gentle scholar reading in a chapel, but a rude married countryman who was out plowing his fields, and who before he consented to teach him put Milarepa through so many tests as to try (quite literally) the patience of a saint. Not only did Milarepa have to put up with Marpa's drunkenness and abuse, but he was made to build a house with his bare hands, then dismantle it—more than once—because his teacher was dissatisfied, and carry the stones back to the quarry before he could begin again. Isn't it possible that some of the scholars Kawaguchi met along the way were simply testing their visitor in the same typically Tibetan fashion and finding him unworthy—too brash, too quick to judge?

Our traveler's behavior on the entire journey from Lhatse to Lhasa is hard to explain. On the one hand he often seems restless, too pressed for time to take in the treasures of Tsang. Sakya he flees in disgust, Shigatse and Engon in disappointment. It is only about a hundred and fifty miles from Shigatse to Lhasa, and anyone in a hurry could cover this distance in a week to ten days (indeed he did this very thing years later). Yet speed does not seem to be his chief concern either, because over the New Year he makes a five-day stop at an obscure village called Ta-mi-la.

New Year's is the most important holiday in Japan, and since the Meiji Restoration it has been celebrated on January 1 rather than by the lunar calendar. This was the wanderer's fourth such holiday abroad, yet even here he continued to perform the odd little secret ceremony he had begun in Darjeeling, and in one of the strangest passages in his book he seems on this occasion to confuse Buddhism with Japanese nationalism.

> I got up early at three o'clock in the morning, and turning east, as I had done every New Year's Day, I began the New Year's reading of the Scriptures. For, as Buddhism teaches us, it is our duty to pray for the health of the sovereign, and every Buddhist reads the Scriptures on New Year's Day, in however remote a place he happens to be, and prays for the welfare of the Imperial Family.

To make the most of it, he gave readings of "the Word" until January 5—apparently at some material profit to himself. Paradoxically, he was now beginning to find less suspicion and more demand for his services as a priest. In the western plains, despite a lax administration, everyone seemed to be constantly on the lookout for spies. This close to Lhasa, people may have been more sophisticated, but they seemed to assume that anyone traveling alone belonged there. In a moment of reflection, he stopped to congratulate himself:

> I had met the highwaymen, and had been robbed of my money, but money was constantly given to me, and my reading the Scrip-

tures earned me so many gifts, that I had now laid by a considerable sum of money, and I was living on the food given me by others.

Nor was he above a bit of charlatanism—not for profit, of course, but simply to bring a hypocrite down a peg or two. At a temple called Mani Lha Khang, famous for its huge prayer wheel, the priest in charge was very rude, reinforcing his rudeness by demanding that Kawaguchi analyze his physiognomy:

> So I told him that I was very sorry for him, for he seemed to be a man who, though often given money and other things, would sustain much loss through other men, and for whom the future would have nothing but debt. Singularly enough this exactly told his past life. . . .

The victim of this little joke, however, was so impressed that he ran straight out and told the richest man in the neighborhood; and suddenly Kawaguchi found himself faced with a much more serious problem, for the man's wife brought him a child that was close to death. Confronted with a request to tell the boy's fortune, it was impossible to bluff his way out of it, and he had to tell the mother that her son would soon die. All he could offer was the religious consolation of reading the Complete Scriptures for him.

The next day, while Kawaguchi sat in meditation, the child's mother came to tell him that the boy was dead, and to beg him to try to bring him back to life. Kawaguchi must have felt there was little point in it; but though he found the small body cold and senseless, he could detect a faint pulse, and he was able to massage him back to consciousness. This was accounted a miracle, though in fact it was little more than competent first aid; to everyone's delight, however, the child survived this crisis to make a complete recovery. And as a result of his success— his first medical "case" since leaving Tsarang ten months before—he was invited to remain as a guest till spring, an offer he accepted on the pretext that he was "glad to stay there over the two months during the cold season, enjoying my reading."

Kawaguchi's behavior, always erratic, now bordered on the bizarre.

He had come halfway from Shigatse to Lhasa in the dead of winter without complaining: why worry about a few more days? True, if he wanted to see the Turquoise Lake, he would have to cross the Khamba La at close to sixteen thousand feet; but the route was well traveled and there were numerous settlements on either side of the pass. Four years of preparation, exile, and hard trekking were about to come to fruition. Why did he hesitate on the brink of success? Did he want to reemphasize the religious nature of his long journey, and demonstrate how little he cared for worldly achievements and possible honors? Or did he simply take a good look at his situation and decide that there was a fair chance of exposure as soon as he set foot in the capital? He was tired, and if he were expelled on reaching Lhasa a forced march in midwinter to the Indian border could well end in disaster. By spring he would at least be in better shape, rested and refreshed.

So, whatever his reasons, he spent the months of January and February as the guest of a local squire. It was a happy interlude:

> Besides reading the Scriptures I often took walks among the hills and valleys and on these occasions many children, with the one I had saved, followed me in my walks quite as if they were my own children. I loved the children so much, or rather was so loved by them, that my only business besides my reading was to take them for walks.

Remembering Kawaguchi's shocked reaction to the monk playing with the boy at Sakya, one can only wonder what another celibate monk, happening upon *this* cheerful winter scene, would have made of it.

---

1. There is, of course, one striking exception to all this: the kingdom of Bhutan, located between Sikkim and Arunachal Pradesh. Dominated by a sect that was virtually wiped out in Tibet by the Gelupa, the Bhutanese fought and won two wars against invading armies of Tibetans and Mongolians. To this day Bhutan remains fiercely independent, and just as fiercely Buddhist.

2. Alexandra David-Neel, *Initiations and Initiates in Tibet*, London, 1970, pp. 19–20.

3. The situation is confused by the Chinese, who use a different numbering system; according to this, the last incumbent was the Tenth Panchen Lama. This system appeals to champions of his political claims because it makes the line as old as the Dalai Lama's.

The Doctor of Sera

On March 14, 1901, Kawaguchi decided that it was getting warm enough to leave his winter refuge and push on to Lhasa. A day or two later he climbed to the Yamdruk Tso. This beautiful and curiously shaped lake lies at around fifteen thousand feet, and for once Kawaguchi must be credited with some excellent geographical observations —though he did underestimate its altitude.

Here he was back on the explorer's trail: Thomas Manning had passed this way in 1811 (disliking the lake, as he had disliked everything about Tibet), followed later by Das and some of the other Pundits. Yet there were still a number of misconceptions about this stretch of water which Kawaguchi would have cleared up had anyone bothered to listen to him. One of these was the name itself, for even the usually careful Das had called it Palti, in fact the name of a village on the western shore near the start of the climb to the Khamba La. Then again, since the best maps of the day still showed it emptying into the Tsang Po, surveyors seem not to have recognized that the lake has no outlet. Being fed by streams rich in minerals and drained only by evaporation, its water is poisonous to drink, though like seawater it supports fish. The Tibetans have traditionally been aware that there is no outflow, and on this have based another of their flood legends: on the southern shore stands the monastery of Samding, presided over by Tibet's only important female incarnation, Dorje Phagmo ("the Thunderbolt Sow"), and it was thought to be only her power that kept the lake from overflowing and inundating the whole country.

There is also a more recent legend about how the lake became poisoned. It was supposed to have had something to do with that monster of depravity Surat Chandra Das, since apparently around the time of his visit the water mysteriously turned red (Kawaguchi felt this had probably actually happened, though he is unable to offer any explanation), and, conveniently forgetting that the lake had been unhealthy before this took place, the inhabitants credited Das with its pollution.

The last of the misconceptions concerned a huge "island" in the middle of the lake, which is in reality a peninsula connected to the mainland by a narrow neck near Samding. Deep water almost encircles this peninsula in the shape of an inverted C, so that at any point along its rim the lake appears quite narrow and, with mountains rising from both shores, has something of the mystery of a Scottish loch.

Another incidental fact about the lake we learn from Das, who, recovering from a dangerous fever as a guest of Dorje Phagmo herself, observed that this was one of the few places in Tibet where the dead were disposed of by choice in water; usually bodies were cut up and fed to the vultures. The reason why corpses were thrown into the Yamdruk Tso near Samding was due to a belief in serpent demigods who inhabited the lake. By nourishing their king, who lived in a crystal palace at the bottom, it was thought that the spirits of the dead had a chance to store up some good karma between death and rebirth.

As Kawaguchi had little interest in Dorje Phagmo (which is hardly surprising, since she is commonly depicted in paintings and statues dancing naked, with a prominent vulva and only bones for ornament, or locked in abandoned sexual embrace as the consort of the many-armed Chaklashambara), we do not learn from him if the incumbent at the time was the same who at the age of twenty-six was so hospitable to Das twenty years before, or if she had suffered any hardship because of her kindness to him. But she was not the first of her line to have befriended an outsider. More than a hundred years earlier, another incarnation had become a close friend of George Bogle's deputy, Dr. Hamilton, who had cured her of some disease or other, at the same time that Bogle was developing his own friendship with the Third Panchen Lama. She was then an attractive twenty-seven-year-old—the more attractive since, unlike most Tibetan nuns (who shave their heads), Dorje Phagmo wears her hair long.

It was only much later that it became widely known that Bogle had married a Tibetan, and the romantic tradition in his family that he had sneaked off with the Panchen Lama's sister, when his only sister was Dorje Phagmo, shows how ill-informed the West has generally been about Tibet. For in spite of what to outsiders appear to be voluptuous representations of her, in life she is required to conform to the strictest moral principles. She is not even allowed to lie down to sleep, but must pass her nights in a posture of meditation. To have made off with this highest female incarnation in the land, and the Panchen Lama's sister besides, would probably have soured relations between Tibet and England indefinitely.

Since he chose to ignore the local celebrity, Kawaguchi found himself free to admire the scenery, and his mode of travel was such that he could enjoy it to full advantage. After spending a night at Palti he continued his journey at about 4:00 A.M. and, following the path a little way up the mountainside, saw the crescent moon and the morning star reflected on the surface of the lake at sunrise:

> Amid the charms of nature I lost all my fatigue and weariness, and I stood quite entranced. Soon the waterfowl were heard on the sands along the lake, and some mandarin ducks were amusing themselves in the water, while cranes were wildly flying about with noisy cries. . . . No pleasure on a journey can be greater than travelling in this way at dawn.

Stopping by a stream to make his tea and have lunch, as the lake water was obviously unusable, he took up with another of that series of jocular traveling companions, a Nepali soldier assigned to the legation guards of the Nepalese minister in Lhasa. "He was one of the most humorous fellows I ever saw, and he was very good company for me." He was also, apparently, absent without leave.

> His love of his mother had tempted him from his duty, but at Shigatze on his way to Nepal his thought turned to his love of a woman at Lhasa and this was so much greater than his love for his mother that he suddenly changed his mind and determined to go back to Lhasa.

How much more attractive Kawaguchi is—sympathetic toward and amused by simple human foibles—when he forgets to be a prude.

In the company of the Nepali soldier he climbed the last pass that stood between them and Lhasa, the Khamba La, and from a hill nearby it seems he had his first view of the holy city, still some fifty miles away. Oddly enough, this claim was eventually to get him into trouble in Japan, where it was used to discredit him by people like Narita Yasuteru, the secret agent who crossed the same pass nine months later but was apparently unaware of any such vantage point (he spoke no Tibetan, incidentally). The Khamba La rises to nearly sixteen thousand feet, and only someone conditioned by long residence to high altitude would even consider detouring to climb a hill, no matter how grand the view. After Kawaguchi's account of his trip began to be serialized in Japan, Narita actually wrote to Das in Darjeeling, through the Tokyo Geographical Society, to ascertain the truth of it. Since this letter even questioned the existence of Sera—Tibet's second-largest monastery— it is obvious that Narita had learned almost nothing during his brief stay in Lhasa, and anyway Das confirmed virtually all Kawaguchi's claims.

By now the joys of dawn travel were beginning to be tempered by sore feet, for the descent from the Khamba La to the Tsang Po is grueling. But in the valley, which is again below twelve thousand feet, he was cheered by the sight of willow trees in bud. He crossed the river by public ferry (a large wooden boat, since it was winter, rather than the yak-hide coracles used in summer) at the same spot where the mad Manning had had to be restrained from leaping overboard through sheer exuberance—and probably where the present-day bridge stands. Shortly afterward he was lucky enough to get a horse to take him to the village of Chu-shur, where the clear, green Kyi Chu—Lhasa's river— joins the sandy Tsang Po.

He was not inclined to linger here, as "I hardly know any town on the way to Lhasa worse and more wicked than this." It was widely known as the sort of place where no traveler could leave his luggage unattended for a moment. Being so close to the capital and on the main road, it should have been a relatively wealthy spot, but Kawaguchi has the satisfaction of telling us that in spite of the free circulation of money "there were more poor men in that town than in most other towns and villages in Tibet."

It was still several days' walk to Lhasa, and though a servant he had acquired deserted him along the way, there were enough travelers and horses to ensure that he made good time by hitching rides. About five miles from his goal, at a point north of the road where the slope of the valley meets the steeper gradient of the mountains, he passed what appeared to be a compact, walled town—in fact the world's largest monastery, Drepung or "the Rice Heap," whose resident population was officially listed as 7,777 (though its numbers might swell to ten thousand). Whatever emotions this famous site may have aroused in him, however, were blunted by the slaughterhouse below it—a rather special one, for it was from here that the Dalai Lama's meat came.

But at last, on March 21, 1901—almost four years after leaving Japan, two years and three months after leaving Darjeeling, and a little over a year after his departure from Tsarang—Kawaguchi rode a borrowed horse into the forbidden city. His persistence had paid off. He was the first Japanese to walk the streets of Lhasa and the first real outsider

The gate of Lhasa (now destroyed).

(remembering that Mongolians and Chinese, as well as some Indians and Nepalis, could enter without hindrance) since the Frenchman Abbé Huc more than fifty years before. But simply getting there was not his chief accomplishment. After all, Thomas Manning had also arrived in 1811, but had not even had the sense to realize he was somewhere worth visiting (his real objective was China), and he was sent back after a couple of bad-tempered weeks. Huc was expelled after two months. Even Das stayed only for a fortnight, seldom venturing out in the daytime. But Kawaguchi was to remain over a year, fourteen months in fact, a full participant in the life of the monastery and university of Sera.

There are really only two previous travelers to Tibet with whom he can be compared. One is the Pundit Kishan Singh, whose four-year marathon included a year in Lhasa where, since he arrived destitute, he had to stay and earn his living. But though we should in no way belittle his achievements as an explorer (being a *bona fide* spy in possession of clandestine surveying equipment, he was in even greater danger than Kawaguchi), it must be admitted that, as a native speaker of a Tibetan dialect and a member of a group of Indian hillmen who traditionally had free access to Tibet, he did have certain advantages. The other is Father Ippolito Desideri, the Jesuit missionary whom we have mentioned several times in passing, and who in the seventeenth century spent five years in Tibet. The similarities between the two men, Japanese and Italian, are striking: they both studied at Sera, both learned to write the language with grace and style, and both thought they knew better than the Tibetans themselves what was good for them and their religion. One feels that Kawaguchi and Desideri would have had a lot to talk about, and that in the end they might have felt more comfortable with one another than with their own coreligionists. For Desideri was eventually forced out of Lhasa on the orders of lesser men in Rome, while Kawaguchi seldom found any ordained Buddhists who met with his approval.

But, for the present, his attention must have been riveted by the Potala, the first sight of which can only be compared to seeing the Taj Mahal or the pyramids for the first time. Though it may lack the grace of the former or the sheer mass of the latter, for a combination of size and a subtle blending of the works of man with the works of nature this thousand-roomed, white and dark red edifice, crowned with the golden roofs of the tombs of the Dalai Lamas and rising seven hundred feet above the valley floor, has no equal in the world.

Of even greater attraction for this traveler who had arrived physically, emotionally, and spiritually at his journey's end, however, was the Jokhang, the spiritual center of the Tibetan faith, a few hundred yards farther on in the heart of old Lhasa. Here was enshrined the image of the Buddha brought by Princess Wen Ch'ing from China when she came to marry King Srontsan Gampo thirteen hundred years before, an image old even then and reputed to have been made in India during the Buddha's very lifetime. As he made his way from the open ground in front of the Potala, down the wide streets containing only the occasional mansion, and into the narrow, crowded lanes of the old city itself, his heart must have throbbed with the same excitement as that of the other pilgrims here from all parts of the country. On the Barkhor, the holy circuit around the Jokhang, he would have seen not only the haughty Lhasa nobles in their fur-lined silks, but nomads and countrymen smelling of butter and yak-dung smoke from the northern and western plains and from Kham and Amdo to the east, most gazing in rapt wonder at the largest city and the holiest place they had ever seen as they absently spun their prayer wheels. Amdo women, their hair carefully braided into 108 separate plaits, nursed their babies beside nomads clad head to foot in sheepskin; ragged monks sat at the base of the walls, reading the scriptures aloud; mad-eyed holy men with calloused foreheads chanted as they moved, measuring their length upon the ground, around the temple; and giant Khampas, their hair lengthened with brightly colored strings wrapped turban-like about their heads, intimidated whoever they could into buying trinkets and newly manufactured relics. Standing by in case of any disturbance were muscular, black-faced police monks armed with fierce expressions and rawhide whips.

But Kawaguchi had eyes for none of this worldly scene as he pushed past the several hundred people praying and socializing in front of the great doorway, between the giant prayer wheels, and into the main hall. So inspired was he, as he too prostrated himself before Tibet's holiest image, that for once he forgot all his prejudices and objections, rejoicing in the knowledge that since the arrival of this statue his faith had been "taught for over thirteen centuries, to the great advantage of Tibet and of Buddhism."

It was a moment of both joy and humility, and here again one is reminded that of all the foreign adventurers who had sneaked into Lhasa, Kawaguchi was the first sincere Buddhist traveling simply for the sake of his religion. In the history of exploration we have no other moment quite like it. The closest equivalent would be Burkhardt or Burton circling the Kaba'a in Mecca, but though both these men were strongly drawn toward Islam, neither of them were members of that faith. While it is difficult to imagine a devout Muslim risking death at the hands of the religious authorities in Mecca merely by being there, or a Catholic running a similar risk at St. Peter's, here in Lhasa in 1901 we have someone who combined the spiritual satisfaction of a pilgrimage with the unabashed thrill of the secret discoverer.

Soon enough, however, more practical considerations brought him down to earth. Here he could hardly beg a night's lodging in a tent or farmhouse in return for reading the scriptures, and though there were plenty of cheap inns in Lhasa, he had no wish to spoil the spiritual purity of his triumphant entry—for he had been informed that these were "not respectable." But back in Darjeeling he had got to know a young nobleman from Lhasa who was the son of one of Tibet's "four Prime Ministers" (by which he meant the four members of the Kashag, the chief executive body of the government), and who had offered to put him up if he ever got this far. Of course he was in on Kawaguchi's secret, but he himself wanted it kept quiet that he had been to Darjeeling, so they each had a hold over the other.

This strange young man, to whom Kawaguchi refers as "the Para Prince," is a shadowy figure. We never learn, for example, why he did not want it known that he had visited Darjeeling. At any rate, Kawaguchi did not find him that day. On inquiring at his father's magnificent mansion, he was given the disturbing news that the youth had gone mad two years ago, but could be found at his brother's house. Not the least put off by this information, Kawaguchi went there and waited for two hours before it occurred to him that a madman was

176

really the last thing that he needed just then. As it turned out, it was one of the luckier coincidences of his trip that he failed to meet his friend that day, since the young man was a thorough ne'er-do-well who was to cause trouble later on, and Kawaguchi's stay in Lhasa might have been very short indeed had he found him. Anyway, with afternoon wearing on and with nowhere to stay, he took the sensible course of heading toward Sera, where his Mongolian teacher, Serab Gyaltsen, had studied for twenty years.

Though smaller than Drepung, Sera is also built at the foot of the rocky hills, but unlike its rival it lies within sight of the Potala, four miles distant. The walk to the northeast is pleasant and level, and as the traveler approaches, the afternoon sun reflecting off its golden roofs holds a crown over the five-thousand-strong monastery. Entering its confines would have been a little like entering the old city of Lhasa itself, though all the buildings that lined the narrow streets here were religious in nature. Like anyone else arriving for the first time, he would have followed the pilgrim route clockwise around the great temples and college chapels; but after the emotional experience of worshiping at the Jokhang earlier in the day, he decided not to complete the circuit and went straight to the largest college, Je Tatsang. Late afternoon was a popular time for Sera's many "warrior monks" to practice in the hills behind the monastery, and he must have noticed some of these burly fellows with soot-smeared faces hurrying off in that direction.

Announcing himself as a monk from the western plains ("I had not trimmed my hair, nor shaved my face, nor bathed for a long time, and I cannot have been much cleaner than a Tibetan, so I made up my mind to pass for one and live among them"), he asked for the dormitory called Pituk Khamtsan rather than the one where the Chinese monks stayed. There were a number of Chinese at Sera, and, having succeeded in passing himself off as a Tibetan at Tashi Lhumpo, he adopted this as the safer course. The head of the dormitory was a kind and simple old man, and the new monk was admitted on a temporary basis without difficulty.

* * *

Of all the many hundreds of monasteries that once existed in Tibet it was the four great Gelupa institutions of Drepung, Sera, Ganden, and Tashi Lhumpo that were the most prominent politically and academically, and it was also in them that the old university system of India had been most faithfully preserved. By the time of their creation, during and shortly after the life of Tsong Khapa, the great age of importation and translation was already well past, and the system of learning they incorporated became virtually immune to change, settled firmly in a Tibetan way of life and housed in Tibetan styles of architecture. In this setting scholars studied the five branches of "logical philosophy" just as their counterparts in India had done a thousand years and more before. And in this setting a lone Japanese shared their life on and off for fourteen months.

Each of these institutions consisted of a number of colleges, or *ta-tsang*: at Drepung there were four, at Sera three, and at Ganden and Tashi Lhumpo two each. Several dormitories, or *khamtsan*, ranging in number of inmates from fifty to over a thousand, were attached to each college. The focal point of Sera's three sections was a temple large enough for all the monks of the college to assemble inside for daily services (where they were given their ration of tea), and fronted by a flagstone courtyard in which dances and processions were held at festival times. In addition there was a main temple, the Choching, where the entire community would gather once a week to share a meal, prepared in a kitchen so vast and cavernous that even the pots in which the tea was boiled were as large as communal bathtubs. Je Tatsang, the college to which Kawaguchi's dormitory belonged, was home, according to Kawaguchi, to 3,800 monks. Me Tatsang was next in size, while Nakpa Tatsang, the Tantric college, had only about five hundred members.

To describe the great monasteries as akin to towns is both true and misleading. Certainly from a distance they look like walled towns, and they are equivalent in size. But once inside there is a difference. For one thing no women live there, though boys as young as five are taken on as novices. Also there is no obvious commercial or agricultural activity: no taverns or tea shops, no restaurants or stores selling general merchandise, no animals being tended, no threshing and winnowing being

The golden roofs of Sera (with the main assembly hall on the right).

done. But this apparent lack of gainful employment does not mean that the monasteries are given over entirely to spiritual pursuits and divorced from secular life. In a courtyard off a back alley one might find thanka painters or sculptors at work creating sacred images; in another carpenters or stonemasons, for buildings have to be maintained and, besides, there is usually something new going up. And while a fair number of the residents devote most of their time to meditation, memorizing texts, and honing their debating skills, others spend much of the day with account books, because like any large organization a monastery requires administration.

Over the years, these communities grew rich in land, worked by peasants and common laborers tied to the estates.[1] Thus stewards and accountants were needed, as well as help during the harvest from the brawnier and less studious monks. All that butter, tsampa, tea, and meat to feed the monks, whether it came directly from offerings or from the estates, had to be organized, distributed, and accounted for. Since the landowning monasteries were primarily religious institutions, and since compassion was an underlying concept of the religion concerned, one might have hoped that that quality would shine through in the treatment of their retainers; yet such was not always the case. In one well-known incident a few years after Kawaguchi's visit, the monks of Sera had gone to collect overdue debts and, when the peasants were unable to pay, had violently seized what little property they possessed. But in this case the victims sought redress from the Thirteenth Dalai Lama, a man disturbed by such excesses, who made a point of dealing harshly with the guilty parties.

To be fair, the worldliness of the monasteries should not unduly surprise us. It is not a comment on the frailty of the Tibetans and their religion so much as on universal human nature that whenever a large and diverse group of men is gathered together it is unlikely that all will be good and holy. About a quarter of all Tibetan and Mongolian males were monks, surely the highest percentage in the world. When Kawaguchi later complained that the only difference between most monks and laymen was that the former shaved their heads and wore maroon robes, he was saying no more than that most men are fallible, not saints.

Sera is a restful place, a place that both comforts and inspires the spirit. Each of the four large temples is painted in that unique Tibetan combination of white with black and soft red trim which is so pleasing to the eye, and the holiest of their chapels are topped with gilded roofs. The pillars of the porticoes are bright with the Buddhist primary colors, while the doors and walls are covered with detailed images of both the gentle and fearsome deities of Tibetan mythology. Inside all is mystery, as the larger chapels are lit only by the dim glow from a skylight and the occasional pinpoint of the butter lamps. The smaller chapels are like caverns, and the fine workmanship of the sculptures is often hidden not only by the darkness but by the layers of white scarves offered by crowds of pilgrims. Outside again, the debating garden where the monks question one another and explore the finer points of Buddhist doctrine is located next to Kawaguchi's Je Tatsang. Surrounded by a high wall and pleasantly shaded by trees, it is a refuge from all concerns but those that have occupied scholar monks since the time of Ashoka. One can well imagine that the weary traveler rejoiced inwardly at finding somewhere at last that both soothed his soul and suited his inclinations, a base where he could finally settle down to the kind of relentless study that seemed at once to be his main occupation and his principal form of relaxation.

* * *

Kawaguchi quickly settled into the routine of the monastery. The day after he arrived he went to a barber priest to have his head and face shaved, since neither operation had been performed for ten months. The barber, however, refused to shave the beard, saying that as beards were rare in Tibet anyone who had one should be proud of it. And so the beard remained—and would in fact remain for the rest of his life. Admission to the college he had found surprisingly easy: it seemed that all one needed was the money to support oneself and the willingness to study for the formal entrance exams (some very determined scholars scraped by on next to nothing). It was for these exams that Kawaguchi now began to prepare, with the permission of the head tutor and the dean of Je Tatsang. Being a new student, he was assigned to a "strangely smelling, dark and dirty room," which he had to share with another aspirant. All students, unless they could afford better rooms, had to live in these squalid quarters for their first ten years; but after his difficult journey it seemed to Kawaguchi a very minor inconvenience. For now he found himself so busy that he scarcely noticed his surroundings, and the complaints about the quality of Tibetan scholarship suddenly stopped; indeed he had to engage two tutors simply to keep up.

Just at this point he was nearly caught out again. One of the members of the caravan with whom he had traveled to Lhatse was at Sera, and the man remembered him, of course, as a Chinese. When summoned before the dean and asked to explain this deception, Kawaguchi managed to get off by pleading poverty, since the Chinese dormitory was more expensive. Luckily, he had made a good impression, and it was agreed that he could stay where he was as long as no one lodged a formal complaint.

And now he was as happy as he could be. A sure sign of this was that he soon overworked and began to suffer from "a great swelling" in the shoulders. This was serious enough to require a visit to a Chinese pharmacist in central Lhasa to buy some medicine; he also had to draw some blood from the affected area. Nevertheless, on August 18 he passed the written and oral exams that admitted him as an official student at Sera. He had reason to be pleased with himself, since he was one of only seven out of forty who were successful.

All in all, it was fortunate that Kawaguchi took the exams so soon after his arrival, for up to this point his only distraction had been a festival held for the well-being of the Manchu emperor during the Boxer Rebellion. But soon he found himself very much in demand among a very special sort of people, the famous *dop-dop*, or the warrior monks of Sera. Huge, muscular young men who blackened their faces both to look fierce and to hide their distinctive hairdos (they let two locks grow out at the temples which, if discovered by the proctors, were torn out by the roots), they spent more time working out than praying and were also employed as bodyguards and policemen during festivals. Few travelers to Lhasa failed to notice the presence of these unique men of the cloth, but none got to know them as well as Kawaguchi did, nor has anyone left us quite so full a description of them. For as always, much as he might protest, there was something in him that was drawn to those outside the pale of orthodox society. If these warrior monks could not be admired for their piety, they at least could not be faulted for hypocrisy, as they never pretended to be more or less than what they were, and the Japanese traveler's heart went out to them. In the end he found them to be valuable and loyal friends.

Their origin as an institution goes back to the days of the warring sects. Though Tibet was never again to be a significant military power after the downfall of the empire, which followed closely on King Trison Detson's death, it was seldom fully at peace either. When the large monasteries were not busy sacking and burning one another, there was often an invader from Mongolia, Nepal, or China to be dealt with, and since many of the monasteries were armed anyway, they helped supply the fighting men. A large, dark, and very popular chapel just off the main hall of Je Tatsang is hung with ancient swords, shields, and armor, now blackened with the soot of butter smoke and incense, as a reminder of those days.

With most of Tibet in the firm control of the Gelupa after the Fifth

Dalai Lama's reign, the Gelupa monasteries—in the way of famous universities all over the world—developed their own rivalries. Sera and Drepung have always had particularly strong feelings about each other; it is even believed that the name "Sera," meaning "the Merciful Hail," is intended as a slight on its larger rival, Drepung or "Rice Heap," hail being something that Tibetan farmers (and especially the rare rice farmers in the lower valleys) fear greatly. Continuing the old tradition of monastic violence, certain factions in the two monasteries were always happy to arrange a raid on one another, and their miniature armies were sometimes involved in more wide-reaching disputes: as late as 1947, for example, the capital itself was taken over temporarily by Sera's corps of warrior monks.

The dop-dop were organized into fraternities, and formed a subculture with its own leaders and rules. These fraternities were not formally part of the monasteries, but as their officials often rose to positions of power their conduct, if not approved, was at least tolerated. The dop-dop usually came from among the poor ("warrior priests have no money to pay for a course of study at the college," Kawaguchi tells us) and those not gifted with a scholarly turn of mind. They earned their living by gathering yak dung, carrying firewood from the river, acting as servants to the scholar monks, playing musical instruments and beating drums during the prayer services, preparing offerings for the deities—but particularly by hiring themselves out as bodyguards to aristocrats or high lamas on journeys. During their free time they went to their training grounds in the hills behind the monastery, where they ran up and down slopes, threw stones at targets, and practiced long-jumping, high-jumping, and fighting with clubs and swords. Occasionally they would put on displays of these skills in return for a feast.

Their conduct, as one might expect, was hardly that of the traditional monk, but they had their own virtues, including a strong sense of honor. Hugh Richardson tells us that "they were characterized not only by generosity within their own group, but often by light-hearted, almost reckless charity to those in great material need, the beggars and the poor." Kawaguchi, having experienced their gratitude at first hand, sums up their character in this way:

They are very true to their duties and obligations. They may look a little rough, but they are much more truthful than the nobles and other priests of the land, who, though kind and truthful at first sight, are deceitful and crafty in seeking their own benefit and happiness. The warrior priests are as a rule not deceitful and cunning at heart, and I have found in them many other points that claim my respect and liking.

He adds that "they are very daring. Having no wives to look after they meet death calmly."

Typical of their code of honor was the manner in which duels were conducted. Just as in the Paris of *The Three Musketeers*, dueling was outlawed—in this case both by the monasteries and by the city of Lhasa—so that it had to take place in secret. Kawaguchi tells us a good deal about it, and, knowing how inquisitive he was (even in slaughterhouses), one suspects that he was present at one or two bouts, perhaps as the doctor in attendance. We are told, for example, that the dop-dop seldom fought over money matters, but that "the beauty of young boys presents an exciting cause, and the theft of a boy will often lead to a duel."

> Once challenged, no priest can honorably avoid the duel, for to shun it would instantly excommunicate him from among his fellow priests and he would be driven out of the temple. . . . A duel being agreed upon, both fighters go to the appointed place, mostly in the evening. They fight each other with swords while the umpires judge their way of fighting. If either of the combatants does anything cowardly or mean, the umpire leaves the fighters to themselves, till one or the other is killed. If both fight bravely till they are wounded, the umpire bids them stop fighting. He tells them to make peace and takes them to Lhasa where they make friends over a cup of chang.

Injuries were, of course, quite common, both during practice and in combat. And as soon as it became known among the dop-dop that Kawaguchi possessed some medical skill, "all hope of peace and quiet was shattered," especially as he treated them free of charge. His medical knowledge came to light one day shortly after the entrance examptams when he heard cries of pain from a nearby window. Apparently there had been a row between two young priests (not warrior priests, judging from the unprofessional nature of the fight), and one had had his arm dislocated after being hit with a large stone.

> When I asked if no doctor in Tibet could set a dislocated bone, they seemed to be much surprised at my improbable question. . . . So going to the wounded boy I easily set his bone, while a Tibetan held his head and left hand. Then I acupunctured the part where the muscle was a little swollen, and the boy was soon cured.

Their ignorance is understandable since, like many other cultural imports from India, the long tradition of Tibetan medicine had become stultified. True, local doctors were knowledgeable about the psychological factors in illnesses and well versed in the medicinal values of indigenous herbs; but they spent an inordinate amount of time during their lengthy training doing nothing but memorizing ancient texts. Just as it was possible to find scholars who after twenty years of study were barely able to write their own names, so on occasion one could find qualified doctors incapable of treating the simplest ailments.

This was of course by no means universally true, as Kawaguchi himself discovered when his own life was saved by traditional remedies. It is also noteworthy that his own reputation in Lhasa was largely based on a remedy he had learned from a "Tibetan hermit" (probably Gelong Rimpoche, the only hermit he mentions having known), and that when he met the Dalai Lama's physician he had trouble—as he admits himself—keeping up his end of a technical discussion. Yet one of Kawaguchi's more notable inconsistencies is that even after these positive experiences he was able to deliver a sweeping condemnation of Tibetan medicine and its practitioners.

Still, it is best to approach the subject with some caution, for it has been caught up in the emotionalism associated with Tibetan culture after the Chinese occupation. Writers whose attitude is that Tibet was a paradise on earth before the invasion would also like to convince us that its traditional medicine offers a miracle cure for virtually any ill-

ness. It is certainly true that recently many Westerners have found
Tibetan treatments more effective than Western ones for colds, fevers,
stomach problems, and hepatitis; and it seems more than probable that
Tibetans in exile have done a good job of building on a solid tradition
and reforming what had become corrupt. But had the average Tibetan
derived much comfort from his own doctors in 1901, it is hardly likely
that Kawaguchi could have achieved the extraordinary reputation that
he did in so short a time.

   Probably the best objective evidence we have of the state of Tibetan
medicine in the old days comes from two foreign residents of Lhasa in
the 1940s: Hugh Richardson and Heinrich Harrer. The sympathies of
both men lie solidly with the old Tibet, yet Richardson, the British
diplomatic envoy at the time, could state categorically:

> Several books have appeared recently [he was writing in 1968] on
> the subject of Tibetan medicine, suggesting that the Tibetans, hav-
> ing preserved intact the teachings of ancient Indian medicine,
> possess an effective medical practice of their own. This would

View of the Chagpori (the medical college on the hilltop at left)
and the Potala from the edge of the old city.

seem to be a false assumption. . . . It would be a mistake to conceive of the few monasteries where such texts are learnt, notably the Chagpori on the edge of Lhasa, which is often called a 'medical college', as training centres whence medically qualified graduates go out to practice their skills among the layfolk.

Harrer, the Austrian mountaineer and refugee who became tutor to the Dalai Lama, tells us that "the people had more confidence in the laying-on of hands and faith-healing than in the ministration of the monks of the schools of medicine." Both men also agree that the British hospital in Lhasa was always busy, the patients being both monks and laymen who had sometimes come long distances to seek cures.

Even so, one feels that in his general condemnation of local medical practices Kawaguchi is, typically, being a little hard on the Tibetans. Both Richardson and Harrer assert that Tibetan knowledge of medicinal herbs was highly advanced, and the Chinese, moreover, have not only preserved but expanded the Mendzekhang, the larger of Lhasa's two old medical colleges.[2]

But, whatever the strengths and weaknesses of this tradition, Kawaguchi soon found himself famous. Despite being the capital, Lhasa was in practice little more than a country town (in 1900 it had a population of only fifty thousand), and as in all small towns everyone minded everyone else's business. Wanting nothing more than solitude and time to study, the reluctant doctor soon had more patients than he could handle, and the more he tried to discourage them, the more they came, for his reputation had spread rapidly among the warrior monks. Though he continued to treat the poor for nothing, the wealthy showered him with gifts, and before long he was fairly well-off, though this was by no means his intention.

It was his dropsy cure that really sealed his fate. This, ironically, he had got from his friend the hermit in the western plains, who must have known a local folk cure not mentioned in the ancient texts, since no one in Lhasa knew how to treat this dreaded disease. A common practice among Tibetans was to choose a doctor by consulting a sorcerer, and when word got around about the Sera physician and his remedy the sorcerers began recommending him—both to make their own predictions look better and in the hope of a reward from the doctor, whom they expected to be grateful. As his fame spread beyond the confines of Sera and Lhasa he would sometimes find a horse sent specially to take him to the bedside of some wealthy patient. "Wherever I went I was kindly received, for the life of the patient was supposed to depend entirely on me."

It would seem that he was playing, albeit unwillingly, a dangerous game, as he was by no means a qualified doctor. Admittedly, his maternal grandfather had been a physician to the court in Kyoto, and the family in Sakai had inherited his medical library along with his books on Buddhism; but while we know that this was the beginning of the future explorer's interest in medicine, there is no way of telling how much time he spent with these books. Nowhere in Kawaguchi's own writings, or in his biography by his nephew, do we learn of any formal training, and one is left with the impression that it was just another of those fields which his insatiable curiosity led him to delve into.

His own comments are as baffling as they are enlightening. "I had read a few books on medicine," or "I had studied the rudiments of medical science (of the old school, it is true)," are typical remarks. The original text makes it clear that it was *kampo* he had studied—a combination of the Chinese and Japanese traditions—which meant that he was able to buy medicines from a Chinese druggist in Lhasa and work out how to use them. But he was also well aware of his limitations, and he had the good sense to insure himself against failure by treating only those he was fairly certain he could cure.

> There are many cases of consumption in Tibet. I gave my medicine to those patients who were in the first stages of the disease, but chronic cases I left without any medicine, to meditation or religious services that they might gain salvation, and die at ease. This, I was told, made some patients fear to come to me, for it was said that those to whom the medicine was given recovered, while the others, whom I taught about death and the future, without giving them any medicine, were sure to die. Some did not like to be told that death was near them....

In a place as small as Lhasa, always on the lookout for some new sensation or new topic of gossip, it was not long before reports about him even reached the ears of the Thirteenth Dalai Lama, and the man now known as the Sera Amchi, the "Doctor of Sera," was invited to diagnose a complaint he was said to be suffering from. The receipt of this invitation must have been a moment of very mixed feelings for our traveler. On the one hand, he could certainly receive no greater honor. Access to the Dalai Lama was very strictly limited. Though Kawaguchi was cynical about incarnate lamas in general, he seemed to hold both the person and the institution of the Dalai Lama in high regard. Both in the worldly sense of a rare experience for an outsider, and in the spiritual sense of an audience with the greatest living Bodhisattva, there was scarcely anything more important that could have happened to him.

Nor was there anything more dangerous. Even if his disguise survived the meeting—and the Dalai Lama was said to speak Chinese— he would from now on be a Lhasa celebrity, always in the public eye. Things were in fact developing a little too quickly for comfort. Kawaguchi had arrived in Lhasa on March 21, passed his entrance exams less than a month later on April 18, and gained a reputation as a doctor so rapidly that he was summoned by the Dalai Lama on July 21.

Thubten Gyatso, the Thirteenth Dalai Lama, was only about twenty-six in 1901, and was still at the beginning of an eventful career that was to last another thirty-two years. His most formative years, his biggest problems, and his greatest triumphs still lay ahead of him. Only three years later, in 1904, he would flee from a British invasion to Mongolia and then to Peking. He did not return until 1909, but his homecoming was short-lived, for within weeks Tibet was invaded again, this time by the Chinese. Taking refuge with his old enemies the British in India,[3] he made a number of friends there, traveled a good deal, and underwent experiences that further broadened his mind, before returning to Tibet more determined than ever to transform his country into an independent state capable of meeting other nations in the world on an equal basis. He was able to make a formal declaration of independence from the Chinese, and though he ran headlong into the entrenched conservatism of his own Gelupa monks, he managed to carry out a number of reforms, both political and religious.

But in 1901, with these events yet to come, he was still the most powerful incarnation of Chenrisig in over two hundred years. His position was never an easy one. For one thing, though he proved a match for them, he was surrounded by courtiers intent on poisoning or otherwise dispatching him. A famous case in point involved a curse that had been inserted in the heel of a pair of boots he was given soon after his accession. Far-fetched as this may sound, it is on record that someone else who wore the boots began getting nosebleeds, and Kawaguchi's account says that the Dalai Lama fell ill whenever he wore them. (The plot was uncovered by the State Oracle in a trance.) How many undocumented incidents of attempted poisoning there may have been is not known, but Thubten Gyatso had just passed an important test by returning successfully from his ritual visit to Lake Lham Tso. Here the young Dalai Lamas are supposed to be able to see the manner of their lives and deaths. For a number of his immediate predecessors there could have been little to see, since they died soon afterward of mysterious illnesses contracted on the journey. Thubten Gyatso, however, managed to end this venerable tradition by putting off his own pilgrimage until he was a shrewd and mature twenty-five-year-old—and by providing himself with loyal cooks.

Kawaguchi's own assessment gives us some idea of what kind of man he was:

> He was bred in Buddhism, and in it he has great faith, and he is very anxious to clear away all corruption from Buddhism and Buddhists in Tibet. . . . He is wise for his age, for, young as he is, he seems to have great sympathy with the afflicted, and is much respected, and indeed almost worshiped, by his people, though much disliked by the evil local governors, whom he has been known to punish, to deprive of their estates, and to imprison for their evil deeds.

In late July, Kawaguchi mounted the horse that had been sent to Sera for him and rode to the Norbu Lingka, or "Jewel Park," the summer resort of the Dalai Lamas. Imposing as the Potala may be, it is not very comfortable, and the tenants had always been glad to leave it during the summer months for these pleasant gardens several miles to the southwest of Lhasa; so the annual processions to and from there had become big events in the Lhasa calendar. The park itself is really two concentric gardens, the outer one usually open to the public (Heinrich Harrer remarked, forty-odd years later, that one only had to be wearing Tibetan clothes to be admitted), and an inner garden surrounded by a yellow wall accessible only to the Dalai Lama and high officials. This inner area is a peaceful place, a refuge with lotus ponds, pavilions, palaces, and cottages, combining the best in the architectural traditions of India, China, and Tibet; the dazzling white façades, the ornate paintings on the porticoes, and the profusion of flowers make it perhaps the single most attractive spot in all Tibet. Yet there is a marked lack of ostentation: the park itself is small and none of the buildings is unduly grand.

A chat with the court physician preceded the formal interview. The two got on well and were said to look so much alike that they could be taken for brothers. He was one of the few Tibetan doctors for whom Kawaguchi had any professional respect, and the latter admits not only to learning a number of things about medicine from him but to being barely able to follow the scientific side of his conversation. Indeed he had to be good. The court physician always bore the brunt of the blame after the death of a Dalai Lama—if for no other reason than to divert suspicion from the real cause. Since the Thirteenth Dalai Lama lived so much longer than any of his predecessors in the previous two centuries, we can assume that his doctor was both technically competent and extremely loyal, as well as skilled in the art of intrigue. Kawaguchi also learned from him an incidental fact which he had already suspected: that the Dalai Lama was not ill, only curious.

When the audience took place, Kawaguchi fortunately made none of his usual fuss about etiquette. He may have doubted whether Thubten Gyatso was indeed the earthly incarnation of Chenrisig, but there was no question in his mind that he was in the presence of a priest of great virtue, and as such entitled to all the prescribed tokens of respect. They were not, of course, alone. With Kawaguchi was the court physician, while accompanying the Dalai Lama were three high monastic officials. Seven or eight other high priests were also present.

The Thirteenth Dalai Lama.

The "Doctor of Sera" was honored with a one-handed blessing. The Dalai Lama praised him for the good work he was doing among the poor and enjoined him to stay for some time. Throughout the brief interview Kawaguchi was more than a little nervous, knowing that the Dalai Lama might address him in Chinese; and he had decided not to keep up the pretense of speaking an obscure dialect: "I would in that case tell him to what nationality I belonged . . . for I deemed it a great honor to be granted an interview with him."

This would have produced an interesting state of affairs, and it is almost disappointing that the meeting passed without incident. Would the hapless impostor have been immediately cast into prison? Or would the broad-minded young Dalai Lama have seized this opportunity to overrule his conservative advisers and try to establish relations with Buddhist Japan, a distant but powerful country that might be used as an ally and foil against Britain, Russia, and China? A moment that could have changed history passed unnoticed by all but one.

A cup of tea, and the announcement that he was being considered for a government appointment, brought the audience to a close. The disguised monk had survived a dangerous encounter. But he was no longer the anonymous scholar who could come and go unnoticed, devoting long hours to the books he had come so far to study. Whatever happened now, his life in Lhasa would never be quite the same.

---

1. Communist sources, which must be viewed with a certain amount of caution, estimate that Drepung controlled 25,000 "serfs" and herdsmen working 185 estates and tending 200 pastures.

2. It is only fair, to the Tibetans as well as to Kawaguchi, to mention that the Mendzekhang did not exist in his time. It was established in 1916 on the site of the former Tangyeling monastery (which had ill-advisedly sided with the Chinese before their expulsion in 1913) as one of the Thirteenth Dalai Lama's many reforms.

3. This retreat in the face of invasion does not imply cowardice, but is rather like protecting the king on a chessboard. Where the Dalai Lama lives, there lives the soul of the country, and without him no invader can really conquer Tibet.

Notoriety and Discovery

The first consequence was a considerable improvement in his living standards. He had already been a subject of discussion among the monks of his dormitory since high-ranking citizens had begun sending for him for treatment; but after his audience with the Dalai Lama it was no longer felt proper for him to live in the usual small shared room, and he was moved to what he called a second-class study: "a cosy structure of two stories with a kitchen and a closet." Ordinarily this sort of room was reserved for those who had taken their geshe degrees, and as it was the best form of accommodation available for all but incarnate lamas, one can see how important this visit to the Dalai Lama was regarded as being.

The new arrangement was not without its disadvantages, however. For one thing, being ensconced in a better room, he was expected to keep himself in better style. "I was now like a poor boy, who had grown up all of a sudden and had been given a house to keep. I was obliged to procure many articles needed for my new condition, all of which I had fortunately enough money to buy." He also needed servants.

But though his station in life had improved, he continued to run his free clinic for the poor, among whom were the more serious of the scholar monks, whose studies prevented them from going out to earn their keep. A small stipend from their college and the occasional offering from believers were not enough to get by on, and though "during catechisms they go to Ta-tsang where they are given three cups of tea for dinner," there were periods of private study when no free tea was available. At times like these they made do with the used leaves discarded by wealthier priests. Of course they also needed tsampa, not to mention fuel, both for warmth and sustenance. Yak dung cost roughly eighteen cents a bag, and while a priest with no need to be careful would probably burn two or three bags a month, an impoverished scholar might have to make a single bag last the whole year.

> The poorest priest has in his room a sheep's fur, a wooden bowl, a rosary and a dirty cushion, which makes a bed at night. In a corner are found a stove, an earthen pan, and a pot or jar, which all belong to the room. A bag hanging in one corner contains the baked flour which supports his life; but it is very rarely full. The most precious items of their property are the text books of the catechism. . . . These books, however, are not their permanent property, for they will sell them as soon as their examinations are over. At night their [bedding] consists of their hood, an underdress and a bed covering, besides an old blanket, which, however, is in the possession of only a limited number. . . . In most rooms of nine feet square, three or four priests often have a pan in common.

Kawaguchi not only treated these penniless men without charging them anything but often contributed to their upkeep, so that he became as popular with them as with the warrior monks.

Yet he was never to forget that practicing medicine was not his original purpose. The court physician seemed to enjoy Kawaguchi's company, and when they got together (there is also a cryptic reference to "frequent interviews" with the Dalai Lama, but disappointingly no details) he mentioned that he was pushing to have him appointed to an official position where the two would share some duties. For various reasons the prospect clearly appalled our doctor in disguise, who tried to talk his way out of it: .

> . . . The physician very plausibly argued that as it was the ultimate object of Buddhism to save men, I might as well stay in the city as a doctor to practice medicine. The doctor, I said, only relieved men of earthly pains, but could hardly do anything toward the salvation of souls. What doctor, however skillful, could save a dying patient?. . . I might heal them of their diseases, but I could not give peace to their souls, while a priest could free them from the most

painful and durable of all diseases. It was more urgent to study how to heal this. Buddha was the greatest doctor. . . .

All in all, his medical practice was playing havoc with his academic life, so when an opportunity presented itself to move into Lhasa and stay as a nobleman's private guest, he jumped at it. He had made his host's acquaintance after successfully treating his mistress for a disease that had been troubling her for fifteen years. The two were, in fact, an interesting couple. The old gentleman was a Gelupa monk and former minister of finance called Chamba Choe Sang. Kawaguchi thought highly of him despite his "ill-famed deeds of love" and felt that his honesty had been his downfall, and that he had been forced out of office by the same sort of scheming courtiers who were always plotting to poison the Dalai Lama.

Chamba Choe Sang was sixty-two years old and seven feet six inches tall (his monk's robe took up twice as much cloth as was needed for an ordinary person). His mistress was a nun of about sixty. Both were rather past it by then, but remained fond of one another and continued to live together. Kawaguchi, however, seems to have stirred their conscience: "While talking with me," he says, "they often repented with tears of the folly they had committed with each other when young." And, as if he needed any further education on the subject, "they taught me how great was the power of charming love, and warned me against it." Yet they do not seem to have been very persuasive, for in the end— just as with Alchu Tulku and his wife—"instead of blaming them for their bad behavior, which brought shame on Buddhism, I rather sympathized with them for it, as they had so many things in common."

The liking was mutual, and the ex-minister, who felt sorry for a scholar forced to spend all his time attending a horde of patients, offered him a small room and a stipend. There were several advantages to this arrangement: not only was Kawaguchi less likely to be disturbed in his new home, but he had unconsciously provoked the jealousy of a number of other doctors whose business he had harmed. If anyone with a grudge against him got hold of his secret, he was done for.

From this point on—probably in August or September, though we are not told when—he began to live two separate lives. He kept his study at Sera, and his servant was always on duty with orders to send patients elsewhere. The boy, who was given an allowance for his own needs, was also supposed to look after the living quarters, since his master would return on occasion to practice debating and take part in prayer services and other communal activities. But most of Kawaguchi's life was now spent in Lhasa, in rooms that sound about as pleasant and romantic as any accommodation could be:

> My new dwelling was six yards by four. It was divided in the middle into two rooms, and being the dwelling of a noble, the walls were brightly colored green with various pictures. The thick carpet had flowers of gold woven in it in the Tibetan style. There was a desk of ebony, as well as a little Buddhist shrine. The accommodation was very complete, and everything was clean.

Of all Asians it is probably the Japanese and the Tibetans who have developed the most appealing interior design. Owing to physical circumstances, most Tibetan houses are of necessity plain and simple, but there is always a shrine, with a colorful carpet or two spread on the low benches that also serve as beds; what furniture there is is often gaily decorated, and pillars and beams are usually carved and painted too. The interiors of the more well-to-do homes are both elaborate and tasteful, achieving much the same sense of balance as their Japanese counterparts, though with different means. Here in this room Kawaguchi was to spend many happy months during the autumn and winter of 1901–1902, usually immersed in study, but more and more often emerging to visit some of his widening circle of friends.

Among these friends were several Chinese, and just how long he had them fooled we never find out for sure. His oldest Chinese friend in Lhasa was a Yunanese named Li Tsu-shu, the owner of the largest of three Chinese medicine shops. Kawaguchi bought so much from him that before he moved into Lhasa he sometimes had to stay at Li's house for a day or two while his orders were filled, and he thus got to know the entire family. He was always receiving gifts of cakes or sweets which he passed on to the children there, becoming as popular with them as he had been with the village children of the previous winter.

Through his friendship with Li Tsu-shu he was to meet another

Chinese called Ma Tseng, one of the most influential foreigners in the capital. Ma Tseng was secretary to one of the Chinese Ambans, the imperial representatives in Lhasa, and symbols of the Middle Kingdom's largely mythical sovereignty over Tibet. Born in Tibet of a Chinese father and a Tibetan mother, he was perfectly bilingual, widely read in both languages, and privy to many secrets concerning the dealings between both countries. He was also extremely talkative, and Kawaguchi so enjoyed pumping him for information that he would often take a break from his studies to go and talk to him at the medicine shop. The two had in common that they were both great travelers, and Ma Tseng had been as far in one direction as Peking and, in the other, Calcutta and Bombay.

Someone he often encountered, though he never became close to him personally, was a current minister of finance (there were at least three such ministers at any given time), Tenjin Chogyal. Although the ex-minister no longer held any formal post, Tenjin Chogyal (who, like Kawaguchi, lived at his house) often consulted him on important topics before coming to a decision. As the Japanese was sometimes present during their informal discussions, he gained some insight into the workings of the Tibetan government. Interestingly enough, it was this Tibetan official who had been sent to turn back the British missionary Annie Taylor, who in 1893 had got to within three days of Lhasa. He and Kawaguchi once had a long chat about why foreigners should be so anxious to reach the capital when they were so obviously not wanted there, Kawaguchi making only attentive but noncommittal comments.

But in every sense the most impressive friend and mentor he acquired was the Ganden Tri Rimpoche of the time. This figure, who in the Gelupa hierarchy actually outranks the Dalai Lama and is technically the leader of the sect, is one of the few non-incarnate lamas to hold the title "Rimpoche." This he achieves solely by reason of his virtue and his learning, as he is expected to study for a further thirty years after obtaining his geshe degree. Chosen alternately from among the former abbots of Lhasa's two Tantric colleges, he occupies a position— usually for seven years—of immense prestige, though his duties are largely ceremonial, prominent among them being his role in the Monlam festival.

In spite of his frequent squeals of protest, Kawaguchi admired a number of Tibetans, from Gelong Rimpoche to the Dalai Lama; but for the Ganden Tri Rimpoche his praise is unreserved. It even seems possible that this wise old man saw through his pupil's disguise almost immediately yet for some reason did not publicize it:

> The highest priest at the first glance at me seemed to know what kind of a man I am.... He hinted, if indirectly, that he felt some fear for me, and I, too, began to fear him. Still, he must have found faithfulness in me, for he taught me Buddhism in its true form, and I felt correspondingly grateful to him, for none of the many doctors, learned scholars, religionists, and hermits with whom I studied Buddhism influenced me half so much....

Kawaguchi had the privilege of knowing him because his host in Lhasa was his half-brother. Though the Tri Rimpoche was then sixty-seven, he still had one of the most formidable tasks of his life ahead of him, for in 1904, when the British invaded and the Dalai Lama fled,

The Ganden Tri Rimpoche.

this venerable priest was left in charge. It was he who carried out all the negotiations with the British and remained the effective ruler until the Dalai Lama returned briefly in 1909. He seems to have had a way with foreigners, and to Kawaguchi's praise we can add that of Sir Francis Younghusband, who "greatly revered" him and thought he "more nearly approached Kipling's Lama in *Kim* than any other Tibetan I had met."

Now there is something rather strange about all this if one stops to consider it. Not long after Kawaguchi meets the Dalai Lama he is invited to stay as the guest of a former high official, and promptly acquires as a tutor the most learned man in this land of scholars. All three Tibetans in question are farsighted men who as often as not find themselves in conflict with a conservative hierarchy of priests. Kawaguchi indicates several times that the Tri Rimpoche had seen through his disguise. Isn't it possible that the Dalai Lama, having also smelled something fishy about this "Chinese doctor" and knowing that he was in contact with the ex-minister anyway, might have instructed the latter to keep an eye on him?

It must also be remembered that the Tibetan government had an extensive internal detective and spy system in operation. Kawaguchi had been well known as a Japanese in Darjeeling, and since any number of Tibetan merchants and officials moved freely between northern Bengal and Lhasa, there must at least have been rumors in circulation about him. Little enough, it is true, was known of Japan at the time, even among well-informed Tibetans. Some Japanese products ranging from matches to hanging scrolls were on sale in the Lhasa markets ("These inanimate goods are more daring than the people who made them," Kawaguchi quips), and the Boxer Rebellion had shed a little more light on this distant country. It was also acknowledged that Japan had unwittingly done its bit for Tibetan nationalism, because since the Chinese defeat in the first Sino-Japanese War, Chinese prestige had plummeted so low in Lhasa that imperial edicts were openly disobeyed and Chinese sovereignty was barely given lip service. If a small number of officials did indeed realize that Kawaguchi was Japanese, they also recognized that it would not be in Tibet's interest to provoke a potentially friendly ally. If he was an agent—their reasoning might have been—he should be given a good impression, but nothing vital. If he was what he seemed to be, then by all means allow him to acquire the knowledge of Buddhism he aspired to, in the hope that he would give favorable reports of his experience which might some day lead to better relations.

Of course this is all speculation, and in the end probably nothing would have come of it. Two years after Kawaguchi's departure, Tibet was invaded by the British, and a few years later from the other direction by the Chinese. Just after the latter invasion the old Chinese Empire collapsed and Tibet was soon able to declare its independence. Amidst all the excitement and comings and goings of armies the solitary monk would have been all but forgotten.

Not all his friends, incidentally, were well known or influential. A man who was to play an important role in his life (and to suffer a great deal for it) was a trader he had met in Darjeeling named Tsa Rongba. One day Kawaguchi went into a shop on the Barkhor—the street in the heart of Lhasa that circles the Jokhang and is filled with concerns both spiritual and worldly—to buy a cake of soap, and thought he recognized the shopkeeper. But it was not until their next meeting that he and Tsa Rongba identified each other, for the clean-shaven Japanese monk studying basic Tibetan in Darjeeling could have borne little resemblance to the bearded scholar and doctor three years and countless experiences later. Once recognition dawned, however, there was real danger, as Tsa Rongba knew him for a Japanese and was astonished to see him in the capital (he even thought he must have spirited himself there by some supernatural power). In order to test his reliability, Kawaguchi suggested that the merchant turn him in and collect the reward, but Tsa Rongba quickly swore by "Cho-o Rimpoche," the image in the Jokhang, that he would do no such thing. Among a people addicted to swearing solemn oaths, this was a serious promise; in fact, of the forty-five Tibetan oaths that Kawaguchi knew, this was the strongest, and he was duly impressed.

Another old acquaintance from Darjeeling was a friend he could well have done without: "the Para Prince," the young man he had unsuccessfully sought out on his very first day in Lhasa. It was only a matter of time before they ran into one another, and it happened one day when

Kawaguchi was idling away a few moments (something one can imagine only with difficulty) standing in the doorway of Li Tsu-shu's pharmacy. The young man spied him and came into the shop, where he seems to have been known anyway. They had a brief chat, but no secrets were given away at the time. Yet knowing him at all was bad luck, since it turned out that he was a congenital liar and usually in debt. His rumored madness was even said to be feigned as a way of putting off his creditors.

There were other chance meetings that must have proved interesting. One day in mid-October he was returning to Sera for the monthly debate. The first snow of the year had just fallen, and as he was watching a group of young novices along the way having a snowball fight—a sight that reminded him that "human nature, after all, is very much alike the world over"—he was overtaken by a rough-looking character who stopped to stare at him.

> I at once recognized in him one of my old acquaintances, the youngest of the three brothers whom I accompanied on the pilgrimage round Lake Manasarovara, who gave my face a sharp parting smack, as already told. He seemed to be quite astonished, even frightened, when he saw me, his whilom companion of humble attire, now transformed into an aristocratic-looking personage, such as I must have appeared to him.

It must indeed have been a shock, and—probably remembering the brawl and the accompanying accusations that occasioned their parting—the man tried to get away. But Kawaguchi detained him and took him along to his impressive two-story study in Sera, where he had tea made and asked him about the family. The monk even brought tears to the rough nomad's eyes when he thanked him for all the kindness he had received during the pilgrimage. Whether he asked or learned anything specific about Dawa he does not say, but we may be quite sure that she later heard of her lama's altered circumstances—and was probably rebuked by her family for not being more persistent.

In November he was back in Lhasa, and on discovering that his friend Tsa Rongba was about to set off on a government commission to India to buy iron for making small arms for Tibet's small army, he seized the opportunity to send letters to Chandra Das and Lama Shabdung in Darjeeling, as well as others to be forwarded to friends in Japan. Again one longs to know what was in this, the second letter he had sent to Das from Tibet. Was Kawaguchi really so naive as to believe that his former teacher had given up spying and was now a simple scholar interested only in anthropological and geographical data? ("Do you know what Hurree Babu really wants? He wants to be made a member of the Royal Society by taking ethnological notes," says Lurgan Sahib in *Kim*. It is possible that Das used this approach to persuade Kawaguchi to send him information.) Did he unconsciously reveal anything that might have been passed on to Calcutta, influencing the British decision to invade in 1904? Some have argued in support of both theories—that Kawaguchi *was* working for the British (though what his motive could have been is impossible to imagine), and that he simply passed things innocently along to Das. Whatever the case, there seems little evidence that anyone took him seriously.

It was also in November that the Para Prince began to make trouble. Kawaguchi was suddenly confronted by a servant demanding the "loan" of a rather large sum. Recognizing this for what it was— blackmail—he at first tried to fend off the young nobleman with a smaller amount, but in the end he had no choice but to pay up.

It was probably this episode that made him feel that his days in Lhasa might be numbered, and whenever he was not actually studying or debating he spent much of November and December collecting books. This was a complicated and fairly expensive process, since any unusual works had to be specially ordered from the various monasteries where the blocks were kept. Luckily, in spite of the substantial sum he had just paid in blackmail, he was still in funds from his doctoring.

To order a book, one first had to get permission from the monastery that held the copyright, and depending on the volume this cost the equivalent of between twelve and sixty-two cents per hundred pages. Then there were printers to be hired, each team consisting of two printers and a sorter. Their wages were two tankas (twenty-five cents) a day. Before long, his collection got so large that it began to be talked about in Sera, so he started keeping some of his books in town to avoid suspicion.

On December 8, without Kawaguchi knowing, a man traveling under the name of Ch'en Liang-yu arrived in Lhasa from Darjeeling for a brief stay. There was no reason he should have been aware of this, except that the visitor was not really Chinese at all but a fellow Japanese—his future critic, Narita Yasuteru, under instructions from and financed by the Japanese Foreign Ministry. Narita's only real accomplishment was to be the first Japanese to take photographs of the forbidden city, but, as we have already seen, he had the presumption to claim later that Kawaguchi had never been to Tibet at all.

New Year's Day, 1902, his fifth since leaving Japan, found Kawaguchi back at Sera. The Tibetan New Year is a great celebration in Lhasa, but of course January 1 passed unnoticed—just as it had done in Japan at the time of Kawaguchi's birth. More settled than he had been the previous year on the road to Lhasa, he arranged his study for the occasion and held a solitary service that lasted until 4:00 A.M. "Then I performed a ceremony in order to pray for the prosperity of their Imperial Majesties the Emperor and Empress, H.I.H. the Crown Prince, and also for the greater prosperity and glory of the Empire of Japan."

At about the same time, the festival season began in Lhasa. First was the two-week Festival of Lights commemorating the death of Tsong Khapa. Kawaguchi was impressed by the solemnity with which the function was observed: "It seemed to me," he said, "as if angels were conducting the service." He was rather less impressed by the custom of begging and even extorting money practiced by the monks at this time of year. It also became the only occasion on which he found fault with his warrior monks: "The nights of the holy service are abused as occasions for indulging in fearful malpractices. They [the monks] really seem to be the descendants of Sodom and Gomorrah mentioned in the Bible."

But if some aspects of the Festival of Lights upset him, the twelve days preceding Monlam, the Tibetan New Year, horrified him.

> The temples are no longer sacred places; they are more like gambling-houses—places where the priests make themselves merry by holding revels far into the night. Now is the time when the

Tibetan priesthood bids good-bye for a while to all moral and social restraints, when young and old indulge themselves ... to their heart's content, and when those who remain aloof from this universal practice are laughed at as old fogeys.

Despite his ill humor, however, he was fortunate to see the Monlam festival at that particular time, for it was an exciting experience, Lhasa's normal population being doubled by a festive influx of both priests and laymen. Had he arrived before the Thirteenth Dalai Lama's reign, he would have found instead a gloomy scene where the flow of people had left the city rather than entered it. The reason, paradoxically, was that during this period the city underwent a symbolic return to purely religious rule by being temporarily under the jurisdiction of Drepung. Over the years it had become traditional for Drepung's chief official, the Shalgno, to use this occasion not only to fill the coffers of the monastery but to enrich himself to the point where he could live happily ever after. Stopping this extortion had been one of the early reforms carried out by the Thirteenth Dalai Lama, and the festival thus reverted to being a time of joy rather than a headlong rush out of the capital to avoid corrupt monks intent on fleecing the populace.

One of its chief attractions was the display of colorful butter sculpture in the Jokhang. This form of sculpture, using a food staple as the medium, is unique to Tibetan Buddhism, and is probably meant to emphasize the Buddhist idea of impermanence, for though it takes a month to create the figures they are exhibited only for a single night, after which they are used to feed butter lamps or to make sacred medicines. As well executed as any sculpture in wood, stone, or clay, their brief life gives them a poignancy lacking in most other forms of statuary. Their creation is attended with a good deal of patience and dedication: to keep its shape, the butter must be worked in an unheated room in winter, with the artist continually dipping his fingers into cold water. Colors are applied not by painting the finished object but by impregnating the butter with powdered color before it is shaped. Each figure is two feet tall or more, and a large number of them are displayed on a triangular wooden frame around thirty feet wide at the base and nearly forty feet high. There is a lively competition among the monasteries to see who can produce the best exhibits, and there were about a hundred and twenty of them in the Jokhang in 1902.

Formerly this had been a public display on the Barkhor (by Heinrich Harrer's time it would be so again), but around 1870 it had got out of hand; there had been such a crush of people that serious accidents had occurred, and so for some years the sculptures were on view only to invited guests. Kawaguchi, who got his invitation through the ex-minister, described the scene as "gorgeous."

But the part of the festival that most impressed him was the oral examinations held for the geshe degrees at the Jokhang. "The learned discourses delivered by examiners and examinees awoke in me high admiration." And for once—betraying his ambivalence about Tibet—he even makes a favorable comparison with Japan:

> The doctors of the highest grade are unquestionably theologians of great erudition, for knowledge of the ordinary Buddhist text-books is not enough for the aspirant to that title; they must study and make themselves at home in the complete cycle of Buddhist works. Perhaps the Tibetan first-class Doctors possess a better knowledge of Buddhist theology and are more at home in all its ramifications than are the Japanese Buddhist divines; for though there are quite a large number of theologians in Japan who are thoroughly versed in the philosophy and doctrine of their own particular sects it cannot boast so many divines whose knowledge completely covers the whole field of Buddhist philosophy.

As for his own studies, Kawaguchi was now relying on a Sera tutor, since the Ganden Tri Rimpoche was busy with his most important ceremonial duties of the year. He felt a sense of urgency, cramming all the work he could into the few hours at his disposal, because he tells us that he had finally fixed a date for his departure. Yet, as when the time came for him to take his leave of Dawa's family in the west, he seems to have had trouble dragging himself away and remained, as before, just a little too long—until events forced his hand.

* * *

The festival finished in early March, and until the end of April Kawaguchi's work continued without interruption; but the return of Tsa Rongba from India with replies to his letters heralded the end of this peaceful interlude. It was a dangerous game his friend had been playing: had the Indian government discovered that he was buying iron for the Tibetan army he would have been arrested in India, while if the Tibetans had discovered that he was delivering letters to and from Das he would have been in very hot water at home. We do not know if he was well rewarded by Kawaguchi for his postal services, or if he was simply hoping for future favors from a man rumored to be soon part of the Dalai Lama's medical staff.

Now, while Tsa Rongba had been in Calcutta he had heard favorable things about the Japanese, for at this time they were considered by many Asians to be a source of hope. True, they were entrenched in China along with the Western powers, but—perhaps believing the Japanese official line or simply eager for an ally against the colonial powers—many Indians and other Asians were willing to accept that Japan really had the good of Asia at heart. One example of this benevolence was that they were supposed to be more chivalrous toward defeated Asians than were Westerners.[1] When Tsa Rongba added this knowledge to the rumors that Kawaguchi had powerful friends and was on the verge of becoming a court physician, he somehow came to the conclusion that it might not be so important to keep his secret after all.

May 13 was a great day for Lhasa but an uneasy one for Kawaguchi. On that day the young Panchen Lama, now twenty years old, arrived from Shigatse for his investiture by the Dalai Lama. Kawaguchi watched the procession with his friend Li Tsu-shu, and on the way back ran into Tsa Rongba, who invited him to tea. There was another guest present, a merchant called Takbo Tunbai Choen Joe, who was in charge of some of the Dalai Lama's caravans to China, and purchasing agent for the Tibetan government there as well. At the time of the Boxer Rebellion he had been in China and had had all his goods confiscated, then returned, by the Japanese, whom he found extremely polite and easy to deal with. Thus like Tsa Rongba he had formed a high opinion of Japan and was even hoping to go there on business, as he was sure that Japanese products would find a ready market in Lhasa.

He must have had his doubts about Kawaguchi, who at times seemed just a bit too diligent to be truly Chinese, and who suddenly found himself confronted with questions about his nationality. Before he could answer, Tsa Rongba replied for him: "This gentleman is a Japanese."

There it was. "Just a few words, and all was over. It was the first time my nationality had been mentioned in Lhasa."

Despair was soon followed by relief, however, since it seemed that the caravan chief was mainly interested in securing the monk's help for some business ventures he had in mind. They parted with the promise from Choen Joe that he would never reveal the secret unless it was absolutely to Kawaguchi's benefit. He should have been sworn to secrecy on the Cho-o Rimpoche, for it turned out that, aside from business matters, Choen Joe was not a man of particularly sound judgment.

But somehow the secret was now out anyway. The very next day Ma Tseng, secretary to the Amban, began to question Kawaguchi as he had never done before. Then Li Tsu-shu's wife told him that the Para Prince had been openly accusing him of being a Japanese spy in the guise of a priest, and saying that he knew all about him since they had met in Darjeeling. As this was the first anyone had ever heard of the young man's visit to Darjeeling, no one knew quite what to make of it all.

On the evening of May 15, a worried Kawaguchi returned to Sera and spent the next three nights composing a letter to the Dalai Lama. Since he felt that this was the best thing he ever wrote in Tibetan, and since it tells us more than anything hitherto about his motives for coming to Tibet, it is worth quoting at length, though its quaint wording in English—a translation from the Japanese—gives an inadequate impression of the original.[2]

> My original intention in coming to this country was to glorify Buddhism and thus to find the way of saving the people of the world from spiritual pain. Among the several countries where Buddhism prevails, the only places where the true features of the Great Vehicle are preserved as the essence of Buddhism are Japan and Tibet. The time has already come when the seed of pure Buddhism must

The first part of Kawaguchi's letter to the Dalai Lama.

be sown in every country in the world, for the people of the world are tired of bodily pleasures which can never satisfy, and are earnestly seeking for spiritual satisfaction. This demand can only be supplied from the fountain of genuine Buddhism. It is our duty as well as our honor to do this. Impelled by this motive, I have come to this country to investigate whether Tibetan Buddhism agrees with that of Japan. Thanks be to the Buddha, the new Buddhism in Tibet quite agrees with the real Shingon Sect of Japan, both having their founder in the person of the Bodhisattva Nagarjuna. Therefore these two countries must work together towards the propagation of the true Buddhism. This was the cause that has brought me to this country so far away and over mountains and

209

rivers. My faithful spirit has certainly [moved] the heart of Buddha, and I was admitted to the country which is closed from the world, to drink from the fountain of Truth; the Gods must therefore have accepted my ardent desire. If that be true, why should Your Holiness not protect me who have already been protected by the Buddha and other Gods; and why not cooperate with me in glorifying the world with the light of true Buddhism?

It is a curious letter in many ways. Did Kawaguchi really believe that mankind, in an age dedicated to the glorification of science, militarism, and the pursuit of pleasure, was "earnestly seeking for spiritual satisfaction"? Did he really think that Tibetan Buddhism, which he spent so much time deriding, corresponded to Japan's mildly Tantric Shingon sect? Did he really look on the Buddha as a personal protector? And was he really at heart a Buddhist missionary bent on converting the world?

On the twentieth he returned to Lhasa and with the ex-minister attended a garden party. Tibetans are great picnickers and enjoy nothing more than getting together to eat and drink in the open air whenever the weather permits. There were a number of his old friends and patients present, including some country gentlemen still in town after Monlam. This festive occasion he described as his "last good time" in Tibet.

> I talked freely with them and spent the whole day in the most pleasant conversation on the subject of the lives of the ancient saints of Tibet and on various other topics. While I was thus passing a pleasant day a very serious thing in regard to my person was occurring at the other end of the city of Lhasa.

Ominously, Choen Joe, the caravan chief, was getting drunk with the Dalai Lama's elder brother—now head of the family, since both parents were dead. Choen Joe, in a mood of convivial intimacy with this eminent person, remembered his promise not to reveal Kawaguchi's secret unless it would do him good, and now thought the right moment had come.

He could not have been more wrong. He had hoped to please, and perhaps get a monopoly on any future Japanese trade, but he was talking to a man who was not nearly as farsighted as his brother. This was someone who would see in Japan not a potential ally but merely a potential conqueror; in a Japanese, nothing but a spy; and in a strictly celibate, vegetarian scholar-physician, only a devious charlatan.

That evening, distraught at the possibility that he had now put himself in danger as well, Choen Joe went to Tsa Rongba's house and had a few more drinks. Though he had resolved to say nothing of what had occurred earlier, he wound up spilling the whole story, leaving poor Tsa Rongba and his wife very uncomfortable indeed, for Kawaguchi had in his possession a letter from Lama Shabdung in Darjeeling which Tsa Rongba had delivered. If Kawaguchi were caught with this, his messenger was bound to suffer for it. Throughout the next day Tsa Rongba sent people to Sera and all over Lhasa to search for him, and he had almost given up hope when Kawaguchi himself turned up and calmly told the horrified couple that he was going to make a written appeal to the Dalai Lama.

Kawaguchi, dissuaded from doing anything rash for the moment, then struggled through a few nerve-racking days in which he tried both silent contemplation and seeking the advice of friends about what he should do. He claims that, if at all possible, he wanted to protect his friends, that he was most unwilling to leave them behind to face the consequences, and that he did everything in his power to make things come right in the end. Yet the fact is that he did escape, while some of his associates suffered torture and imprisonment (his tutor at Sera was not released until the Younghusband expedition of 1904), and he obviously felt very guilty about it.

But the best advice he could obtain under the circumstances told him to leave. No other solution, he thought after hours of meditation, seemed possible: "If I stay in this country it will be harmful to the people whether I present the appeal or not; and on the other hand if I leave the country it is no great loss to [them]." He then went to the Ganden Tri Rimpoche and asked cryptically if he thought it was a good time to go on a pilgrimage, for the health of some people he knew. The wise old man gave his judgment with a knowing smile: yes, they would get better if he left.

He was thus fairly certain what his course of action should be, but he was still not sure whether to try to get his letter delivered to the Dalai Lama. Kawaguchi was proud of the document, but he was also proud of being Japanese, and he wanted to depart honorably rather than in full-scale retreat. At the same time, he was still worried about his friends, and so he next called on the ex-minister and the nun to tell them everything, even offering to let them arrest him so as to protect themselves.

Lending credence to the speculation that perhaps the Dalai Lama, the former minister, and a few others might have known the secret all along (and indeed have been actively protecting him behind the scenes), his host showed no surprise at the revelation. But he was staunchly opposed to a public confession in the form of a letter to the Dalai Lama, and also rejected Kawaguchi's offer to turn himself in. In fact, when told that if he took that course he would simply be thrown into prison, starved, and perhaps poisoned, even Kawaguchi admits he had second thoughts. The ex-minister for his part advised him to leave Lhasa as soon as possible and not to worry about them, but he did agree that if the Tri Rimpoche's advice were different he would abide by it. When Kawaguchi told him in turn that the latter had already been consulted, all doubts vanished: "If his judgment agrees with yours then it is the will of the Buddha, the breach of which will cause you certain evil." It is hard to avoid the impression that his friends in high places did not feel confident enough to protect him from the conservatives, and wanted to hustle him out of the country before he caused any more trouble.

Now he was decided. He would go, and he would not deliver the letter. His next worry was his luggage. This, of course, was not just the usual belongings but all the books and manuscripts that had inspired his journey in the first place. There was quite a pile of them in his room by now, and he packed them up and took them to Li Tsu-shu's house with a story about going off to Calcutta to try to get the money to buy more. Here was another friend who probably knew who he was but helped him all the same.

His library at Sera was yet another problem. Luck was with him in this entire venture, however, for the city was entirely taken up with the festivities accompanying the investiture of the Panchen Lama. No one noticed what Kawaguchi was up to in Lhasa itself, and as there was hardly anyone left at Sera, the hours he spent packing his books, without pausing to sleep, attracted no attention there either. Nor apparently did all the gifts he left behind for everyone from his servant to his tutor and guarantor. Finally he went to the great hall of Je Tatsang and read out his farewell prayer in front of the image of the Buddha. This prayer, along with his undelivered message to the Dalai Lama, provides a long-overdue glimpse of what some of those private "26 Desires" must have been.

> I, Ekai Jinko, bound by the chain of deeds done in the previous world, have not been able to accomplish the union and conformity of the Japanese and Tibetan Buddhists, and am now obliged to leave the country. May the good cause of the present day be the beginning of success, and of the union of the Japanese and the Tibetan Buddhists at some future time, and also of illuminating the whole world with the light of Buddhism.

He then paid a last visit to the spot he loved best in all Sera, the tree-shaded debating garden; and here a very strange thing happened. Standing in this peaceful, walled-in refuge, final doubts overtook him, and as he stood there in confusion, this man who had mocked folk beliefs from Muktinath to Lhasa suddenly heard a mysterious voice telling him in Tibetan to go. He heard it not once but again and again; he even searched the garden to see if anyone was hidden there. Perhaps he was finally on the verge of succumbing to Tibet, as he tells us "this strange voice had much to do with my final determination."

Back in Lhasa it took him two more days to collect the remaining volumes he had ordered from various booksellers. Then—the finishing touch—everything was wrapped in three fresh yak hides ("with the fur inside and the still bloody and greasy side out"), a common enough packing material in Tibet but still an odd one for a vegetarian with Buddhist texts as baggage to employ. Odder still was the fact that Kawaguchi—now presumably the object of growing suspicion—was allowed to complete his preparations without interference, even though attention was focused elsewhere at the time. Only one last-minute setback occurred: the Chinese merchant with whom he had been scheduled to leave had been scared off by Ma Tseng. But Li Tsu-shu arranged for his books to be sent on later via the Chinese legation under his own name, while his wife hired a porter for him, a personable Tibetan called Tenba; and Kawaguchi went to bed on May 28 fairly confident of setting off the next day.

1. Kawaguchi had no way of knowing at the time that the favorable impression the Japanese were making on Tibet in the wake of the Boxer Rebellion was partly attributable to another monk, Teramoto Enga. Teramoto was then in Peking, and it was through his influence that Russian soldiers were evicted from the Tibetan monastery there, allowing the community of eight hundred monks to take up residence again. He had also distributed food to the monks.

2. A well-educated Tibetan recently shown a copy of the original was amazed to see his language written so well by a non-Tibetan.

Escape

The Tibetans observe an interesting custom when seeing people off. Instead of bidding farewell at the start of a journey, friends of the traveler wait for him a few hours down the road, with a tent and the inevitable picnic, and everyone says a last good-bye after the journey has technically begun. In Kawaguchi's case, in spite of the secrecy of his departure, he got the best of both worlds: a Chinese vegetarian lunch at the home of Li Tsu-shu, and then a Tibetan send-off from a few friends waiting at a favorite picnic spot, the pleasant grove in front of Drepung.

But between the two he was given a final fright when he was accosted near the Jokhang by a policeman. To allay suspicion he was wearing not traveling clothes but a rather grand monk's robe borrowed from his host in Lhasa, and the policeman, recognizing him and thinking that the rumored appointment as the Dalai Lama's physician had come, simply wanted to congratulate him in the hope of a donation (Lhasa's thirty regular policemen lived on donations which were really more in the nature of protection money). Greatly relieved, the monk responded with a tanka and a one-handed blessing.

Apart from a clerk in the Chinese medicine shop, we are not told who was waiting to see him on his way, but from their behavior they were undoubtedly Tibetans rather than Chinese. They had equipped themselves with a pot of chang, though they knew of Kawaguchi's own abstemious habits, and they probably had a much better time than did their rather nervous guest of honor. For before him lay an uncertain journey along the Yamdruk Tso to Gyantse, and then straight south to the checkpoints between Phari and Yatung, the latter being the border town beyond which lay Kalimpong and Darjeeling. At any time, he knew, he might be overtaken, arrested, and dragged back in chains to Lhasa. As his carefree friends drank to his health he changed into traveling clothes and asked them to take the borrowed robe back to the ex-minister.

Accompanying him was the porter Tenba who had been hired at the last moment and who was to prove his worth by always securing good lodgings along the way, either by telling the truth (that his master was the "Doctor of Sera") or by lying (that he was an incarnation) as the situation demanded. Kawaguchi, preferring to travel anonymously, disapproved of both methods at first, but they soon accommodated themselves to each other's style as the monk learned to temper his objections just enough to encourage Tenba's fabrications. In the end this servant became a useful ally, and the act they put on together at the border posts was to procure a passport in record time.

Within three days of leaving the capital, they had recrossed the Tsang Po by ferry and climbed to the top of the Khamba La on horseback. Here Kawaguchi bade farewell to distant Lhasa as he had greeted it on coming, from that controversial viewpoint. They then spent the night in the village of Palti where, since Tenba had gone ahead to announce his arrival, describing him as a famous physician, he was obliged to treat several patients.

With the festivities in Lhasa lasting another ten days, there was reason to hope that no one would notice his absence, or have the means to do anything about it, for some time. All the same, Kawaguchi was taking no chances. At Palti he began what became a routine, setting out just after midnight and keeping on the move until nightfall. Poor Tenba, who must have been close to exhaustion from carrying all the luggage for up to eighteen hours a day, was also terrified of traveling in the dark, so it is little wonder he always made a point of finding the best possible accommodations. On that day they marched all the way around the northwestern side of the lake to reach Nagartse by noon, and after lunch—much to Tenba's disgust—pressed on.

The route now diverged from the one he had used to approach Lhasa fourteen months before. Between them and Gyantse stood the Karo La, a gloomy pass at well over sixteen thousand feet where the snow falls even in summer, and where a few years later was to occur what is still the world's highest known military engagement as the Young-husband expedition pushed on toward Lhasa. Kawaguchi was lucky enough to obtain horses for the crossing, and the most strenuous part of it was getting a frightened and sleepy Tenba out of bed and on the road soon after midnight. But, just five days after leaving Lhasa, they reached Gyantse, where they decided to take a break for a day or two to see the famous temple and buy whatever they would need for the journey across the Himalayas.

Gyantse is the third largest city in Tibet, and when a British trade agent was posted there after the Younghusband expedition, it became the Tibetan town best known to the West. An attractive and well-preserved market town, it is dominated at one end by a fortress on a high rock outcropping, and at the other by the impressive Palkhor Chorten and monastery. In Kawaguchi's day there were about fifteen hundred monks in residence, mostly Gelupa but also some from the Ny-ingmapa, Sakyapa, and Kargyupa sects. There are unique chapels in this monastery of Indian and Chinese design, and the Palkhor Chorten, a stupa dating from the time of direct Nepali influence on Tibetan art, has large Newari eyes gazing in the four directions on the outside and typical wall paintings within. Gyantse's daily market, where they collected their provisions for crossing the Himalayas, is still in existence; but Kawaguchi was in a hurry, so we get only a very cursory description, lacking even the usual remarks on the particular vices of the local inhabitants.

The day they left they covered twenty-five miles before arriving at Tenba's home village, where "my man had a good carouse that night." It must have been a relief for him to have his family to talk to, though in the end whatever doubts and fears he may have had seem only to have increased, for Tenba's brother thought his master was a European. Probably as a result, when they resumed their journey Tenba began to suggest alternative routes by which they could avoid the checkpoints in Phari and the Chumbi Valley, but Kawaguchi staunchly refused: he preferred to take his chances with the border guards rather than with the bandits of Bhutan. Besides, he was not entirely confident of Tenba's loyalty.

They were now climbing the northern side of the Himalayan range, and despite the fact that they were heading south and the summer was advancing, it was getting steadily colder. The river valleys and farmlands of U and Tsang were far behind them, and though they were still technically in Tsang, here the high steppes were barren, if starkly beautiful, with the snow peaks spread out before them.

As they made toward Phari an experience from the western plains was repeated when "a band of ill-favored, savage-looking men, four in number, stood in my path, made a profound bow, and asked me to do them a favor." It seems that they were salt traders on their way from the north, and, having lost forty-five of their yaks to bandits, they wanted a divination to tell them in which direction to search. As he had done when confronted with a similar request (though from brigands rather than traders), he went through the motions and, not really knowing what to tell them, suggested they go north.

Tenba, who seems to have realized just how bad his master's sense of direction was, had been continually trying to lead him off the main road, but when the traders overtook them the next day with the news that they had recovered their lost goods and animals (and with a present of two tankas and a white scarf) the servant suddenly developed a new respect for him, and gave no more trouble. Yet ironically Kawaguchi himself was now beset by doubts about which route to take. Without telling Tenba what he was doing, he went into silent meditation to decide, and the result confirmed his earlier decision to make for the border gates along the main road.

The trouble with this route was that the Tibetans and the Chinese between them had come up with what must surely have been one of the most laborious border-crossing procedures ever devised by man. Part of the problem was that the Chinese attempted to assert their authority here by garrisoning the frontier, making it necessary for documents to be produced in both Chinese and Tibetan. But more important was that the system actually accomplished what it set out to do, which was to discourage any travelers but those on essential government business or trading missions.

Present-day travelers who find themselves irritated by delays in consulates, immigration offices, or international airports might take some comfort in the knowledge that others have been put through an obstacle course consisting of five separate checkpoints, where bribery and delay were so much the order of the day that they amounted to official policy, and where once the poor contestant reached the final hurdle he had to double back again to the third. The first border gate was at the town of Phari, where one had to produce "a witness, who for a consideration swears that the traveler is going into India on business for a short time, intending to come back." After delays of up to a week from officials reluctant to attend to any work unless it was made worth their while, the applicant—if successful—could proceed twenty miles or so to the second gate at Chumbi Samba. The third, at a place called Pimbithang, usually caused no problems the first time through; but another certificate was needed from the fourth gate at Tomo-Rinchen-Gang, and from there one proceeded to the strictest examination of all at the border town of Yatung. Provided everything was in order and the local official was satisfied with his gift, the now weary and discouraged traveler would get a note which he had to take back to the fourth gate. There he would get the paper countersigned, pick up some more forms, and move on to the third gate, where he was supposed to collect a document in Chinese. Then, burdened with papers, he returned to Yatung, where if all went well he would finally be authorized to leave the country. The whole process took a minimum of a week to ten days, even for officials on pressing government business. For others it could take weeks or even months.

Phari, the first checkpoint, has been described as the highest town on earth, located at well over fifteen thousand feet (though Tsharka in Dolpo must be another candidate). Kawaguchi describes the district as the "coldest, wildest, most barren place between Lhasa and Darjeeling," where even in summer a constant fire was needed to ward off the chill. There is an oppressive air to the town, crouched beneath an unfriendly-looking castle, for not only is the surrounding plain bleak and windswept but all the houses are black, being constructed of turf cut into bricks, the only building material locally available. Strangely, Kawaguchi does not comment on the feature that would always first impress Europeans there: its filth. Phari must surely have been the only town in the world with so much accumulated rubbish in its streets that trenches had to be dug through it to reach the doors of some of the houses—while the inhabitants of others simply gave up and used their second-floor windows as entrances.

It was customary to keep travelers waiting in this uninviting place for as long as possible (in order to fleece them as thoroughly as possible), and normally Kawaguchi could have expected a delay of at least four or five days. But here, confronted by an officious innkeeper who refused to put them up without full details of who they were and what their business was, Kawaguchi and Tenba went into their act, which was by now a well-rehearsed routine. The former refused to answer any questions concerning his person or his business except to say that he was from Sera on a pilgrimage, while Tenba kept trying to interrupt. Realizing he might learn something useful from the servant, the innkeeper took him to another room and soon discovered that his master was a famous doctor, and very probably the court physician, on a mission of the utmost importance. The reluctant doctor was then persuaded to treat one of the landlord's relatives—a young girl suffering from melancholia (hardly surprising in such a place).

His next problem was to find a "witness" to guarantee his return. Witnesses in Phari were professionals who usually charged high fees for their services, which, considering the risk entailed (they were, after all, technically responsible for the behavior of those they vouched for), would seem to be no more than their due. We do not know what happened later to the witness procured by Kawaguchi; but when Tenba and the innkeeper revealed that the present client was the court physician—over Kawaguchi's ineffectual protests—the man agreed to offer his services free of charge.

They all then proceeded to the gatehouse, the first administrative stumbling block. And sure enough, even though the innkeeper and the father of the girl he had treated took the officials aside and explained what an important person they were dealing with, they were reluctant to hold a "conference" (though everyone was present and doing nothing), and the expected delay seemed likely to occur. At this point he took matters into his own hands. "'If I wait till tomorrow,' said I in great excitement, 'give me a note mentioning that though I arrived here on this date there was no time to open the conference, and you detained me here three days.'"

Impressed by this unusual demand, the official in turn wanted to know the exact nature of his pressing business, and here Kawaguchi finally resorted to an outright lie. "'I may say this much. There is in Lhasa a patient of great eminence; I am hurrying on the road to get the medicine for him.'" The implication was quite clear: the Dalai Lama was gravely ill but wanted the matter kept secret. Anyone who held things up would have serious trouble to face later on.

"'Dear me! I never came across such a case,' said the chief official, greatly surprised and turning pale." Possibly as a way of testing his claim, Kawaguchi was then asked to have a look at someone else who was ill, while the official and his colleagues went into urgent consultation. Before he was finished with the patient, Kawaguchi had his passport. His "private circumstances" had made them waive the usual rules; he had cleared the first hurdle. Even so, it was 4:00 P.M. by the time he got the document, and he was obliged to spend the night in Phari.

In the morning they left as early as possible. A shallow but very cold stream caused Kawaguchi some problems, and he noted how soft he had become after the comforts of Lhasa. But he was certainly cheered by the ease with which he had obtained his first papers, and he chided Tenba for not appreciating the beauties of nature that surrounded them, and for grumbling about the steady rain that now accompanied them. A drawing in Kawaguchi's book, with Tenba looking uneasily at the road while his master gazes off at the scenery, probably captures the moment perfectly, and it is easy to imagine the thoughts of poor burdened Tenba, who was asked not only to carry a heavy load along a slippery trail for twenty miles but also to enjoy himself. That night they slept in a garrison town where, however, "the duties of these soldiers did not oblige them to examine the passports of travellers."

Since leaving Phari they had been moving to a lower, wooded area, and were now far enough into the Himalayan range to be affected by the monsoon, for it rained constantly. The second gate, at Chumbi, was straightforward. Here he had only to present his passport, and since it specified that "no impolite treatment was to be accorded to the bearer" he met with none, and proceeded to the third gate at Pimbithang.

It had been a long way between Phari and the second gate, but from now on the border posts would all be within a few miles of one another. Pimbithang presented no problems for the time being; these would come after he had completed the procedures at the next two gates and returned. The prospect of delay was uninviting, and while he was passing through he kept an eye open for some means of making his second visit easier. If only he could smooth the way a little . . .

The answer appeared in a form tailor-made for his talents: a Tibetan beauty who came to him seeking treatment for hysteria, and who happened to be the wife of the Chinese official in charge of the Pimbithang gate. She must have reminded him strongly of Alchu Tulku's wife:

> She was a rare beauty and had almost unlimited influence over her husband. Military officers are of course entrusted with power to command soldiers; yet in their families, the wives are often the officers and their husbands are ready to obey their command like private soldiers. So much I was told by a soldier, who understood that his chief officer was a greatly henpecked husband.

In such an isolated post a friendly doctor would have been a pleasant novelty, and it was presumably Kawaguchi's bedside manner that was the principal factor in his success, for long before any real results could have been apparent the lady overwhelmed him with gratitude. He of course refused any payment for his treatment, and the more she insisted the more adamant he became. Finally, with great reluctance and almost as if granting her a favor, he asked if it might be possible on his return to have his papers furnished immediately, regardless of when he arrived, as they were usually only issued between 11:00 and 11:30 A.M. Nothing, he was assured, could be easier to arrange.

It was only two miles to the next station at Tomo-Rinchen-Gang, and by leaving Pimbithang at three in the morning he arrived early enough to get the gatekeeper out of bed and demand the document required at Yatung. Just as the sleepy official was grumbling about there being no precedent for this sort of thing, Tenba came in on cue and let slip that his master was the famous "Doctor of Sera." To the further inquiry— was he also the Dalai Lama's physician?—the reply was suitably vague, and the note was delivered immediately.

Only a mile or two farther on was Yatung, the castle and garrison town that was the last inhabited place in Tibet before the wide strip of no-man's-land leading to the Jelap La, Sikkim, and British India. Kawaguchi was particularly worried about Yatung because he knew that a number of people living there were old acquaintances from Darjeeling.

It must have been a cosmopolitan little town, inhabited not only by Tibetans and Chinese but by Europeans and Indians as well. One of the Europeans was the British missionary Annie Taylor, who had made that brave attempt to reach Lhasa ten years earlier and had been turned back by Kawaguchi's friend the minister of finance. Another was Randall Parr, a customs officer employed by the Chinese. Nicknamed "tide waiters," since they usually resided in treaty ports, these European officials were notorious for finding ways of enriching themselves, and were only there at all because Chinese customs duties after the Opium Wars went not to the Chinese government but to pay war reparations. Parr seems to have been a cut above the average tide waiter. Younghusband thought highly of him (colonial officials usually despised them), and he was to make inquiries on Kawaguchi's behalf a couple of years later concerning the fate of his friends.

The officer Kawaguchi had to deal with in Yatung was one of those people to whom he took a violent dislike, which increased in retrospect since the lies this official told later were one of the chief causes of trouble for his friends in Lhasa. He bore the title of Chyi Kyab, or supervisor, and his name was Dargye. Originally he had been a coolie chief in Darjeeling, and he seems to have risen through government ranks by devious means. "Like all upstarts, his speech is more arrogant than that of a Minister President in Lhasa, and it was thought almost certain that if I should call at his mansion to see him, I should be driven out from his gate."

But word of the "Doctor of Sera" and his urgent business had preceded him. He was granted an interview and immediately went on the offensive, first demanding (as he had in Phari) a formal note explaining the reason for any delay. Then when Dargye asked for a full account of his activities Kawaguchi calmly agreed—on condition that everyone else was sent out of earshot and he was given a certificate "signed and sealed with the chief's stamp" saying that he had been compelled to divulge a secret "which no one knows but the Dalai Lama." Suddenly humble, the Chyi Kyab agreed not only to cut through the red tape but to allow Kawaguchi himself to remain at Yatung while his servant did all the running back and forth between there and Pimbithang.

> To get a note from the supervisor Dargye was not an easy task. This man has a bad reputation as a taker of bribes. His personal appearance is disgusting. When I told him I had secret business from the Dalai Lama, he instantly prostrated himself and bowed low again and again. I was surprised at his entire change of manner; but as I believe that, in every country, those who are haughty to their inferiors are also servile to their superiors and are usually hateful knaves, my feeling was only deepened by the sudden change.

It was still morning when a reluctant Tenba was sent back to Tomo-Rinchen-Gang and Pimbithang to obtain the final passes: in Tibetan from the former and in Chinese from the latter. There was no trouble at Tomo-Rinchen-Gang, but by the time he arrived at Pimbithang it was half-past one, two hours after the normal deadline for conducting business. So Tenba, as instructed, called on Kawaguchi's friend, the wife of the Chinese officer in charge, and she in turn went with him to the guardhouse and told her husband to produce the document at once. When she met with halfhearted resistance, "she lost her temper and exposed the true character of a Tibetan woman. Whereupon, the henpecked husband yielded to her demands and gave a note to the servant, who came back with it about four o'clock in the afternoon."

Now, poor Tenba had been almost constantly on the move, in the rain, since 3:00 A.M.; but his day was not over. Kawaguchi was determined to push on a further eight miles, where there was said to be a house they could shelter in. It was a long trek from Yatung to Nakthang—the first town in Sikkim—and he was afraid that if they stayed put they would never make it all the way there in one day. The following exchange ensued:

> "How about going there?" asked I of the servant.

"It is almost impossible for me to walk," replied the servant, who was weary and exhausted.

"As the servant of a master who has urgent business," said the supervisor, in a somewhat scolding tone of voice, "it is extremely rude and impolite to say it is impossible to go."

"Pardon me," replied the servant, shrinking almost like a rat among cats, "you are right, Sir."

And so they began the five-thousand-foot ascent of the Jelap La, the pass that marked the real border between Tibet and Sikkim. The steady climb in the rain left Tenba in such a pitiful state that his master unbent to the point of carrying half the luggage. Still several miles from their destination they came upon a tent. There were already five people inside and there was really no room for two more, but Tenba forced his way in, sat down, and refused to budge. Kawaguchi himself compromised by sitting up all night alternately meditating, reading the holy texts, and congratulating himself on getting through the five border gates in a record three days. He seems not to have spared a thought for the fate of the poor officials whom he had duped along the way, once it became known who he really was.

*   *   *

Reaching the crest of the pass after another long climb the next morning, Kawaguchi, who had entered Tibet at Tsarang three years before—at least in cultural terms—stopped to look back nostalgically toward Lhasa and compose some lines of poetry, while Tenba stood shivering nearby. It was June 15, 1902.

On the other side they soon came across a paved road, something unknown in Tibet and a sure sign that they had left the country. And now they began to relax a little, to slow their pace, for though the going was as hard as ever there was no longer any need to hurry. The monsoon was in full swing here in the southern foothills of the Himalayas, the road was slippery, and they sometimes descended into valleys where it was hot and oppressive.

Three days out of Tibet they arrived in the town of Boetong, only a day's walk from Kalimpong. Here Kawaguchi was accosted in English by an old friend from Darjeeling, a man who had taught Tibetan in the government school there and who was now the postmaster of Boetong. In spite of having taught the language, his Lhasa dialect was so rusty that the two found it easier to talk in English; yet the hapless Tenba had already heard enough to realize finally his master was a "Japanese Lama." Tenba had never, of course, even heard of Japan, but on being told by the postmaster's wife that its name, "like the rising sun, gleams even to the remotest part of the world"—something her husband had read in the paper—it suddenly dawned on him that it could be very dangerous indeed for him to return home.

Kalimpong, which they reached the next day, was known at the time as the "harbor of Tibet," though its really prosperous days were only to begin a few years later, after the Younghusband expedition. Tibetan merchants, following the same route Kawaguchi had taken, were allowed as far as this little hillside town, where they exchanged their wool for Indian cotton and manufactured goods. Had it not been a well-appointed trading terminus, Kalimpong would probably never have been more than a second-class hill station, a poor stepsister to the more glamorous Darjeeling. At only four thousand feet it is not high enough to be really cool in summer, and its summer residents tended to be the less affluent British, unable to afford the rarer atmosphere of its neighbor, whose lights could be seen—and envied—across the Tista Gorge on a clear night.

But the real center of Kalimpong had nothing to do with Sahibs and Memsahibs: it was the market, which was to become one of the most famous in the Himalayas. Here could be found not only Tibetans but swarthy, short-haired Bhutanese, looking wild and rough in their woven knee-length *khos*; the more elegant Sikkimese in their own characteristic kimono-like robes of wool or silk; the martial-looking Nepali Rais and Limbus, caps jauntily askew and kukris in their belts. But the only true cutthroats in the market, waiting like sharks to buy as cheaply and sell as dearly as possible, were the Marwari merchants from Rajasthan, undoubtedly the world's most obese and oily vegetarians. To serve the spiritual needs of Kalimpong's various inhabitants were Hindu temples and Christian churches transplanted from rural England, as well as Tibetan, Sikkimese, and Bhutanese temples—so there was no shortage of places for Kawaguchi to stay as he waited for his precious manuscripts to arrive from Lhasa.

And while he waited he finally had to face the problem of what to do about Tenba. The unfortunate porter was scared to death of returning to Tibet now that he knew his master's true identity. But he had two children and his wife was pregnant, so that he either had to go back or settle down in Kalimpong or Darjeeling and send for his family. Impressed by the divination that had led the salt traders to their missing yaks, he asked Kawaguchi to perform another to help him decide what to do, but he was refused on the grounds that their personal connection would influence the result. Finally a local lama gave it as his judgment that Tenba should return home; Kawaguchi then outfitted him for the trip and paid him thirty-five rupees (about eleven dollars), which was virtually all the money he had left except what he owed as freight on his luggage. The story, as far as Kawaguchi could ascertain from later inquiries, had a happy ending, for Tenba seems to have suffered no harm from his contact with the Japanese intruder.

Once Tenba had been taken care of and the baggage had arrived, it was time to push on to Darjeeling. Though it was not far, the trip involved crossing the gorge of the Tista River, and this was the worst time of the year to do it, especially for someone coming from the healthier climate of Tibet. At the bridge over this wide and turbulent river one is only a couple of hundred feet above sea level, and the fevers that could be picked up in the surrounding jungle during the steamy monsoon season were a common menace. Indeed it was almost certainly a Tista fever that had finished off an earlier Tibetologist, the Hungarian Csoma de Körös.

Two days after leaving Kalimpong, Kawaguchi found himself again at Das's villa in Darjeeling after a round trip lasting three and a half years and covering an estimated 2,400 miles—most of which he had done on foot, except for the initial train journey to the Nepali border. In going as far as Lo, Dolpo, and Kailash, and living in disguise for more than a year in Lhasa and Sera, he had far surpassed any of Das's own achievements. Though exposure, starvation, and altitude had nearly killed him, he had not suffered any prolonged illness during the whole expedition; yet he now came down with a Tista fever so severe that he thought the end was near. "I . . . thought how lucky it was to die here at Darjeeling, for then my death could be announced to all my friends, whereas if it had occurred in Tibet, no one would have heard of it."

He did not die, though he came very close to it. The crisis passed in three days, but so debilitating had the fever been that it was another five before he had the strength to try writing a letter home, and a full month before he had any real energy. The weight he had put on in Lhasa as a prosperous monk disappeared, and he became thin and haggard. But now at least he was able to rest, to receive guests, and to reflect on what he had accomplished.

There is one very curious feature of this episode. Kawaguchi mentions careful attendance by Das as one of the reasons for his recovery, yet Das himself was never to admit to meeting Kawaguchi in Darjeel-

Kawaguchi in Darjeeling after his illness.

ing after his trip—only later, in Calcutta. Isn't it possible that in his "careful attendance" the aging spy had something more on his mind than his former student's health? If delirium makes people babble away without remembering what was said, then Das may well have sat by his bedside with a notebook and pencil taking down all the latest Lhasa gossip as well as wilder theories about what the Russians were up to in Tibet, without the sick man ever knowing. And because Kawaguchi never knew, and Rai Bahadur Surat Chandra Das was not about to say, there is no way of telling what was revealed and written down during those three days, or how much of it was passed on to Calcutta.

Anyway, the calm that followed these harrowing days lasted only as long as the monsoon season, when all communication between Phari and Darjeeling was closed. No one ventured on the journey at this time of year for fear of the very fever that had almost killed Kawaguchi. But in October, when the caravans began coming through, his peace of mind was at an end, for the very first brought news that his friends in Lhasa were now in prison, that every house he had frequented was constantly watched by detectives, and that Sera had been sealed off. Much of this he put down to exaggeration, but he realized something must be going on, and when a Lhasa merchant he knew turned up in Darjeeling he rushed to him for information.

What he learned was that, though things were not quite as bad as the wildest rumors suggested, they were bad enough. The former minister and his mistress had been arrested for a short time, then released; the Ganden Tri Rimpoche was too important to have been affected; but Tsa Rongba and his wife, as well as Takbo Tunbai Choen Joe (who had leaked the secret to the Dalai Lama's brother in the first place), were all in prison and said to be undergoing torture, as was his elderly teacher from Sera.

It seems that much of the trouble had been caused by the Chyi Kyab at Yatung, that "upstart" official to whom Kawaguchi had taken such a strong dislike. He had cooked up some fantastic story about how the "Lama who was rumored to be a Japanese was in truth an Englishman and brother to a high official of the British Indian Government," and even that he had spirited himself out of Tibet using magic powers. Admittedly, the ease with which he had passed through the notorious border gates did seem little short of miraculous; but Kawaguchi knew that this official was merely using common superstition to save his own skin, while other, honest men were languishing in jail.

At first, apparently, he thought of sneaking back into Tibet via Nepal to see what he could do on the spot. Whether he was dissuaded from this or simply came to the conclusion that it would be a noble but hopeless gesture we are not told; obviously all Tibet would now be on the lookout for him. He also toyed with the idea of going to China and petitioning the emperor for help, but China's status in Tibet made this, too, seem a pointless exercise. In the end he decided to go back to Nepal and try to win the government over to his side.

Odd though the decision may seem at first, there were several good reasons for it. Though small, Nepal was regarded in Lhasa with considerably more respect than China, largely because of its Ghorkha troops, so there was reason to believe that a communication from the Nepali government in favor of his friends might have some effect. He also hoped that his own status as a Japanese priest might smooth the way since Nepal was now showing an interest in Japan, and had even begun to send students there to study. Just how much he really thought he could accomplish in this venture is difficult to judge, but it is certainly to his credit that he at least tried to do everything he could.

But he was now broke. After paying off Tenba and the freight on his baggage, he had arrived in Darjeeling with only two rupees, and though living off Das's hospitality ever since, he had run up some small debts. Quite unexpectedly, however, a fairly large sum of money arrived from Sakai, his hometown, donated by acquaintances. It could not have been better timed.

Das wanted him to stay and put his thorough knowledge of Tibetan grammar to use by writing a complete grammar of the language, to be appended to his dictionary. But the monk was unable to concentrate on anything of this kind, feeling guilty for sitting around in comfort while his friends in Lhasa suffered for their kindness. He was now largely recovered from his illness, and with the weather in the Indian plains cooling to the point where it would be safe to travel even though he was still a bit weak, he left for Calcutta—as a first step on the way back to Nepal—in November.

Back to Nepal

Yet the road to Nepal was to be a long and devious one, as our traveler spent the next several months crossing and recrossing northern India, stopping moreover to socialize along the way. These haphazard movements can only be explained by his having no idea how to get himself into Nepal legally (or precisely what to do when he arrived), and also by his encountering fellow countrymen for the first time since 1897.

In Calcutta he stayed again at the Mahabodhi Society, where he ran into a former classmate from Tokyo (from the days when he had been rector of the Gohyaku Rakanji and studying simultaneously), and discovered in himself a phenomenon not at all uncommon in Japanese who have spent long periods abroad: an inability to speak a word of his own language. But he soon recovered, and when he did one can imagine the flood of words, held back for five years, that poured out of him. Then when a former teacher also turned up at the Mahabodhi Society on December 14, he seemed to forget why he had come to Calcutta in the first place: the next day all three of them headed back to Darjeeling for the famous view of the Himalayas from Tiger Hill, and to write a little poetry about the mountains. They did not return to Calcutta until the end of the month, though by then Kawaguchi had at least developed a plan for getting into Nepal.

The idea was to go to Delhi and there try to arrange an introduction to the maharaja of Nepal through a Lieutenant General Oku, who was in Delhi representing Japan at the great Durbar held in honor of the coronation of Edward VII, Emperor of India. Since it was more or less on the way, however, they thought they might stop off at Bodh Gaya, and, before long, they had become a regular Japanese tour group, for while changing trains at a place called Bankipur Kawaguchi met yet another old acquaintance: a Reverend Fujii, also bound for Bodh Gaya on a visit to an aristocratic Japanese priest (Count Otani Kozui, who later made his own name as a Central Asian traveler). This leisurely progression toward Delhi and beyond shows that at least in his sense of time and urgency Kawaguchi had become completely Tibetan.

At Bodh Gaya his Japanese companions brought pressure to bear on him, urging him to stop wasting money and risking his life in a useless cause, and to go home where a hero's welcome awaited him. What was the fate of a few ignorant Tibetans compared to the honor of Japan? His first duty, they argued, was to return and tell the world about his exploits. To his credit, the explorer himself remained unconvinced. But the other three refused to let him go to sleep that night until he had made some concession; and eventually he agreed that if he could get the general and his delegation to forward a letter directly to the Nepali government appealing to them in turn to petition the Dalai Lama on behalf of his imprisoned friends, then he might forgo his own trip to Nepal. This for the moment satisfied them.

The extent to which he had lost touch with Japan was revealed as soon as he reached Delhi: the Japanese military were obviously horrified by the figure he presented, more like some local beggar than a member of their race. Nor was Kawaguchi feeling up to the occasion. For some reason he had had no opportunity to eat the day before, and, owing to the festivities, hotels in Delhi were so expensive that he had walked all the way to the tented site of the Durbar from Delhi Station. Once there he failed to get anywhere near the general, seeing only an underling, Colonel Yui, who made it clear he thought him a disgrace. He was then given a lecture on international diplomacy, told that it was important for Japan and England to remain friendly, and that official representatives of the emperor's government had no intention of risking an international incident by catering to the whims of a private adventurer. In the end Colonel Yui added insult to injury by ordering him out of the tent before someone suspected him of being a spy come to make a report. To make matters worse, it was now approaching noon and poor Kawaguchi—who throughout the interview had been offered nothing to swallow but his pride—was obliged to beg these people for something to eat. With bad grace he was given two pieces of bread and a cup of tea. He was still so weak with hunger and disappointment, however, that he was unable to walk any distance, and eventually they bundled him into a horse-drawn cab just to get rid of him. All in all, it was not an experience to make him look forward to his return to Japan.

Yet remarkably, and rather admirably, he did not give up, but instead turned back to Calcutta. There by some means or other (he hints at bribery) he obtained a letter of introduction to the prime minister of Nepal from an old Bengali gentleman who was the former principal of a school for young noblemen in Kathmandu. On January 10, 1903, he then left for the unpleasant little border town of Raxaul, just across from Birganj (the railway line had been extended from Sagauli since he was last in these parts). Somewhere in all this activity his sixth New Year since leaving Japan passed, the first on which he makes no comment.

Whether by design or accident his timing was perfect, for a royal hunting party was near Birganj, and both the king and the prime minister were present at this sporting event instead of miles away in Kathmandu. His letter of introduction did the trick at the border: he was allowed into the country and told he could await an audience with the prime minister.

It seems to have been the custom at the time to appear for these appointments at 10:00 A.M., only to wait fruitlessly until five in the afternoon. After a couple of days of this the rather ill-dressed monk was ushered into the presence of Chandra Shamshere Jung Bahadur Rana, prime minister and effective ruler of Nepal, on his evening walk—and was taken for a peddler.

> I had the singular satisfaction of his accepting from me a certain object of Japanese fine art. The Prime-Minister King seemed very well pleased with my present, and even offered to pay me its price. Whatever the King's offer meant, I insisted on its being a present on my part.

Someone must then have whispered in Chandra Shamshere's ear a word about who this strange little man was, noting that he had passed undetected through Nepal four years earlier and had just returned from Tibet; for he was escorted into the royal apartments for a more formal audience with the prime minister and the figurehead king, Prithvi Bir Bhikram Shah (he mistook the latter for a minister of state, not realizing his error until later in Kathmandu). As long as this wandering monk had placed himself in their hands they might as well see what he could tell them. Though there was a Nepali community in Tibet, and the Nepalese undoubtedly had a number of spies there, they probably had none so highly placed as Kawaguchi was rumored to have been, and they were as anxious as the British to know if their neighbor to the north had concluded a secret treaty with Russia. Kawaguchi, however, had little to say on this point: he believed that there had been no treaty, that public opinion was against it, but that most officials favored it.

In addition, the prime minister was naturally curious to discover how his visitor had managed to sneak through Nepal on his way to Tibet; but Kawaguchi had learned his lesson. He was not going to get his Nepali friends into the same kind of mess his Tibetan friends were already in, and he excused himself by saying that his English was not up to any adequate account. He cunningly added that in Kathmandu there were Tibetan-speaking officials to whom he could relate the whole story if permission to travel there were given, obviously preferring not to reveal the real object of this visit to Nepal so close to the border, where he could be promptly expelled. Far better, he felt, to wait until he had reached the capital and perhaps ingratiated himself a bit. Finally he was asked what had transformed Japan into so great a power. "I, of course, answered that it was the result of education and patriotism."

Throughout this interview and later meetings it was obvious that the Nepalese side had no idea what to make of Kawaguchi. Was he a beggar? A spy? A sincere holy man? Was he worth keeping around? And in the last question we find a likely reason why he was ever taken seriously at all, for in Chandra Shamshere Jung Bahadur Rana our monk encountered one of the master schemers of the age, a medieval Asian potentate (in spite of the ornate European-style uniform) with a tortuous and many-faceted mind. As a historical figure he is not easy for the modern reader to evaluate, there being two distinct views of him taken by historians. "A firm, wise leader, he brought order to the coun-

Chandra Shamshere J. B. R. and his wife.

try at a time when it was badly needed. He gave the country a sense of
security and a great deal was accomplished during these years." This is
a typical entry based on the British standpoint, one well disposed
toward a graduate of Calcutta University and a later contributor of
troops to both the Younghusband expedition and the Allied cause in
the First World War. Nepali historians, not surprisingly, take a somewhat different point of view: Chandra Shamshere was an unmitigated
disaster whose only purpose was to perpetuate a system in which a
single extended family treated the entire country as its personal estate.

Given the circumstances, it seems unreasonable to have expected any other sort of man. For when Jung Bahadur Rana had killed off his rivals and imprisoned the royal family in the Kot Square Massacre of 1847, it did not put an end to intrigue and sedition: it simply meant that the Ranas turned their plots upon themselves. In 1885 members of the neglected Shamshere branch murdered their uncle, Prime Minister Rana Udip (and any other Jungs they could find in a blood-soaked night and day reminiscent of the earlier massacre), and then somehow legitimized what they had done by adding "Jung Bahadur Rana" to their own names. Bir Shamshere, the eldest, took over the prime ministership and ruled—with relative restraint—from the Lal Durbar Palace (today a part of the Yak and Yeti Hotel) until his death in 1901. He was succeeded by his brother Deb, a complete anomaly, who in his brief reign of three months took the first steps toward abolishing slavery, and established an elementary school system. He had also already built an impressive drinking-water system in the Terai for the benefit of travelers.

As welcome as these measures might have been among the population at large, they were abhorred by other members of the Rana family, and poor Deb Shamshere had the misfortune of having an ambitious brother, Chandra, waiting in the wings—who soon hustled him off to internal exile in a remote eastern corner of the country. From there he slipped away to Benares, always a focus for Nepali political exiles, where in 1903 he made an unsuccessful attempt to assassinate Chandra when he was passing through.

Though Chandra Shamshere is generally credited with abolishing slavery in Nepal, he did nothing about it until 1926, and one of his first acts on taking power was in fact to reinstate the system his brother had just begun dismantling. Another was to do away with the elementary schools set up by Deb. Indeed many of the hallmarks by which his reign is remembered in Nepal—rigid control, cunning, and a gift for playing factions off against each other—were already evident early on. Kawaguchi, however, meeting him after only his first two years in power, seemed to neither know nor suspect any of this, and merely assumed that whatever he got from the Ranas was the result of his own persistent efforts. In practice, though, anything that came his way had been assessed solely in terms of its advantage to the Rana regime.

At the end of the first interview Kawaguchi was told to present himself again the next day at 2:00 P.M., but when he did so he was kept waiting until five—when Chandra Shamshere saw him only long enough to tell him he was busy. If he wished he could try again at the hunting preserve tomorrow. On the way out he was roughly treated by the guards, which made his servant (a shadowy figure, and obviously much less engaging than Tenba) think Kawaguchi was being made a fool of; the monk was beginning to have his own doubts, too. Anyway, on the following day he hired a horse-drawn cab and made his way to the hunting grounds, where a great shikar was being held, with four or five hundred tents pitched on the southern edge of the Terai. This is the strip of lowland jungle that was once almost as formidable a barrier to the south of Nepal as were the mountains to the north. (In fact in summer when it teemed with malarial mosquitoes it was probably an even greater obstacle, and it had made a shambles of the only attempted British invasion of Nepal.) Today much of it has been turned into farmland, but in January 1903 the Terai was a hunter's paradise, and with the season in full swing it presented a scene now probably lost forever.

> The royal tents sheltering the Kings and their multiple consorts, the Princes and Princesses, were conspicuously beautiful to look at, while the sight of those of the Ministers of State and others, variegated in colors of red, white, blue, and yellow, dotting the woodland, was both grand and picturesque.

He was refused admittance, but he did get a glimpse of the prime minister on his elephant and was told (or at least assumed he was told) to come again in the morning. "My servant again tried to make light of my credulity; but I scolded him into silence." His own confidence, however, was dwindling, and as a matter of policy he now decided to make a thorough nuisance of himself until the promised audience was granted. The next morning he smuggled himself into the royal enclosure at 6:00 A.M.

There followed probably the lowest moment of his entire trip: worse even than nearly drowning and freezing to death, worse than being robbed and almost starving, worse than Dawa's attempted seductions and being flattened by her family in a brawl. For then he was on his own and responsible to no one but himself. Now he was trying to act on behalf of others who at that very moment were suffering for his sake, and failure meant so much more than any personal shortcoming.

Unable to locate the royal tent, he was discovered by tough Gorkha guards, dragged to the front entrance, and unceremoniously dumped outside. There, soldiers swore at him; onlookers laughed at him—a common beggar was all he seemed. Their treatment was more than even this "professor of resignation" could take, and though he had often wept for joy during his trip, he now broke down for the first time and shed tears of sorrow, frustration, and self-pity. At least after the rejection in Delhi he had had another course to turn to. This looked like the end. Later, he consoled himself with a poem:

My suffering surely I with ease must bear
    Compared with all the tortures which my friends
Now undergo, for my sake prisoners made,
    In distant regions far above the clouds.

Yet, as in Delhi, he did not give up, and around 11:00 A.M. he was able to collar the Lord Chamberlain, who was passing by; and, worrying perhaps that a mistake might have been made after all, this official ordered someone to take Kawaguchi to the prime minister's tent. Chandra Shamshere now seemed bemused by the whole affair, and his curiosity about this uninvited guest revived. He replied in the affirmative when asked for a passport to Kathmandu, then good-naturedly offered him some money, which was refused. Kawaguchi's pride in this instance came close to exasperating the premier, who now demanded to know just what he wanted in Nepal. Still unwilling to give his real purpose away, the monk fell back on an ulterior motive: "I wished to secure," he said, "a complete collection of the Sanskrit text of the Buddhist Scriptures in existence in Nepal, offering in return to forward the Japanese edition of the same on my return home."

It was possibly the one perfect reply. Religion was, and still is, a powerful force in this part of the world, and the risk of offending the miscellaneous gods they worship or their sometimes unlikely representatives is not taken lightly. And while the Ranas had never shown any particular affection for Buddhism, there was little sense in humiliating one of its priests, more especially since he came from a country reputed to be rich and influential. There was still a chance that he could be working for his government, and even if he wasn't he might have some information worth knowing. Anyway, he seemed harmless enough.

So a truce was called. With nothing to lose but a few Buddhist texts (and Lord knows what Kawaguchi thought these high-caste Hindus would want with a reciprocal set of Buddhist scriptures in Chinese), the Nepalese granted this odd but determined little monk a passport and ordered him to present a list of the texts he wanted to the regent in Kathmandu. Chandra Shamshere himself would return in twenty-five days. "Henceforward I became a sort of special traveller under royal protection, for a police official was detailed to escort me to Kathmandu." He neglects to mention that his escort was also probably supposed to see that he did no more free-lance exploring.

Quite apart from anything else, this scripture trading was important for Kawaguchi's own future. First, it enabled him, on returning to Japan, to collect sufficient funds for another visit to India and Nepal. Perhaps more important, with this deal as precedent he managed to arrange a similar one with the Panchen Lama in India, two years later, which resulted in an invitation to Tibet.

But for the time being he was on his way to Kathmandu. It was exhilarating to be on the road again and his spirits rose. He had overcome opposition from both friends and foes among his fellow countrymen, had somehow found favor with the rulers of Nepal, and was at last getting somewhere. His immediate task was to cross the eight miles of the Terai jungle. Though warned about tigers, he rather enjoyed the prospect of seeing them; in fact when he got to Bichagori, the spot where he had heard a tiger roaring on his last trip, he decided it was rather lonely now without one.

> The same as once before the moonlight sleeps
>   On Bichagori fair; but whence is heard
> Upon the stream the savage tiger's roar?

He was also impressed by the water system along the trail, which he had failed to notice before. There were no springs or other natural sources of drinking water in the Terai, so reservoirs had been build at two-mile intervals, each connected to the next by iron pipes—a system constructed at his own expense by the philanthropic but hapless Deb Shamshere in accordance with the dying wishes of his wife. Stone tablets in Nepali, Tibetan, English, Hindi, and Parsi described its history, and parts of it are still in operation today.

It was too early in the year for anything but stray rhododendrons as he climbed through the bracing winter air toward the Chandragiri Pass, which he crossed into the Kathmandu Valley on the evening of January 21. On arriving in the capital he went straight to the palace of Bhim Shamshere, another of Chandra's brothers and acting regent in his absence. Bhim, however, who was fond of a pipe or two of ganja in the evenings, put him off until the next day, and all Kawaguchi got from the visit was two new "bodyguards." But on leaving the palace grounds he found that his old friend the Chiniya Lama had heard of his arrival and had sent one of his sons with a horse and servant to fetch him to Boudha.

How the news reached the lama remains a mystery. It is safe to assume that this prominent figure, who—according to Kawaguchi's nephew—had been privy to the secret four years earlier, was nervous, to say the least, on hearing that his guest had returned; but Kawaguchi's comment on his reception is characteristically unenlightening, saying only that they immediately renewed their friendship, and that the lama "received me with a right royal welcome and placed me under fresh obligations by his great hospitality." One would love to have eavesdropped on their conversation. All we know for certain is that Kawaguchi spent the rest of his first night back at Boudha holding a service for his father who, he had learned, had died in December 1899 while Kawaguchi was in Tsarang. His death prevented the honest old bucket maker from ever recognizing his wayward son's achievements, and one wonders if he ever forgave him for not carrying on the family business. On the morning after the service—presumably not held in the Chiniya Lama's temple next to the house, which is dedicated to Padmasambhava—Kawaguchi's friend took him to his appointment with Bhim Shamshere.

It is a pity that we never learn in which particular palaces the ensuing interviews took place. Most of these curiosities, or at least parts of them, still survive. Some are public buildings, others are ministries, one or two are hotels (though the most famous, the old Royal Hotel, has been torn down and replaced with a replica housing the Election Commission), several are banks, another a library, one is an orphanage, and a few are still private residences crumbling down around their ancient inhabitants. Though some of these palaces remain impressive, it is all but impossible today to imagine the opulence they represented until 1950. Tired, excited, nervous, and undoubtedly suffering from slight culture shock as well, about all Kawaguchi noticed was the strange mixture of East and West they incorporated, reminding him probably of Meiji Japan.

The Japanese monk was the perfect courtier at this first interview, beginning by complimenting Bhim Shamshere on having a country so like Japan. He then underwent another grilling on developments between Tibet and Russia, and finally came to the true purpose of his trip, which was of course to persuade the government of Nepal to intercede with Tibet on behalf of his friends. He also asked about the scriptures,[1] and met with a friendly and enthusiastic response on both counts. Then, on the spot, Kawaguchi seems to have made a major decision about his future, because when Bhim Shamshere told him they would probably be unable to assemble a complete edition during his stay, he made the sudden announcement that he was determined to revisit Nepal in two years' time, "and that I should be most pleased to receive the remainder of the Scriptures on the occasion of that second visit, I taking home for the time being such portions of them as could be collected during my stay." We are offered no explanation for this apparently impulsive decision, but the idea must have been at the back of his mind since Delhi, or perhaps even Bodh Gaya. For he had become accustomed to the traveling life, showed no homesickness for Japan except in his poetry, and undoubtedly began to remember, as his inevitable departure approached, more and more of the things that had bothered him at home. It was all very well to write fanciful poems to an idealized Japan while freezing on the plains of western Tibet; the reality could be quite different. He had had a hint of this in Bodh Gaya and

Delhi, where it should have been painfully obvious that he was as out of step with the rest of the country as ever. And so the prodigal was already planning his next escape.

*　*　*

Darjeeling and Boudhanath were probably the two best spots outside Tibet for news of that country, and as he awaited Chandra Shamshere's return Kawaguchi became increasingly distressed at the rumors he kept hearing. Finally he found a trustworthy lama who was passing through on a pilgrimage and from him had tidings at once painful and encouraging. The good news was that the ex-minister had still been free six weeks before when the lama had left Lhasa, and though there was talk of his rearrest, it was probably untrue. But poor Tsa Rongba was in a very bad way. He was reportedly being tortured every other day and was frequently interrogated. Though the merchant knew little about Kawaguchi beyond his nationality, the secret he had at all costs to keep was that he had carried letters to Das: if this became known he would be lucky to escape with his life. Touchingly, from what he told the lama (who had spoken to him as he stood in chains outside the courthouse), Tsa Rongba did not blame Kawaguchi at all but "bore his sufferings patiently in the belief that his tortures were due to the sins of his former lives." There was no news whatever of his former tutor from Sera, who seems simply to have been clapped into a prison and then forgotten. Helpless until Chandra Shamshere's return, Kawaguchi spent much of his time composing poetry about his friends.

Finally, on February 9, Kawaguchi and the Chiniya Lama rode into Kathmandu, through a rare snowfall, for the long-awaited audience with the prime minister. Though impressed with the size of the palace and the grounds, Kawaguchi again fails to identify it, but presumably it was Jung Bahadur's old Thapathali Durbar, a grand if somewhat ill-proportioned building near the banks of the Bagmati. Here Chandra Shamshere lived while the huge Singha Durbar (which when completed would be the largest palace in Asia) was under construction.

Kawaguchi perhaps preferred not to remember the palace's name, as the interview went very badly indeed. No beggar or peddler, they had decided, could possibly have gone so far unless he were working undercover, and before he was even allowed into the audience hall the foreign secretary and others grilled him on everything from his official rank in Japan to the route he had taken into Tibet. Kawaguchi, for his part, kept insisting that he was only a simple priest, and he refused to answer the latter question at all without a promise of immunity for anyone whose friendship he had profited from. To his surprise, when they were eventually ushered into the prime minister's presence, he noticed among the provincial officials the puzzled face of Harkaman Serchan, the Thakali subbha, who, if he recognized him at all, remembered him as a Chinese pilgrim. This was one of the very people he was trying to keep out of trouble.

Chandra Shamshere's earlier tolerance had vanished, and Kawaguchi was berated for not having given any details of his former visit. The prime minister softened somewhat when Kawaguchi replied that he would do so in return for some guarantee that no harm would come to those who had helped him, but Chandra still refused to believe that the Japanese was anything but a spy. A point that came up repeatedly was the question of how he could have afforded a six-year jaunt without official funds from home, since no one believed that he had really paid his own way. "Never did I feel more disgusted with what they call politics and diplomacy than on that occasion," Kawaguchi wrote later of his exposure to the Rana mentality. He was curtly dismissed and told to return in two days' time with the truth about his "mission."

On the ride back to Boudha, incidentally, Kawaguchi committed another of his geographical gaffes when he caught sight of Mt. Gauri Shankar and called it the highest peak in the world. Though Everest had been measured long before, there was still so much mystery about this part of the world that a spectacular but relatively minor (23,434-foot) mountain like this was believed by some to be higher. True, it does dominate the view east from the Kathmandu Valley while Everest itself is only just visible from the valley's rim, but Kawaguchi's confusion went deeper still, for at one point he refers to "the famous Gaurishankara, or Chomo Lhari, often called Mt. Everest." Here he was talking about three different mountains, all widely separated, since Chomo Lhari is in Bhutan.

The Chiniya Lama thought Kawaguchi should simply lie his way out of it, admit to being the Japanese spy that he wasn't, and be done with it. To this suggestion the often righteous monk replied with his "Theory of Lying," which disclosed yet another unexpected side of himself:

> Stratagems or temporary plans . . . may be used in war, or in circumstances like war, or among rascals, in order to avoid difficulties for others as well as for ourselves. . . . The civilization of Nepal permits the people to hear reason and truth. How could I insult the Governor with falsehood?

He was, of course, well off the mark politically here, since "reason and truth" were the last things Chandra Shamshere and his family would be willing to let "the people" hear.

On February 11 he duly appeared at the palace again, where he found both the prime minister and the king in attendance, and it was only now that Kawaguchi realized who the latter was. The two descriptions he gives us of Chandra Shamshere and King Prithvi Bir Bhikram Shah together are interesting if only because no other outsider saw them simultaneously at this time and left an account of the occasion. In neither audience did the king say a word. It may be remembered that the monarchy was retained by the first Rana prime minister, Jung Bahadur, essentially to legitimize his own dynasty. But, while it served this purpose, the monarchy was always a threat, as the Ranas were never popular and the throne could easily become a rallying point for the discontented. All that was needed was a strong and well-liked king for the Ranas to be in trouble. Chandra Shamshere had not been in power long when Kawaguchi saw him, and he seems to have at least been going through the motions of consulting the king on state matters. Relations were to worsen, however, and before his death in 1910 Prithvi Bir Bhikram Shah made one brave, if unsuccessful, attempt to limit the power of the Ranas (it would be left to his son Tribhuvan to finally overthrow them in 1950).

In the solemn presence of these two men, the Japanese monk was asked once more to reveal his secret. But this time for some reason his claim of innocence was accepted, and attention was switched to his petition. Here, at long last, was the moment he had waited for. He told the rulers of Nepal what, if circumstances had allowed, he would have told the Dalai Lama: that any fault was entirely his own, that if the Dalai Lama so wished he could send experts to Japan to ascertain what sort of man he really was, and that he himself would find some way to bear the cost. And miraculously, inexplicably, the tide turned. His determination, his refusal to back down, and possibly his sincerity had won the day. Chandra Shamshere asked for copies of the petition in Tibetan and Nepali, and a list of the scriptures he was looking for, promising that as much as possible would be collected within fifteen days.

At that point a very strange thing happened. Chandra Shamshere called Kawaguchi near and began to talk to him in English, in conspiratorial tones. He said that what he had to tell him was so secret he was not to write it down, even in his diary. Kawaguchi gave him his word. Tantalizingly he mentions this episode in the Japanese version of his travels—without going into details—but he diplomatically omits any reference to it in the English edition; and though he claims that the ensuing conversation went on for two hours, nobody has ever discovered what it was about. One suspects, however, that the prime minister merely planted some information as a test to see how trustworthy this monk really was.

On the ride home, during which he composed a few lines about the "highest" mountain in the world, Kawaguchi was in a much more cheerful frame of mind. His trip to Nepal seemed to have been crowned with success. The most powerful man in the country had listened patiently to him, had acquiesced to all his requests, and had even taken him into his confidence. Though he would not learn the fate of his petition for another twelve years, he had at least placed it in the hands of the people he thought most likely to bring it to the attention of the Dalai Lama. He had done all that was in his power to do, and while he waited out the next two weeks he put himself above suspicion by climbing to the cave of Nagarjuna, on a hilltop northwest of Swayambunath, and remaining there in meditation.

Finally, on March 12, he was given his scriptures and hustled out of the country, no doubt to the relief of the Nepalese, who may still have wondered whether they were dealing with an undercover agent or an overzealous monk. So Kawaguchi headed south, satisfied that at least no unfinished work remained to delay the journey to Japan, where apparently his arrival was awaited with some excitement. According to Das the two met again in Calcutta, but Kawaguchi told him nothing of the results of his visit to Nepal. Whether this indicates a lingering dissatisfaction with what had gone on in Kathmandu or a new caution toward Das (particularly in the light of whatever Chandra Shamshere had told him privately) must remain a mystery.

After preaching to Japanese residents in Calcutta he moved on to Bombay, where he gave another sermon to fellow countrymen—and received sufficient donations to be able to buy a ticket home. On May 20 his ship, the *Bombay Maru*, docked at Kobe after an uneventful voyage. It was a month short of six years since he had left in the opposite direction.

The adventure was over and it had been grand. He had met pilgrims and saints, beggars and highwaymen, incarnations and kings. He had traveled thousands of miles on foot, been reviled and honored, lived in squalor and comfort, and had accepted his share of hardship with Buddhist equanimity. As a penniless wandering scholar he had succeeded where expeditions had failed. But now he faced a different test. He was not an easy man at the best of times, and armchair geographers were likely to resent him. He had been only too glad to get out of Japan before. How long would he last this time?

1. Like archaeological sites in Asia, the significance of these scriptures was discovered by a succession of foreigners. They were first noted in 1824 by Brian Hodgson, who was either Secretary or British Resident in Kathmandu from 1820 to 1843. Hodgson, who was also the first Westerner to procure a complete *Kangyur* and *Tangyur* from Tibet, collected the Sanskrit scriptures in Nepal and sent them to the Asiatic Society in London.

Interlude in Japan

Japan is not an easy country to come home to. This has been the recent experience of thousands of Japanese businessmen and their children, as well as students and ordinary travelers, who in the latter part of the twentieth century have gone to live abroad and thus for several years or more have broken away from the culture and language that hold them so tightly bound at home. They find to their discomfort that anyone who has spent time away, and as a result has associated closely with foreigners, is regarded as not altogether Japanese; and instead of being admired for his mastery of a foreign language and ability to bridge cultural gaps (skills that the average Japanese seems actually proud to lack), he is all too often held in some suspicion. There are today special school programs for returning children whose parents have been stationed abroad, and their main emphasis is on cultural reassimilation, or "wiping out the foreignness." If the students happen in the process to forget the English, French, or Chinese that may have been their first language, so much the better.

In 1903 few Japanese besides diplomats, soldiers, and those charged with bringing home specific ideas and techniques considered beneficial to Japan had been abroad for any length of time, so that Kawaguchi was really one of the first independent representatives of this modern type. And while Europe by this time was well accustomed to greeting its homecoming heroes of Africa or other far-flung parts of the world with acclaim or condemnation, Kawaguchi was the first comparable explorer to return to Japan from unknown regions.

He received, initially, a hero's welcome. On the Kobe docks he was greeted by friends and mobbed by reporters. The journalists felt they were onto a front-page story, and Kawaguchi himself seemed to enjoy talking so much that they kept him going for five hours on the spot—and were still hungry for more. His impatient friends finally got him back, but not before he had agreed to more interviews with the *Mainichi Shimbun* of Osaka and the *Jiji Shimpo* of Tokyo, which were conducted at a villa in Kyoto and which turned into the kind of marathon session that today would be called an intensive debriefing. They went on for eighteen days, four hours a day, with the reporters dwelling on the more spectacular episodes of his adventure and not bothering to pin him down about trifling details like precise dates and routes. The results soon after began to be serialized in both papers in 155 parts as *Chibetto Ryoko Ki,* or "A Tibetan Travel Diary."

Here was immediate evidence that Kawaguchi had not lost his old talent for offending people, since by talking only to journalists and un-diplomatically ignoring the academics he managed to raise the hackles of the Tokyo Geographical Society. Had he given his first lectures in their presence, paid court to them as he had to Bhim Shamshere, or even allowed a few of their members to sit in on the interviews, things might have been different. But a slighted academic is about as under-standing as a woman scorned, so trouble from the Geographical Society was only to be expected.

Nor had he any intention of restoring good relations with the Oba-ku sect, and it was soon obvious that in some ways travel had not mellowed him appreciably. For when he was offered a robe of honor by the head of the sect, who now seemed anxious to make amends and welcome him back into the fold, he amazed everyone by refusing it on the grounds that it was too grand for someone of his lowly rank (bearing in mind his off-and-on-again status as an active member of the community). This was an acute embarrassment to the sect, which seemed to fear public criticism if it failed to honor its suddenly most celebrated member, and it implored him to accept. With typical reasoning Kawaguchi now replied that he would only agree to do so on condition that he was allowed, yet again, to renounce his ties to the order. The hierarchy must have scratched their shaven pates and thrown up their arms in despair. Couldn't he tell that this was a peace offering, beneficial to both sides? Why couldn't he just take what was offered and be grateful like any normal human being? True, they had quarreled years before, but couldn't he see that it was now best for all concerned to let bygones be bygones? In retrospect, it is perhaps reassuring to see Kawaguchi's overscrupulous behavior at Sakya and elsewhere in Tibet extend to the well-scrubbed monks and monasteries of his homeland. And simultaneously one is made still more aware that the homesickness in the poems was for a world that existed only in his imagination.

Then one of his early lectures turned sour in a way that was only partially his fault; for his attempt to explain to a (supposedly) Buddhist audience the selection process of the Dalai Lamas and other incarnations was greeted with skepticism and open disbelief. Knowing how badly Kawaguchi suffered fools (a category that included virtually anyone who disagreed with him), it is no surprise that his reply, in which he improvised on Buddhist theory and quoted the story of a scientist who had dismissed the idea of reincarnation until doctors told him he was dying, offended more listeners than it enlightened. It was particularly unfortunate that the specific example he used, that of a well-known proponent of the new scientific age called Professor Nakae, was not entirely sound. He had simply taken a vague remark of the professor's—that he hoped to meet again and supervise his students after death—and interpreted it as a sudden conversion to a belief in reincarnation.

Soon a mysterious article appeared in a popular Tokyo newspaper, the *Yorozu Choho*, saying that people in the provinces were being taken in by a charlatan named Kawaguchi who claimed to have been to Tibet, and that Tokyoites ought to know better than to be fooled by him. When the reporter was tracked down, he admitted quite candidly that he was a former student of Professor Nakae's and that he had written the article only to avenge what he regarded as a slight on his mentor. Worse was to come.

Though not an uncommon practice at the time, Kawaguchi's decision to leave the writing of his travel diary to the reporters who debriefed him was the biggest mistake he made on his return. This was typical of someone whose reluctance to face facts was often conspicuous: one remembers his inability to extract himself from situations where even he knew it was time to leave; or his peripatetic movements in the period that followed his convalescence in Darjeeling. He simply seems to have been swept away by events on returning to Japan, and to have spread himself too thin; for the publication of the newspaper articles and the subsequent book were to lead to almost instant controversy, and though he countered skillfully in person, the written word would remain when he was not there to defend himself, and the controversy lingered on.

As soon as the articles began appearing, there was an outcry from the Tokyo Geographical Society, and Kawaguchi was bluntly called a fraud. One can imagine its stiff-collared members, sunk deep in armchairs and sipping whisky, saying to each other: "The fellow's mad. Talks of some animal that looks like a hairy bull and is almost the size of an elephant. Honestly. . . . Says they cut up corpses and feed them to the birds. Just a morbid imagination. And an entire country led for hundreds of years by the same man reborn again and again in different bodies? Amusing, of course, but in this day and age . . ." By this time Kawaguchi was lecturing in Tokyo, where his brother Hanzui put him up. After one lecture he was hustled away to confront a roomful of newspaper executives at the *Jiji Shimpo* office who were understandably upset. According to the Geographical Society there were no less than twenty-five specific points on which he could be faulted, all of which proved that he had never been to Tibet at all. These points were said to have been brought up by someone in the army—someone whom the Geographical Society refused to name but who, they claimed, *had* been in the country in question.

This claim was a surprise to Kawaguchi, who knew of only two other attempts by Japanese to reach Tibet. Both had been made by Buddhist priests, and both had been unsuccessful. Indeed the determined Nomi Kan had died in this endeavor, while Teramoto Enga had been turned back to await a more favorable time (he eventually reached Lhasa in 1905, and later met the Thirteenth Dalai Lama during his exile in Mongolia). It seems most likely that the shadowy figure objecting to Kawaguchi's report was Narita Yasuteru, the Japanese spy who had visited Lhasa for a couple of weeks in December 1901 disguised as a Chinese. Since he had been on a secret mission financed by the government, everyone was anxious to keep his identity hidden, and though he went so far as to write to Chandra Das for details about his rival, he did not use his own name on the letter, dated July 30, 1903, but that of a

Mr. S. Inoma of the Tokyo Geographical Society.

Meanwhile, Kawaguchi managed to placate the newspaper executives with the suggestion that both his case and the case for the Geographical Society be printed side by side in the paper so that the public could judge for themselves. But the hot and muggy summers of Tokyo can be relied on to cause irritability, and one can assume that the simple monk who had dared and succeeded where no other Japanese before him had even come close was getting a little fed up with all this. For relief in a sweltering city, his thoughts must often have turned to the snowy plains he had left behind.

Opinion in the Geographical Society itself then split over what to do about Kawaguchi. One faction felt he might be telling the truth after all, and that since they could not produce a champion of their own it was virtually impossible to refute his claims convincingly anyway. Opposed to this approach was a group headed by the society's secretary, who considered it a point of honor to defend in a public debate the issues they had raised. But feeling that it would somehow compromise the dignity of the society if he appeared there in his official capacity, he offered to resign first. This put Kawaguchi in the unaccustomed position of restoring sense to the situation by inviting the secretary simply to come as he was. In the end the debate was conducted in a fairly friendly atmosphere in front of assembled scholars, and the monk did such a good job of answering each of the twenty-five points that everyone was impressed. It is a pity, though—for Kawaguchi's reputation, and public knowledge in general—that a more sustained inquiry was not carried out, and that this mine of information about Tibet and the trade routes of western Nepal was worked only by a team of journalists unable to separate prejudice and poetic license from reality.

At any rate, by this time answers began coming back from India. The society had written formally to the government of India, which confined itself to confirming that a Japanese called Kawaguchi was known to have entered Tibet and gained a considerable reputation at Sera. Chandra Das's reply was rather more interesting. Narita's letter had specified that he had no intention of "injuring any man's reputation," and no direct reference to Kawaguchi was actually made, but Das would have had little difficulty identifying the object of his interest.

Not only was his former pupil the only Japanese he knew who had been to Tibet, but he was aware that the fractious monk could be expected to stir up trouble wherever he went. On all the questions raised (Was Lhasa really visible from the Khamba La? Could Kawaguchi really have successfully practiced medicine in Lhasa? Was there really a place called Sera?) Das supported Kawaguchi. Yet it is also revealing that he neglected to mention that his former student had stayed at Lhasa Villa after leaving Tibet, and indeed had been desperately ill there, saying only that they had met twice in Calcutta: in the winter when Das was given a report on Kawaguchi's travels, and later in March after the return visit to Nepal. The shrewd Pundit knew when he was dealing with another spy, and preferred not to arouse suspicions in Tokyo that he had pumped a sick and delirious monk for information. Playing safe, he merely noted that at the time of their first meeting Kawaguchi was still seriously considering making the long journey back to Lhasa via Nepal to try to assist his friends.

But Das's most enlightening remarks were not about what Kawaguchi had or had not specifically done, but about his character. In making the sensible suggestion that the society should work with the explorer to produce a new map of Tibet, he wrote that "he is a truthful narrator, but he is not a scientific discoverer." Even more important: "You will have to sit down with him for days, otherwise his imagination will run away with him. He has a poetic turn of mind. This you will have to check, because the Geographical Society wants stern facts and figures." Das spoke from personal experience. In the same letter, however, he made another comment that would have delighted Kawaguchi had he ever heard it, and though as a prediction it never came true it is the warmest appreciation we have of his accomplishments both as a Buddhist and a traveler. For in claiming that "in Japan he will take the place Hsuan-Ch'uang had taken in China after his return there from India in the seventh century," Das placed Kawaguchi precisely where he would have most liked to be in the world of exploration. He always in fact resented being called an "explorer," preferring to think of himself as a pilgrim traveling in search of higher truths, and it is ironic that praise of this sort should have come not from a fellow Buddhist but from the worldly Das.

The dispute with the Geographical Society had no sooner died down than there was a fresh attack from the *Yorozu Choho*. This was a small-format four-page tabloid that had come into existence twelve years before and had achieved wide popularity through its twin policy of printing anything sensational and keeping its price low. It was thus the forerunner of today's notorious Japanese "Sports Papers." Readers of this particular report were told that the celibate monk was making a good deal of money from his lectures and spending it on a Shimbashi geisha nicknamed "the Tibetan."

Now, while the Geographical Society's aspersions were at least worth countering, this was pure slander. Yet it could hardly be ignored. Fortunately by this time he had strong supporters as well as detractors, and there was no need to climb into the ring himself. A more respectable paper took up his cause and sent a friendly reporter to interview him—and inform him that the ultimate source of the scurrilous article lay in his references to polyandry among the Tibetans. A respectable geisha is supposed to be satisfied with a single patron, just as a respectable wife is meant to be content with one husband, and a joke in rather poor taste was going the rounds about a notoriously promiscuous geisha in one of Tokyo's entertainment areas: hence the nickname. Hearing about it, the *Yorozu Choho* had simply used a little imagination and linked Kawaguchi with her name. The story was crude, deliberate, and ignorant, and merely added to his growing sense of disaffection.

In March 1904, *Chibetto Ryoko Ki* ("A Tibetan Travel Diary") was published in book form in two volumes by Hakubunkan. Three editors handled the work of revising the articles for publication, but there is no evidence that Kawaguchi himself took much part in this or in correcting their text: he was too busy planning his next trip. While they were about it, his editors encouraged him to have the manuscript translated into English. A reporter from the *Japan Times and Advertiser* named Takahashi (whose contribution was never acknowledged) was hired to do the basic translation, which was then brushed up by a Professor Lloyd, an Englishman. Funnily enough, if this had been rushed into print Kawaguchi might well have found himself with a best-seller on his hands.

For in March that year, while the translation was being done, Colonel Francis Younghusband and his forces were camped on the plain of Tuna, a day's march north of Phari, on their way to Lhasa in one of the most contentious episodes of British colonial history, as debate over the objectives of the mission continued in both London and Calcutta. Kawaguchi was later to claim that he stopped publication of *Three Years in Tibet* (its eventual title) because by that time reports from British journalists accompanying Younghusband were already coming out, and his own work would seem superfluous.[1] On the other hand, Peter Fleming, when researching his *Bayonets to Lhasa*, unearthed evidence that a copy of the translation reached the War Office in London as early as May 1904—three months before Younghusband reached Lhasa. Was this a draft of the English version (perhaps copied out by Professor Lloyd) or, as seems more plausible, had someone at the British embassy in Tokyo been on the ball and arranged for the newspaper articles to be translated—particularly the parts dealing with Russian activities in Tibet? Whoever was responsible for its appearance in London, it remains unlikely, in any case, that the document had any tangible influence on events by then well under way.

* * *

The story of the Younghusband expedition has been told too often to bear a detailed retelling here. The political maneuverings in London and Calcutta, as well as the conflict between the sympathetic, broadminded Younghusband and the myopic, dithering General MacDonald, belong to another tale altogether. Yet it is worth sketching a rough outline of events, for this invasion drastically altered the way Tibet related to the outside world. More important for our story, it would bring some of Kawaguchi's friends (notably the Ganden Tri Rimpoche, who was left more or less in charge, and his half-brother to whom he turned for advice) face to face with Europeans for the first time. And, most positively, it was finally to secure the release of those still imprisoned.

A preemptive move in the "Great Game" preoccupying the Western powers, this operation was the outcome of both distrust and frustration: distrust of Russia promoted by Lord Curzon, viceroy of India since 1899, who feared it might gain a foothold in Tibet; and frustration felt by a colonial heavyweight toward a hermit state that refused to treat with it. Kawaguchi's unwitting part in abetting the British cause has been touched on already; but, as Peter Hopkirk's *Trespassers on the Roof of the World* reveals, the archives of the Foreign Office provide enough material to explain the expedition, without referring to an Asian wanderer's footnotes. And the activities of Russia's own agent in Lhasa—a Mongolian close to the Dalai Lama, whom Kawaguchi wrote at some length about—were just as openly discussed in the papers of St. Petersburg (the Appendix has more to say about this).

From its outset the campaign was marked by mutual incomprehension, neither side really knowing what the fighting was about, and the victorious sometimes sickened by their victories. This was typified in a battle that occurred four months after Younghusband made a difficult midwinter crossing via the Jelap Pass, in the opposite direction to Kawaguchi's hurried flight. In April 1904 his troops engaged a reluctant enemy on the plain of Guru, north of Phari. Outgunned and almost surrounded, the Tibetans simply walked away, turning their backs on the rifle fire. Eventually the British and Indian soldiers laid down their guns without waiting for orders and went about collecting the wounded survivors. The mission then pushed on until held up in Gyantse; fought two high-altitude engagements at the Karo La—that eerie and often snowbound pass leading to the Turquoise Lake—and finally entered Lhasa in August 1904, only to find that the Dalai Lama had interrupted a three-year retreat and escaped, leaving the Tri Rimpoche in his place. Younghusband remained in Lhasa for seven weeks. A treaty was hashed out and signed, Dr. Waddell and accompanying journalists had a field day, and on September 23, just a couple of weeks before Kawaguchi boarded his ship to return to India, the whole party marched back toward the border. Before long, most of the treaty was repudiated in London, and the Tibetans were left wondering why the conditions they had struggled to reject were never put into effect.

For Kawaguchi, no doubt discouraged to read that soldiers' boots with guns and mules had marked the paths he too had passed along, the expedition also brought comforting news. First was a letter from Captain Randall Parr, the Englishman in the employ of the Chinese customs at Yatung, who wrote through a Miss E. R. Scidmore of Yokohama to inform Kawaguchi that to the best of his knowledge all of his Tibetan friends, including his teacher and the merchants, had been released. Though this letter came as a great relief, it was curiously dated March 17, 1904, and would thus seem to be a little premature: the treaty was not signed until early September, and it was only the day after the signing that there occurred the much-reported scene where Kawaguchi's teacher and another unnamed acquaintance (both Younghusband and the journalists displayed a formidable ignorance regarding the identities of the Tibetans they dealt with) were set free, along with two others imprisoned for assisting Das twenty years before.

Kawaguchi's anxiety on their behalf was confirmed by Younghusband's own description of the prisoners: "All were in abject fear of the Tibetans, bowing double before them. Their cheeks were sunken, their eyes glazed and staring, their expression unchangeably fixed in horror, and their skin as white and dry as paper." According to Edmund Chandler, the *Daily Mail* correspondent, "We who looked on these sad relics of humanity felt that their restitution to liberty was itself sufficient to justify our advance to Lhasa." This may have been overstating the case—after all, there were 2,700 Tibetan casualties—but the rescue of these men was certainly one of the few positive achievements of an enterprise curiously devoid of results. (Incidentally, it can hardly have done Kawaguchi's credibility much good when Younghusband went on to state that he trusted the Tibetans "would never again imprison men whose only offence was friendliness to British subjects.")

Accompanying the British side as interpreter was a Captain Francis O'Connor, a Tibetan-speaking gunnery officer whom Younghusband describes as "never so happy as when he was surrounded by begrimed Tibetans, with whom he would spend hour after hour in apparently fruitless conversation." It was to him that Younghusband credits the release of the prisoners, and soon afterward he wrote directly to Kawaguchi—the letter must have been forwarded by Das—with the welcome news. This reached Japan just in time for the monk to read it before departing on his second trip. Unfortunately his later relations with O'Connor, who was destined to play an important though un-

Kawaguchi's Sera tutor and another associate. The accompanying handwriting says: "Photograph of Mr. Kawaguchi's teacher and helper imprisoned and punished by the order of the Lhasa Government and released by the British Mission while at Lhasa on the insistence of the British Commissioner and of Capt. O'Connor. This photograph is sent to Mr. Kawaguchi by the hand of the fearless traveller Mr. Teramoto as a token of his esteem from his well-wisher Capt. O'Connor."

willing role in Kawaguchi's future, would never be characterized by friendliness or trust.

Only much later, in 1909, did Kawaguchi learn for certain that his friend the former minister of finance had not spent long under lock and key. His half-brother, the Ganden Tri Rimpoche, was a scholar rather than a diplomat and must have been hard-pressed to deal with the British. Feeling that the ex-minister was one of the few people he could trust, he had him released to assist in the negotiations. And it was rumored afterward that this elder statesman was responsible for saving Lhasa, since he was the only person among the Tri Rimpoche's advisers who counseled coming to terms rather than continuing a hopeless resistance in the face of a modern army. According to popular opinion, if the British had been sufficiently provoked, they might well have shelled and otherwise wreaked havoc on the holy city (indeed at one point when the negotiations were not going well Younghusband did turn his artillery on the Potala as a threat).

* * *

The year and a half that Kawaguchi spent in Japan—from May 20, 1903, to October 11, 1904—was a busy time; so busy indeed that, as we know already, he gave scant attention to the publication of his book. There were lectures in universities, schools, and even prisons. Everything he had brought back with him was organized, cataloged, and photographed, and there was much more to it than just books in obscure languages. From Tibet he had brought thankas, teacups, statuettes, and women's jewelry and clothing; from Nepal, a miscellany of objects ranging from Buddhist images to saligrams, those ammonite fossils of the Thak Khola region. But essentially his sojourn in Japan had only one object: to return to Nepal and India, and if possible Tibet; and most of his energy was directed to this end. True, he had found some useful allies and had been briefly treated as a celebrity, but fame had never interested him. More than offsetting any benefits was the narrow-mindedness of his reception in professional circles. He cannot have been blind to the irony of having fought constant suspicion from Tibetans, whom he regarded as Buddhist brothers, only to return home to find his experiences among them ridiculed and discredited.

More disturbing still was the sense of being beyond the pale, of having placed himself outside the protective circle of "us Japanese." "Convention" has a central and pervasive significance in Japanese society, and no amount of poems dedicated to the emperor could disguise his unconventionality. For years he had not even spoken his own language. He had gone to Tibet, not under orders or for the glory of Japan, but to pursue a personal vision of Buddhism. He had lived with a largely unknown people, spoken their undoubtedly barbaric language, eaten their horrible food, and not bathed for years on end. He was very nearly a foreigner himself. His position was in some ways not unlike that of a high-caste Hindu who returns polluted from studying in Europe, though in the Hindu's case there are at least ritual means by which the taint can be erased. And much as some individuals may have admired Kawaguchi's courage and accomplishments, they were probably more than happy to see him leave again. Knowing the sort of prejudice, both overt and unspoken, to which he was exposed at this period also helps explain a lot of the inconsistencies and oddities in his published writing.

So he made plans to escape, plans first laid in Kathmandu. Instead of the five hundred yen he had gone with the time before, he expected to have about twenty thousand. The money, though, was not quite so easy to come by as he had hoped. The Russo-Japanese War had broken out, and a good deal of patriotic fervor had been generated in a country determined to show it could defeat a Western nation. Sending an eccentric monk on an obscure spiritual quest was not much to make a fuss about. Kawaguchi nevertheless felt it was particularly important to go at this time. For one thing—and here he was able to marshal the forces of national pride behind him—he had promised the ruler of Nepal a corresponding set of scriptures, and he wanted—as a member of his race—to show he could be trusted. Another reason was perhaps more important personally: if he let the war delay him, it would seem obvious to those who had always been suspicious, particularly in Nepal, that he did in fact have some connection with the government and the military.

One interesting part of his preparations resulted from a lecture he reluctantly gave on Tibetan flora in July 1904. His reluctance was due to feeling he knew too little about the subject, but even this knowledge was more than his audience of botanists possessed. The outcome, anyway, was a crash course in plant collecting and preserving, and a gift of a complete set of tools. Thus during his second visit to Tibet he spent a good deal of time obtaining specimens, which he eventually brought home. For some reason, however, little was done with his collection until much later, and plants were still being identified and cataloged as late as 1980.

Finally, at the end of September 1904, just as Younghusband was leaving Lhasa with a hard-won treaty that was never put to use, Kawaguchi was ready to leave Tokyo. He had considerable funds with him and no less than thirty crates of luggage, which included such marvels of Japanese science as a mechanical pump, a model of a wind-powered rice mill, and, of all things, two swords. On October 11 he boarded his ship in Kobe, bound for Calcutta.

It is unlikely he watched the receding coastline of Japan with the same sense of deliverance he had felt before. By now he was probably indifferent to most criticism and unmoved by praise, and with that special smugness reserved for those who have had unique experiences, he could regard the skeptics as beneath his notice. Yet he undoubtedly felt relieved to be off, for he had developed a taste for life in less familiar parts and, like adventurers the world over, found his homeland confining. It was to be another eleven years before he saw it again.

1. For an analysis of *Three Years in Tibet*, see the Appendix.

The Quiet Years

Landing at Calcutta in November—minus his sutras, model rice mill, and Japanese swords, which somehow wound up in the Mitsui Bussan warehouse in Bombay—Kawaguchi may have hoped he would be granted a Nepalese visa without delay, allowing him to make a comfortable midwinter trip to the Kathmandu Valley. But he was in for a long wait; and since he never liked wasting time he began to study Sanskrit at Calcutta University.

In 1904, though the Indian Congress Party had been formed twenty years before, the independence movement was still in its muddled infancy. Japan, it may be remembered, was at the time considered a source of hope by many Asians in colonized countries. Even so, Kawaguchi found himself rather shocked by the following conversation he had with a Bengali student at the university.

"Why doesn't Japan just take over India?" asked the student. "Surely India would be worth having."

"You can't really mean that," replied the monk.

"I certainly do mean it."

"But don't you see, you are asking the wrong question," Kawaguchi explained. "You should be asking why we don't help your independence movement."

"Independence is only a dream."

"Not if you put your heart into it. Where there's a will there's a way."

"We'd rather be a colony of Japan."

"But why?"

"Because then we could leave the fighting to you and sit back and enjoy ourselves."

"You mean you would simply allow yourselves to be slaves?" Obviously to a citizen of an independent country this sort of attitude made no sense at all.

"It would be easier to live under Orientals than Westerners," replied the student, pursuing his specious theory.

"No, no, you're completely wrong. And besides, what makes you think that Japan has any intention of getting into a war to take India? We only fought China and Russia because we were under pressure."

By no means all Indians, or even all Bengalis, thought along the same lines as this student, and when word of Kawaguchi's attitude reached the ears of the famous Bengali poet Rabindranath Tagore, he was invited to stay as his guest. This was the beginning both of a friendship that was to last many years and a minor form of cultural exchange, since, at Tagore's request, Kawaguchi arranged for a Judo instructor to be sent from Japan to work at the poet's new Shanta Nigetan University; he also found a Japanese painting teacher for the Tagore household.

In the meantime, a major disaster almost occurred in Bombay when the warehouse there burned down. According to the first reports, his books had been destroyed—one of the few material losses that would have seriously disheartened him—but it turned out that only the boxes had been damaged: the sutras themselves were safe and sound. His luck was holding. Not long afterward his visa finally arrived, and by late February 1905 he was able to leave by train for Raxaul. There he rejoined his luggage and hired some porters for the eight-day trek up to the capital. Nepal is at its best in this season, just before the hot months: the rhododendrons are in full bloom, the weather is still cool and pleasant with little chance of rain, and the snow reaches further down the mountainsides than at any other time of year, enhancing distant views. This was the third time he had followed this trail through the Terai up to the Chandragiri Pass (which he crossed early in March), but never had he been so free of worry. For over two years in Japan and Calcutta he had taken little exercise, so it must have felt good to stretch the legs that had carried him from one end of Tibet to the other.

Once settled at Boudha, he was received again by Chandra Shamshere Jung Bahadur Rana. Their meeting must have taken place in the

Singha Durbar, the sprawling monstrosity that had been under construction during his previous visit. Five stories tall, with seventeen hundred rooms around seventeen courtyards, and Italianate fountains in the gardens, this vast edifice had been built in the astonishing time of eleven months, at a cost of two and a half million rupees. (Much later in his reign, Chandra Shamshere resold the palace to the government, which had paid to build it, and pocketed the profit.) The achievement seems even more remarkable when one considers that all the glass for its windows, the marble for its floors, all the chandeliers and European furnishings, had to be carried across the Chandragiri Pass from the plains. The façade of the palace, which is all one is usually shown in photographs, was like the tip of an iceberg, and some idea of its size can be gained from the fact that, when sixteen of its seventeen sections burned down in 1974, the fire raged for three days and nights.

It should have come as no surprise that the rest of Kawaguchi's San-

The Singha Durbar.

skrit scriptures were by no means ready. Chandra Shamshere had been extremely busy during the two years since he had last seen his visitor. Not only had he barely escaped an assassination attempt by his deposed brother Deb while passing through Benares, but he was preoccupied with keeping Lord Curzon out of Kathmandu. The viceroy had repeatedly expressed a desire to visit, but the Ranas were justifiably afraid that it might be used as a means of increasing British influence or as an excuse for plotting with the king. It was scarcely in the Ranas' interest to let too many people know how brutally the country was administered, since misrule had often provided colonial powers with a convenient reason for suppressing independent states. Chandra Shamshere had gone out of his way to please the British by supplying Younghusband with troops; he had also tried placating Curzon with a hunting trip to the Terai, at a safe distance from the throne. And so, while juggling these tricky issues, he can be excused for letting a collection of Sanskrit texts for a tiresome priest slip his mind. Yet, when confronted with Kawaguchi—and undoubtedly remembering what the Japanese forces had just done to the Russians—he was cautiously polite, assigned a minor relative who was interested in such things the task of putting the books together, and allowed Kawaguchi to stay at Boudha with the Chiniya Lama in the interim. But he was careful to keep an eye on him.

This was something the prime minister was very good at doing. He ran a secret police system even more extensive, and certainly more sinister, than Lhasa's. There was a strict curfew every night in the towns, informers were everywhere, and even Nepalese citizens from the Terai were not allowed into the Kathmandu Valley without a pass, which was not easy to obtain. Given these strict controls, it seems that Kawaguchi was virtually confined to Boudha, with the occasional foray into Rana Kathmandu, an artificial world to the east of the old city stretching roughly from Narayanhiti in the north to Thapathali in the south, its palatial residences linked by a network of broad boulevards. Even today this is the least inspiring part of town; eighty years ago it must have seemed utterly remote from the real life of the valley.

The search for the books, on the other hand, would have taken place in the heart of things: not in libraries and bookshops (discouraged in

Chandra Shamshere's time), but in obscure temples and attics in the oldest parts of Kathmandu and neighboring Patan (which can make a fair claim to being the world's oldest Buddhist city). Much as had happened in Tibet, a number of Buddhists works had been saved from the Muslim invasions of India by their removal to Nepal; and these rare manuscripts, many of which remained untranslated from the original Sanskrit, had kept well in this northern climate. But, though the scholar in Kawaguchi must have been pleased to lay his hands on them, the traveler can only have been frustrated at being barred from that part of the search he would most have enjoyed: barred from the streets lined with weathered brick buildings and intricate wooden window frames; from the Buddhist courtyards with their murky shrines and stupas, ancient images and rites; from the pagoda temples often shared by Hindus and Buddhists, with their curious erotic carvings; and from the great festivals, so old that, despite their Buddhist trappings, no one really knew their origins. Instead he spent his time quietly at Boudha under the Chiniya Lama's wing, and, without anything else to do, he immersed himself again in Sanskrit.

Finally, in December 1905, he gathered up all the volumes he had accumulated and, with mixed feelings, returned to India. He had succeeded almost too easily in his aims. He had made good his own promise, and he was weighed down with precious manuscripts (some so precious, in fact, that a law was subsequently passed making it an offense to take such books out of the country). Yet he had really hoped to continue on to Tibet; the old trade route, after all, ran right through Kathmandu on the way to Nyalam (or Kuti, as the Nepalese called it) and thence to Tingri and Lhatse. The trouble was, his presence and purpose in Nepal were too well known for him ever to have slipped away unnoticed. And formal permission would never have been granted since the prime minister was too eager not to offend the British who, after their recent armed passage in Tibet, felt it was their privilege to decide who crossed its border. (If Kawaguchi had actually been working for them, it seems unlikely they would have stood in his way, for the watered-down version of Younghusband's treaty did not even allow the British a representative in Lhasa, and a well-placed agent would certainly have been welcome.)

Quite by accident, Kawaguchi's arrival in India coincided with one of those periodic visits from British royalty that such a fuss was made about. The visitor this time was George, Prince of Wales, who was later to become George V. Since it was principally a hunting trip, the whole affair would simply have been an irrelevant extravagance to Kawaguchi if Francis O'Connor (previously interpreter to Younghusband and now, by reason of the treaty, the British trade agent in Gyantse) had not used the occasion to revive the old game of trying to manipulate the Panchen Lama at the Dalai Lama's expense. One feels he should have known better, and it is rather sad to see this promising young linguist who so enjoyed the company of Tibetans, and who could have been a talented cultural liaison, get embroiled in colonial ambitions.

His aim seems to have been to establish the same sort of personal relations with the Sixth Panchen Lama that Bogle had enjoyed with the third. It had been frustrating for the British expeditionary force to have fought its way to Lhasa only to find a substitute to negotiate with (Kawaguchi subscribed to the theory that the Dalai Lama had left with Russia's agent in Lhasa, and that he would have made straight for St. Petersburg if the Russo-Japanese War had not intervened). And with no access to the Dalai Lama, who was to remain absent in Mongolia, China, and eastern Tibet for years, O'Connor was hoping to bring off a coup of sorts by getting Tibet's other famous incarnation on his side. So he had promptly invited him to India, to meet the prince.

But if O'Connor and company expected the young Panchen Lama to be putty in their hands they were sorely disappointed, for while he may have been curious to see how India had fared under British rule, he was in no way anxious to have the same thing happen to Tibet. The annexation of the Buddhist kingdom of Burma was another lesson he bore in mind. Despite what the British had to show in the way of railways, schools, and hospitals, national independence was too great a sacrifice to make; and the Panchen Lama was no simple opportunist willing to trade a promise of personal favors for the freedom of his country. Besides, he knew very well—even if O'Connor did not— that he was in no position to do any such thing, as Tibetan custom and belief placed temporal power in the Dalai Lama's hands, not his. Though from this point on there was to be trouble between ambitious officials in Shigatse and their counterparts in Lhasa, the unfortunate Panchen Lama would never be a motivating force in these disagreements, only an unwilling tool.

If O'Connor's hopes drew a blank with the Panchen Lama, he fared no better with his own side, and he was reprimanded for trying to go over the heads of senior officers. To make matters worse, his guest somehow heard of Kawaguchi's presence in India (perhaps he had been clamoring for an audience) and expressed an interest in meeting this citizen of an independent Buddhist state. O'Connor and his colleagues were duly horrified, and disconcerted too. They had invited the Panchen Lama to curry favor, not to cause offense. Yet even less did they want this visit to result in ties between Japan and Tibet. O'Connor presumably saw his career in ruins if events should take this turn.

So Kawaguchi again found himself the focus of misapprehension, suspected once more of being some sort of political agent. The British had no way of knowing how he had been humiliated by representatives of his own government the last time he had had any contact with them, two years before in Delhi. What's more, the prospect of a special relationship between Tibet and Japan was not, in fact, unrealistic, though it had nothing to do with Kawaguchi and the Panchen Lama. A connection had been established as an outcome of the Younghusband expedition, when, after fleeing to Mongolia, the Dalai Lama was approached by the pan-Buddhist priest Teramoto Enga, and later, in Peking, when he talked to diplomats at the Japanese embassy—talks that eventually resulted in part of the Tibetan army being trained by a flamboyant soldier of fortune called Yajima Yasujiro. But O'Connor was unaware of all this and, suddenly faced with a meeting that threatened to put a premature end to his career, he came up with the absurd compromise that the two Buddhists could meet—so long as they did not speak.

The encounter took place at Bodh Gaya in O'Connor's presence, at the end of 1905. If either O'Connor or Kawaguchi remembered the former's letter, telling him of his friends' release, neither mentioned it. It must have been an odd meeting, with the Japanese monk perhaps expected simply to prostrate himself and leave, the Panchen Lama eager to learn about Buddhism in Japan, and the British official biting his nails. First to break the unnatural silence was the lama with a flood of religious questions. Kawaguchi made no reply at first, turning his thoughts, perhaps, to the last two occasions on which he had seen this young Tibetan: both had been processions—one in Shigatse, and one in Lhasa at the time of his investiture, which had helped divert attention from Kawaguchi's escape. But eventually the lama lost patience with this ridiculous situation and told O'Connor outright that he wanted a conversation with this man about religion in Japan. It was a difficult request to turn down if friendly relations were to be maintained, particularly when O'Connor's excellent Tibetan would allow him to keep track of things anyway. So permission was given, on condition that they stuck to religious topics.

This they undoubtedly did, for the Panchen Lama had been deeply absorbed in Buddhist studies since childhood, and Kawaguchi, of course, was also in his element. The two got on well, Kawaguchi restraining himself from expressing the sort of extreme opinions that had often annoyed other Tibetans (something marginally easier to do with a Gelupa monk than with a Nyingmapa); and in the end they met for several days running. Presumably, if O'Connor was able to follow their conversation in all its ramifications, he was soon bored, and one feels that having to sit through it was almost as harsh a punishment for his unauthorized scheming as anything meted out by his superiors.

Now, in the course of these talks Kawaguchi happened to remember the exchange of sutras that had enabled him to reenter Nepal, and though it is hard to imagine what he could still be lacking in the way of scriptures, he proposed a similar deal to his new friend. The reply amounted to an invitation to visit Shigatse. Poor O'Connor must almost have dropped through the floor at this ("But we were only talking about religion, as we promised. . . ."). All the same, he probably realized that as long as this meddling monk was living in India his movements could be checked; and, anyway, it would in fact be another eight years before Kawaguchi took advantage of the invitation.

Something else the two priests were able to agree upon was the sorry state of Bodh Gaya. Today, of course, the site of the Buddha's enlightenment is a well-endowed religious center, due largely to the exodus of pious Tibetans to India since 1959, but also to their subsequent prosperity and the spread of Buddhism to the affluent West. Yet at the beginning of the century it was virtually a ruin, visited only by a few pilgrims from Ceylon, Tibet, Burma, and occasionally Japan. These pilgrims must have been confused to discover that even the main Buddha statue had been transformed into one of Shiva. Vishnu might have been a slightly more understandable compromise, but, finding the site neglected since the days of Buddhism's decline before the Muslim invasions, a Shaivite sect had taken it over. An attempt at restoration by the Burmese king in 1847 had faltered, because the matter of jurisdiction remained unclear, and in 1884 the government of India had decided in favor of the Shaivite Mahanta. Partly as a result of Kawaguchi's meetings with the Panchen Lama, however, a committee was formed for the repair and upkeep of Bodh Gaya, with the Panchen Lama as chairman, the raja of Sikkim as vice chairman, and Kawaguchi as an active member. There was a later meeting with Lord Minto, Curzon's successor, who promised support and funds; unfortunately, Minto may not have understood some of the complications involved, since he eventually withdrew his support, and Kawaguchi resigned from the committee in a huff. He was never a very good organization man.

* * *

In March 1906, after a month of further Sanskrit study at Tagore's Shanta Nigetan, north of Calcutta, Kawaguchi moved to the ancient city of Benares on the holy Ganga. Here, at the Central Hindu College, he would spend the next seven years honing his Sanskrit skills and trying to make sense of all his manuscripts.

"Now it is a strange thing, but things that are good to have and days that are good to spend are soon told about, and not much to listen to; while things that are uncomfortable, palpitating, and even gruesome, may make a good tale, and take a deal of telling anyway," says Tolkien somewhere in *The Hobbit*. Much the same can be said of the monk's long interval in India; a sedentary, if ultimately rootless, scholar, he passed his days pleasantly enough though very little actually happened. His few material needs were taken care of, and whenever he tired of studying there were holy places to visit nearby. But apart from the abominable heat in April and May, and the humid, unhealthy monsoon season from June to September, there were no real trials. Apparently he was quite poor, though not bothered by the fact; but in 1909 some visiting Japanese were so shocked by his living conditions that they decided to take up a collection and send him some funds. Since national pride rather than real compassion was behind this, Kawaguchi wrote to his brother Hanzui trying to turn the donation down, saying that he was quite content with his lot and if things got too bad he could always go to the Himalayas and live there for next to nothing. But the money came anyway, and with it went some of his old determination, for from then on he took to escaping the heat—not in a hermit's cave in the mountains—but in Darjeeling. This gave him an opportunity to renew his friendship with Surat Chandra Das, whose Tibetan grammar was about to be published; and it was Kawaguchi who corrected the proofs, which were in a type too small for the aging Bengali's eyes.

Kawaguchi in India in 1909.

Kawaguchi in Lumbini (1911?).

In 1909 he also took some time off to prepare the manuscript of *Three Years in Tibet* for publication, with assistance from Professor Unwalla and the prominent Theosophist, Annie Besant. But nothing broke the level surface of his life until 1911, when a brief moment of excitement occurred. Leading a group of Japanese visitors, which included the current head of the Obaku sect (with whom he was now apparently on good terms), he was stopped at the Nepalese border, not far from their destination, the Buddha's birthplace at Lumbini. Kawaguchi's casual approach to border procedures (none of his party had entry permits) soon had them all in trouble. Fortunately, someone must have kown that the monk had once been in contact with Chandra Shamshere; and in due course, chastened by their little adventure, they were allowed to proceed—now treated as special guests.

* * *

Meanwhile, in contrast to Kawaguchi's otherwise routine existence, the Dalai Lama was beset with problems. In 1909 he had returned to Lhasa, just ahead of a Chinese invasion force. His exile had been prolonged by his efforts to negotiate with the last of the Manchus about irregularities along the Tibetan border. These talks, however, had done little beside convincing the Chinese that this Dalai Lama meant to be more assertive than the previous seven, and they decided to try and reestablish their authority in Tibet while there was still a chance. As a result, it was only another two months before the Dalai Lama appointed a new Ganden Tri Rimpoche to replace the man who had served him so faithfully, and fled again—this time south to his former enemies in British India. He had meant, in fact, to go only as far as Yatung, and to attempt to negotiate there while he was still on Tibetan soil; but he was closely pursued by Chinese troops, and so he pressed on to Kalimpong, then Darjeeling, where he set up court for the next three years. During this period abroad he was to acquire a good deal of knowledge about India and its Buddhist holy places, and develop a close friendship with the Tibetan-speaking Englishman Sir Charles Bell; and with his knowledge of China from previous years, he became by far the most widely traveled and experienced Dalai Lama in history.

Since Kawaguchi now spent his summers in Darjeeling it was inevitable that he should seek an audience, which apparently he obtained. But we are never told exactly what took place; his only comment—that "while in India I got to know both the Dalai Lama and the Panchen Lama"—leaves us just as much in the dark as his earlier remark about "frequent interviews" with the Dalai Lama in Lhasa. One can't help feeling cheated, since they were meeting under very different circumstances: the lama was now much better informed about the world, and about Japan as well, having met both unofficial and diplomatic representatives of that country in Mongolia and China. What, one wonders, did he think on seeing the "Doctor of Sera" again without his disguise?

The brevity of Kawaguchi's reference suggests that the exiled leader gave him a chilly reception, and Kawaguchi's avowed friendship with the Panchen Lama was a likely cause. Relations between the two lamas were strained. Through no real fault of his own, the Panchen Lama had become a surrogate for others' dreams, courted by the British, pushed forward by his attendants at Shigatse, and paraded by the Chinese. In 1911, for example, in a Chinese attempt to install him in the Dalai Lama's rightful place, he was invited to Lhasa and housed in the Norbu Lingka. When he then rode around the city with the Chinese Amban in a palanquin during the butter-lamp festival, the outraged populace dropped old socks and mud on the unfortunate young man's head. He seems to have been as innocent in politics as Kawaguchi claimed to be, and ended his days a rather tragic figure, kept virtually prisoner in China after yet another dispute between Lhasa and Shigatse in 1922. The Tibetan historian Shakabpa contends, however, that correspondence between the two incarnations remained cordial, and that all their misunderstandings were due to unscrupulous officials; but at this point, in Darjeeling, the Dalai Lama may well have suspected Kawaguchi of being one of them.

Kawaguchi himself, unrealistically, may have hoped that their meeting would result in an invitation to Lhasa, and his disappointment was probably keen. He was getting bored and a little impatient. While he had originally traveled in order to study, traveling had become an end in itself. His last real journey had been to Nepal back in 1905, and even that had been unsatisfactory. But Tibet was too unsettled, its leadership too ambiguous, for even this simple monk to try taking up the Panchen Lama's offer. He considered giving up and going back to Japan, yet, beside the fact that he knew no one there who could help him with his Sanskrit, he felt compelled to stay in India, however vague his prospects, because the lure of Tibet continued to attract him.

Then in 1911 the Manchu dynasty was overthrown by Sun Yat-sen's Kuomintang, and many of the Chinese troops in Lhasa mutinied and went home. Nevertheless, it was to take over a year of intermittent fighting in the capital, which destroyed about a third of its buildings, to dislodge the rest. Before the fighting ended, the Dalai Lama returned to Tibet, staying at Dorje Phagmo's monastery on the Yamdruk Tso until the last of the occupying forces departed and he was able to reenter Lhasa, amid great rejoicing, in January 1913. The Panchen Lama made a point of coming from Shigatse to greet him on the way, thus restoring personal relations, even though their respective advocates remained on unfriendly terms.

At last, with the declaration of Tibetan independence, a form of stability prevailed for the first time since Younghusband marched on Lhasa, almost a decade before. To Kawaguchi it seemed the waiting might be over, and he sent a trusted Tibetan friend called Pontso from Darjeeling to Shigatse to contact the Panchen Lama and see if the invitation still stood. The answer was positive, so he immediately sent to Japan for another set of scriptures, which—perhaps to allay suspicion— he had not ordered earlier. And as long as he could leave India undetected, he was on his way.

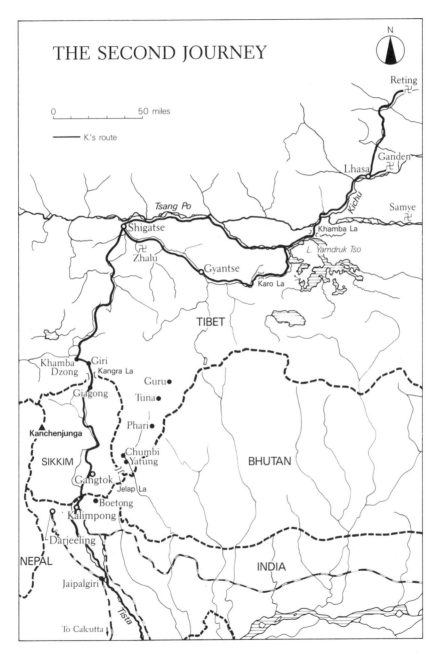

THE SECOND JOURNEY

0   50 miles

K.'s route

N

Reting

Ganden

Lhasa

Samye

Tsang Po

Kichu

Khamba La

Shigatse

L. Yamdruk Tso

Zhalu

Gyantse

Karo La

TIBET

Khamba
Dzong

Giri

Kangra La

Guru ●

Giagong

Tuna ●

Phari ●

Kanchenjunga

Chumbi
Yatung

BHUTAN

SIKKIM

Gangtok

Jelap La

● Boetong

Kalimpong

Darjeeling

NEPAL

INDIA

Jaipalgiri

Tista

To Calcutta

Sentimental Journey

Kawaguchi was later to publish two separate accounts of this second trip to Tibet. The first, *Nyu Zo Ki* ("Record of a Journey into Tibet"), was serialized in the Tokyo *Asahi Shimbun* after his return to Japan. A strange, uneven, and often superficial narrative covering the entire eleven years of his second absence from Japan, it includes sections on his restricted visit to Nepal and his meetings with the Dalai Lama and Panchen Lama in India, terse travel notes interspersed with wild flights of fancy, and observations on the changes he found in Lhasa and the changes in his own attitude toward religion in Tibet.

The second, *Setsuzan Uta Ryoko* ("Poetic Travels in the Snow Mountains"), is completely different. Here, as the title suggests, he allows his poetic fancy free rein. Written in Shigatse, the work says nothing of his stay there or in Lhasa, and about one third of it is verse. There is a fair amount about the scenery and local customs of Sikkim, but in general it rambles rather aimlessly. In neither account do we find the carping and petulant tone of *Three Years in Tibet*, though he still cannot quite bring himself to approve of Tibetans and their religion—in spite of (or perhaps because of) his being so drawn to both.

As in his earlier work, he again proves to be a sharp observer of people and social traits, but as a geographer he is more hopeless than ever. Most obvious and frustrating to the non-Japanese reader—or to the Japanese reader trying to relate the journey to a map in English or any other language—is the lack of any system for transliterating place names, most of these being rendered quite differently in the two books. Some of the discrepancies were pointed out, and the accepted romanized version supplied where possible, by the editor of the 1981 Kodansha edition of both volumes (*Daini-kai Chibetto Ryoko Ki*); others, however, defeated him, and the reader sometimes feels lost in a semi-mythical land.

Both accounts ultimately raise almost as many questions as they answer, and to form any clear picture of his return journey it is necessary to supplement them from his nephew Akira's biography. Using his uncle's unpublished journals, Akira not only gives a much better organized description of it but refers to a number of important aspects of the journey that Kawaguchi himself left out—for, oddly enough, Kawaguchi's published versions omit most of the adventures, as well as his most significant accomplishments.

*　*　*

This trip differed considerably from the first, fifteen years before. For one thing, the traveler himself was a good deal older. In 1899, when he left Darjeeling, he had been thirty-three. Now he was forty-eight, and had been leading a placid life for the past eight years. His route this time would be nothing like as difficult, but it was still far from being a simple mountain stroll, including as it did a midwinter crossing of a pass nearly seventeen thousand feet high.

More important, he was returning to a very different Tibet. With independence formally declared, even the myth of Chinese suzerainty was now gone. No longer were there any Ambans in Lhasa, powerless in themselves yet a threatening reminder of power waiting in the wings. Troublesome Chinese troops and officials no longer manned the borders. Tibet now belonged to the Tibetans. The British had come and gone, confirming what had once been the Tibetans' worst fears, yet the nation's religion was intact, the mood of the country more fiercely nationalistic than ever. And with the threat from the British to the south removed, the Dalai Lama had no more need of the Russians in the north.

Nor would Kawaguchi be entering a still unknown and inhospitable land, though Tibet, by the standards of the rest of the world, could scarcely be called an open country yet. Shortly after Younghusband's march on Lhasa a team of British surveyors, with the permission and backing of the government in Lhasa, had traversed the terrain from

Gyantse to Gartok, verifying earlier clandestine surveys and filling in blanks. The map of western Tibet was completed a few years later by the Swede Sven Hedin, who, in two extended journeys, visited any remaining unexplored ground. There were British trade agents stationed in Yatung and Gyantse, and another making regular visits to Gartok in the far west. More surprising still, there were said to be Japanese living openly in Lhasa, Sera, and Drepung. Even Kawaguchi himself was going this time, not as a secret traveler, but as an invited guest.

Not that the trip would be entirely devoid of excitement: the British had backed up their policy of controlling who went in and out of Tibet with a law calling for a fine of five thousand rupees (then roughly equivalent to $1600) and six months in prison for anyone caught crossing over from India without permission. This was a minor inconvenience compared with what he had had to face the last time, but the embarrassment would certainly have been considerable had he been apprehended. The British just then were particularly annoyed with the Japanese, for at least three were known to have escaped their supervision in the year since the Dalai Lama's return to Lhasa. Two, like Kawaguchi, were Buddhist priests: Aoki Bunkyo, who had gone by way of Nepal, and Tada Tokan, who had gone via Bhutan. Somewhat more alarming was Yajima Yasujiro, a veteran of the Russo-Japanese War, who had taken the Chumbi route and was now reputed to be employed by the Dalai Lama's government in training the Tibetan army. The government of India would not wittingly let yet another of these wily Orientals give them the slip. For such reasons, Kawaguchi donned his disguise before leaving Calcutta and planned a route through Sikkim, avoiding population centers at a season when no one in his right mind would have attempted the high Himalayan passes.

*   *   *

Thus it was that on December 20, 1913, a prosperous-looking Tibetan monk boarded the train in Calcutta for Jaipalgiri, a few stations short of Siliguri. He caused some comment among fellow passengers: he did not quite look the part. Perhaps it was the beard, or maybe he needed a few months of accumulated grime to be convincing as a Tibetan. But passengers on Indian trains are prone to comment on

278

virtually anything, so there little real cause for worry.

Since he never tells us just how it felt to get into the old disguise and face the challenge of the Himalayas again, we have only the tone of his poetry to go on. Judging from this, he had not a care in the world. In Jaipalgiri, at one of those outdoor tea shops that are still such a friendly feature of travel in India, he sat under a banyan tree with his trusty servant Pontso—the same who had run messages for him all the way to Shigatse—and composed poems to the white peaks beyond, which though still distant were clearly visible in the crystal morning air:

> The sky, the snow mountains,
>   Reflected in the Tista,
> Are but a symbol of my happiness.

They were joined at Jaipalgiri by Tashi Tsering, like Pontso a Darjeeling Tibetan. Although he was to form the third member of their party, he never—unlike the amiable Pontso—really emerges as a distinct personality.

The Tista is quite wide here, and the three crossed by ferry to a smaller station, where they took a branch line up the east bank. Alighting at the base of the foothills south of Kalimpong, they found an attractive scene: the mountains as ever in the background, and Bengali women in the foreground, singing as they harvested the rice.

> Voices of peasant women,
>   Singing as they work,
> Mingle with the sounds of cattle;
>   And, over all, one hears
> The great peaceful voice of the snow-covered peaks.

That evening, they walked two miles farther on and slept under a banyan tree.

The next few days were a trial. The baggage carried by the Tibetans was heavy; Kawaguchi, though unencumbered, was in poor physical condition; no one was quite sure of the way; and it rained. Winter always seems to produce a few days of rain in the Himalayas. Farther north and higher up, these rainstorms can be dangerous blizzards, but in the foothills they are simply cold and uncomfortable. The only compensation was the beauty of the misty scenery, and the hot tea that Pontso and Tashi Tsering stopped to brew at every opportunity.

On December 25 they camped only three miles south of Kalimpong. The town, with its promise of warmth and comfort, must have been a temptation to all three travelers, but each of them had friends there, and to make their presence known would have been to end the venture before it had properly begun. Even so, there was no way around, so on the twenty-sixth Kawaguchi sent Tashi Tsering ahead with the bulk of the luggage while he and Pontso waited till the light was fading to slip through the town. He saw two or three acquaintances in the streets, but kept his own face hidden and was not recognized.

Later that day they got lost, and when darkness fell and Pontso went to search out the road, Kawaguchi thought he heard the roaring of a tiger uncomfortably close. If he was correct, the tiger was a well-fed one, for the party passed uneaten—only to encounter the bridge that led across the Tista into Sikkim. Then, as now, the bridge had guards on it at all hours. The travelers tried waiting until late at night, then crossing as silently as possible, but still they woke the guards. Luckily, Pontso was able to convince the latter that they were local Tibetans, and they proceeded to enter this small Buddhist mountain kingdom, which—thanks to the machinations of the British—was now independent only in name.

The New Year, 1914, found them lodging in a pigsty at a rent of a rupee and a half per week. Kawaguchi had thought it wise to stop a few days and check on the state of the passes to the north, but the Nepali Hindu immigrants who inhabited this southern part of Sikkim observed the caste system so strictly that those outside it were not even allowed inside a house. The news from the north was anything but encouraging. The rain of the previous month had been heavy snow farther on, and though the high passes were relatively clear, to reach them would be a tough undertaking. Kawaguchi decided to leave the bulkiest and most important part of the luggage with a friend called Tinley Sambo in Gangtok, a Tibetan who had once been given some grammar lessons by him.

In spite of the hardships, Kawaguchi, like almost every traveler before or since, was enchanted with Sikkim. It is a pity that in the end he was able to see so little of it. He stopped occasionally at a village, but had to skip completely the royal capital of Gangtok, as well as monasteries that he would certainly have found interesting. Nevertheless, he was moved by the physical beauty of the people and their gentle manners. There were, as mentioned, a number of immigrants from Nepal in the foothills, but the majority of the population at lower altitudes belonged to the original Lepcha tribe, while the aristocracy and high-altitude inhabitants were of Tibetan stock. Though Kawaguchi grants the men a certain nobility, it was the appearance of a Sikkimese girl herding cattle that most impressed him. She seems, in fact, to have overstimulated his imagination somewhat. Her face, he tells us, had the grace and fairness of complexion of an ancient Japanese noblewoman, while her white wrap-around dress reminded him of the clothes worn in ancient Japan. The politeness and modesty of the Sikkimese also recalled his homeland. Might there be some connection between the two peoples? Sikkimese houses were raised off the ground, and the crosspieces at the ridge-ends of the roofs made them look rather like Japanese shrines. They even used pillars made of cherry wood. . . . Reluctantly, he lays the question aside as impossible for him to solve.

They were now climbing fast, and on January 6 found themselves in a potentially dangerous snowstorm. Pontso, who obviously thought a lot of his master's prowess as a monk, asked Kawaguchi if he could not perform a small miracle and improve the weather. Whatever his own estimate of the possibilities, he told the two credulous Tibetans to go to sleep: he would do his best. He then set himself to meditating . . . and by morning the snow had stopped. All three of them had a good cry together.

Still, the snow that had already fallen made the going difficult. On the seventh, they saw some large letters in white paint, which proved to be verses from the Bible, emblazoned on the cliffs. Kawaguchi was impressed with the zeal of the missionary responsible, but allowed himself to feel that such religious graffiti tended perhaps to spoil the natural surroundings.

On January 8, still five days from the actual border, they came to the last manned post and found that the official in charge was an old friend from Darjeeling. There could be no hiding now, but the man obviously thought that anyone who had come this far must be traveling legally, and did not press Kawaguchi for papers, cautioning him instead about the rigors of the desolate regions ahead. This was certainly no idle warning, for two days later another blizzard struck while they were camped in a cave. So severe are these high-altitude blizzards that the greatest danger is of being suffocated by snow blocking one's nose and mouth. Moreover, fourteen or fifteen incautious travelers had died there only the year before in an avalanche. That night there was another meditation session, and again the blizzard died down.

The snow, of course, had not improved the trail, which was narrow and slippery, with a long plunge on one side. But the next night they were able to enjoy a little luxury, for though the whole region was uninhabited, the Indian army had built a bungalow where they were able to stay, with a good warm fire in the fireplace. By the following day, the thirteenth, they were approaching the Kangra La, and all three were suffering from altitude sickness. Pontso, who was probably the most experienced traveler among them, got a severe case of the shakes, which Kawaguchi treated with a large dose of Hotan. Happily, this did not produce the same spectacular effects as in Kawaguchi himself many years before, and they were soon able to continue.

On the fourteenth, they found that the 16,900-foot Kangra La was free enough of snow to be passable, and they entered Tibetan territory. The pass marked, more or less, an end to the adventure on this journey. Henceforth, Kawaguchi had no need to pretend to be anything other than what he was, and with no more obstructive Chinese about, there were only friendly Tibetans to deal with. At the outpost called Giri, where they spent their first night in Tibet, there had until recently been a hundred and fifty Chinese—soldiers and their families—now gone without a trace.

Khamba Dzong, the first real settlement, is a cold and lonely border post, but the fort itself is an impressive building, built on a rocky elevation and similar in appearance to the fortress at Gyantse. The scene of earlier, abortive discussions between Younghusband and the Tibetans, it would eventually become an important staging area for six of the seven attempts made on Everest from the Tibetan side between the wars. There was a small market where they could replenish their supplies, but owing to the isolation of the place everything was almost double the normal price.

At Khamba Dzong, Kawaguchi was subjected to a thorough questioning by local officials, but this time all he had to do was tell the truth. Furthermore, no longer in disguise, he was able to strip off and have a good soak in an inviting hot spring—the kind of luxury that would have been taboo on the last trip, when his only total immersion had been a dunking in an ice-cold river. His Tibetan companions were quite amazed by this performance; though aware of the curative powers of hot springs, they themselves were content to soak only the ailing part of their bodies. The air was so cold that the steam from the water froze in the air, making flower patterns on the surrounding rocks, but there is no poem celebrating the occasion.

For all their probings in southern Tibet, the British had never followed the road north of Khamba Dzong; no map was available, and Kawaguchi's party had only hearsay—inevitably vague—to guide it. The night after the bath they spent in a sizable village of part-time herders and farmers, but here they learned that ahead lay not only another high pass but a stretch of thirty-two miles with neither houses nor tents. This meant they had to leave before dawn—on foot, since it was so cold that they were afraid of freezing to death if they rode yaks. With two Tibetans accompanying him, there was little chance, at least, of Kawaguchi taking one of his wrong turns.

The only hitch occurred on the nineteenth, and it was minor. An overzealous official back in Khamba Dzong began to fret as to whether the procedures followed would satisfy his superiors in both Shigatse and Lhasa, between whom relations were strained; and he dispatched three horsemen who, overtaking the travelers, asked them politely to stop thirty miles short of Shigatse while one of them went ahead to make sure everything was as it should be. The delay was not long, for on the evening of the twentieth the same horseman galloped in from Shigatse to say that they could proceed.

Anxious to get to Tashi Lhumpo as soon as possible, they attempted to make it in one day. By 8:30 that evening they had arrived at a village half a mile west of the monastery, but, finding themselves exhausted, decided it might be better to arrive rested and in good order the next day. They accordingly tried to obtain lodgings; the village, however, had "no custom" of putting up strangers, and they were obliged to move on to the great monastery itself. The trip from Calcutta had taken only a month.

Kawaguchi was to remain in Shigatse for six months, until July 27, when he departed for Lhasa. The Kawaguchi we see in Tibet this time is far mellower than before. We are treated to no complaints about the low level of scholarship, or the behavior of the monks. He had, after all, endured eight long years in Benares largely in the hope of coming back here, and the experience seems to have taught him something. The only trouble with this new and more tolerant Kawaguchi is that, with nothing to complain about, he has little to say at all.

At Tashi Lhumpo he stayed at one of the smaller monasteries, which he describes as clean and comfortable. He spent his time translating newspaper and magazine articles from Japanese and English for the Panchen Lama, studying, collecting plants, writing his "Poetic Travels in the Snow Mountains," and reviving his medical skills. His reputation as the "Doctor of Sera" had survived his absence, and he was quite busy. Although in payment he was offered everything from ceremonial scarves to horses, he would only accept old manuscripts or Buddhist images. Plant collecting also seems to have fulfilled a twin need for physical exertion and scholarly activity. On the journey, he had devoted a lot of his time to this botanical pursuit and, having servants to prepare tea and meals, had mounted and preserved his specimens during the periods of rest. Now he often took long walks in the hills on the lookout for new plants to add to his collection.

The heaviest part of his luggage, left behind in Sikkim because of the snow, included not only the sutras but some painted screens, vases, and even children's picture books in Japanese. He had expected everything within a month, but on March 18 there was still no word, so he sent Pontso back after it. The next day, Pontso returned together with Tinley Sambo, whom he had met on the way, but without the luggage. This had been caught in a snowstorm north of Gangtok and eventually taken back to the Sikkimese capital to await a better day. It had fared no better the next time, and was at present in northern Sikkim, trapped in snow too deep for horses and mules to negotiate. In the end a gang of porters was sent to fetch it, poor Pontso at their head, and everything finally arrived in April, when Kawaguchi was at last able to offer his belated gifts to the Panchen Lama.

There was a problem, however, in obtaining the Tibetan scriptures promised in return. The Panchen Lama intended to present him with the entire Narthang collection, but there was a current shortage of suitable paper. Books that were meant not for reading but as objects of veneration—as the majority were—were printed on a paper so thin as to be useless for prolonged study. A better quality of paper could be obtained in Nepal or Bhutan, but the price of all paper was high in Shigatse at this time, for a uniquely Tibetan reason: the Panchen Lama was sponsoring the construction of a huge statue of Maitreya, the Future Buddha, which was to be stuffed with fifty complete copies of the scriptures. Assuming that "complete copy" meant both the *Kangyur* and the *Tangyur*, this would amount to over fifteen thousand

The Sixth Panchen Lama and his advisers.

volumes. Thus when Kawaguchi discovered in July that his way was clear for a visit to Lhasa, he decided to shelve the question of books for a while and leave at once for the capital.

Having been invited to the country not by Lhasa but by Shigatse, he was very lucky to get permission to proceed, but once it was granted he was given every assistance, including five horses, a mule, servants, and a special passport that allowed him to obtain good lodgings, firewood, and water along the way. He was, in other words, traveling in much the same style as a government official.

Of the three possible routes from Shigatse to Lhasa, he took—perhaps for sentimental reasons—the same one as before: the middle road, which followed the Tsang Po for much of the way, then ascended to the Yamdruk Tso. This time there were no stops or delays; he does not even seem to have turned aside to meet people he had encountered previously. The whole trip, in fact, burdened as he was with a small caravan, had a more businesslike and less spontaneous air about it—though he did a lot of plant collecting again, sending Pontso out on the more difficult rock and tree climbs and staying up until eleven or twelve every night preserving and cataloging anything new. After only eleven days on the road, the party arrived at Lhasa on August 7. Kawaguchi spent the first night at the Nepalese legation off the Barkhor, and the next day moved into the house of the aristocratic Ser-chung family, where accommodation was paid for by the government. He had become acquainted with the head of this family during his previous visit, though his name does not crop up in *Three Years in Tibet*.

The Lhasa of 1914 was a city very different from that he had entered in 1901, but one doubts if he noticed the changes at first, for here, in contrast to Shigatse, he walked amidst crowding memories. Everywhere he went, everyone he met, every scene, must have reminded him of those heady days when he went disguised, a fugitive. Now, at last, there were no rumors, no innuendos. The people he had worried about and asked about for all those years were here, and could tell him face to face what had happened.

He found to his intense relief that his best friends, those likely to have been most in danger, had all survived, even prospered. The court physician, who had tried so assiduously to get him a government appointment, was now a member of the Kashag, the Dalai Lama's highest advisory body. The former finance minister, Chamba Choe Sang, about whom he had perhaps been most concerned, was alive and well, living in honorable retirement and still thought of by many as the man who had saved Lhasa by his discreet advice to the Ganden Tri Rimpoche.

Kawaguchi learned now for the first time that the written petition he had asked Chandra Shamshere to forward had indeed reached its destination, and had played at least a marginal role in the release of the ex-minister; it must have been gratifying, after years of uncertainty, to know that his trip to Nepal had not been in vain. He tried to apologize to the old man for the trouble he had caused him, but the latter would have none of it: his sufferings, he said, undoubtedly stemmed from evil done by himself in past lives (a feeling so often expressed by Tibetans that it is difficult to believe they are anything but completely sincere).

The Ganden Tri Rimpoche himself, of course, had never been in trouble. He had presided over the affairs of Tibet in the Dalai Lama's name from 1904 to the beginning of 1910, when he had finally been allowed to retire and pass on his title to a successor (the usual term of office, it may be remembered, was only seven years). He had been an ideal regent: impressing everyone with his piety, neither desiring nor corrupted by power, and gratefully handing over the reins on the Dalai Lama's return.

Conspicuous by the absence of any mention is the merchant Tsa Rongba; we can only speculate and hope that he was the second of Kawaguchi's friends released along with his teacher from Sera. And what happened to the Chinese druggist, Li Tsu-shu? Chinese residents who had not been connected with either the government or the military were allowed to stay on in Lhasa, but his name is absent from Kawaguchi's account of this period; nor was he ever mentioned as having been in any difficulty.

There were some interesting new friends to meet, too, as Kawaguchi was undoubtedly curious about his successors, the Japanese who had followed in his footsteps. One of them, the priest Tada Tokan, was at Sera, halfway through a long course at the same college

Kawaguchi had been associated with. The two men in fact had met in Darjeeling two years before, when Kawaguchi had introduced Tada to Chandra Das. Tada was a quiet man immersed in his books, who in later years wrote nothing and said little about his Tibetan experiences. A fanatical scholar, for days at a time he would forget even to eat. He occasionally came calling at the Serchung villa, and when he did so—his biographer tells us—Kawaguchi, who was quite prosperous by now, always ordered nourishing meals for him, including plenty of meat, since the privations of monastery life were evident in his appearance. This generosity, overriding Kawaguchi's own strictly vegetarian beliefs, must have impressed Tada deeply for him to have passed it on at all. It also suggests that Kawaguchi had himself developed a more easygoing attitude by this time.

The other Japanese priest, Aoki Bunkyo, was at Drepung. Like Tada Tokan, he was a member of Jodo Shinshu, one of Japan's Pure Land sects. This in itself would not, of course, have bothered Kawaguchi, who was contemptuous of sectarian differences and happily wore the robes of two or more sects at the same time. But their meeting at this point was unfortunate, for some Tibetan sutras that Kawaguchi sent back to Japan were later claimed by Aoki in the name of the Higashi Honganji in Kyoto, thus involving the two men in what was to become a long, complex, and unseemly legal battle over their ownership.

The most interesting of the three Japanese then in Lhasa was the man Kawaguchi had least to do with, since Yajima Yasujiro was a professional soldier. Yajima, it seems, was a competent fellow, but flamboyant and thoroughly nonconformist in a way rivaling Kawaguchi himself. He let his hair, for instance, grow down to his shoulders—unthinkable in a post-Meiji Japanese male, especially a military man. The Kawaguchi collection of photographs even includes a curious shot of him got up as a very convincing Tibetan lady, complete with baby; this was the disguise he had used to enter the country. But he is remembered kindly by the Tibetans, for during his six-year stay he adopted Tibetan ways and himself married a local woman.

* * *

In August, when Kawaguchi arrived, the Dalai Lama was in a

religious retreat and seeing no one, and it was not until September 29 that he obtained an audience. He found an older, wiser, and infinitely more confident ruler—yet, as with every other such meeting since the first, he has next to nothing to tell us about the occasion, which was apparently mostly ceremonial. He presented His Holiness with a large vase, a silk scroll, a chest, and a wooden inlaid box. In return, he asked that some old manuscripts be collected and given to Tokyo Imperial University as a sign of friendship between Japan and Tibet. One is curious to know what the ruler of a now fully independent Tibet thought of this Japanese impostor's earlier escapades, and if he had in fact suspected him. But Kawaguchi refuses to enlighten us, and Sir Charles Bell, in his definitive biography of the Thirteenth Dalai Lama, makes only the briefest mention of this persistent Japanese visitor.

The five months Kawaguchi stayed in Lhasa seem to have been lived at a less intense pace than his former visit. If he practiced medicine at all it was on a very limited scale, and most of his time was spent seeking manuscripts to fill the gaps in his collection, socializing with friends old and new, and making long botanical excursions. Yet he proves, in his own way, as alert an observer as ever. He kept his eyes and ears open for political and social changes over the previous ten years, and his observations are particularly valuable in that he was the only outsider who saw Lhasa and set down his impressions just before the Dalai Lama's departure and again just after his return.

The capital was enjoying what one might call a "Lhasa spring," an exciting time of trying out the new independence and learning to cope with its problems. A tendency to euphoria, however, was offset by the discovery that some of the old economic assumptions no longer held. The China trade, except for the perennial tea, was all but cut off; and the tax tribute from Mongolia, which had declared its own independence at the same time as Tibet, was no longer getting through, even though the Mongolians were willing enough to pay. Moreover, the effects of the recent fighting were still evident, giving much of Lhasa a bombed-out look.

But there were some marked material improvements. The streets were much cleaner and healthier. Indiscriminate urinating and defecating were no longer the order of the day, and Kawaguchi was amazed to see public lavatories being constructed. Another surprising change he noted was the appearance of a few two-wheeled carts, though so far only for government use. Previously, the only wheel had been the prayer wheel.

Polyandry was going out of style among the younger aristocrats, though the polyandrous families of their parents remained. Polygamy, on the other hand, was now more fashionable—as was licensed prostitution, with a consequent increase in venereal disease. These innovations Kawaguchi put down to the recent fighting and a new, militaristic male assertiveness. Others arose from a new tendency to look south toward British India rather than east toward China. He particularly welcomed the fact that white face powder from Calcutta was finding its way to Lhasa and gaining in popularity among the ladies of noble families, who no longer went about with faces fashionably blackened, but washed them and attempted to look as fair-complexioned as possible. Among the more stylish males, Chinese clothes were out, having been replaced by drabber Western styles. It was probably around this time that the still popular homburgs and cowboy hats came into fashion as a means of protection from the intense high-altitude sun. Even the standard greeting—sticking out the tongue—was beginning to be replaced by bowing.

None of these minor social changes, of course, had reached beyond the confines of the capital itself, and even there they did not filter down to the common people. Monastic life was still much the same, though the Dalai Lama was actively attempting to improve both the academic standards and the general behavior of the monks. Kawaguchi notes with disapproval that the proctors of the three great monasteries were still accompanied on their forays into town by attendants who—in the manner of retainers during the progress of a Japanese feudal lord—beat anyone who did not bow immediately. On the other hand, the particularly cruel and un-Buddhist custom of having whip-wielding guards present during the Dalai Lama's public audiences to thrash people for the slightest breach of etiquette had been done away with. The guards, who had even been known to blind people, remained only as a ceremonial feature.

It is this kind of on-the-scene, street level reporting that has always been lacking in accounts of Lhasa. So it is all the more unfortunate that Kawaguchi was getting old—that he could neither stay in Lhasa for the next ten years, nor continue his visits at regular intervals. Not until Alexandra David-Neel's visit in 1923 would there be another first-hand report, and not until Heinrich Harrer in the 1940s would another foreigner get to know the Tibetan capital so well.

During the five months of his stay he did make one extended trip, to the Reting monastery about eighty miles north of Lhasa, since he had heard a rumor about some very old Sanskrit manuscripts there. Reting, having been founded by one of Atisha's followers, was a logical enough place to find books from India. It was also very beautiful; Kawaguchi ranked it with Mt. Kailash and the Potala as one of the three most beautiful spots in Tibet. The entire monastery was thrown open to him, since he came with the express permission of the Dalai Lama, yet he failed to find what he was looking for. The abbot thought the manuscripts had probably been lost in a fire that had occurred some four hundred and fifty years earlier. Similar fates were said to have befallen Sanskrit works at both Sakya and Samye, and Kawaguchi reluctantly concluded that there were no other Sanskrit volumes left in Tibet.

On the way back, he stopped at a small temple whose head priest was credited with being able to see into the future. Finding no one about, he entered the sanctuary, where he was disgusted to see the central figures of the Buddha and Chenrisig surrounded by more erotic images than he had ever seen in one place before. Retreating in some confusion, he left without meeting the priest, feeling that the spirituality of anyone who lived in such a place would be questionable at best.

Despite this reminder of his old shocked intolerance, there had been a distinct advance in his own thinking and in his understanding of Tibetan Buddhism. Never does he reach the easy acceptance of Tibetan beliefs shown by so many Westerners—and Japanese as well—in recent years, yet neither is there the shrill rejection of anything that Japanese Buddhism had not prepared him for. He still chides the clergy in general for their worldliness, but more lightly now, as if the years have taught him something about human nature. And while nothing could ever make him approve of some of the more "indulgent" practices of the older sects, he at least seems to admit that they serve a purpose beyond simple hedonism. He tells us that meat, liquor, and sex are regarded as "poisons," but that a select few who have been thoroughly prepared can indulge in them with the object of rising above them. He even goes so far as to describe a ceremony in which the semen of a lama is drunk, mixed with wine and spices, by his disciples. He still considers this *hidoi* ("outrageous" is perhaps the best translation), but previously he had been too shocked even to mention such things.

* * *

Kawaguchi probably sensed that this would be his last visit to Tibet. Although he complained little of the trials of the journey, to cross those high passes must have taxed his strength to the utmost; any further visits would require him in the meantime to keep his body, and above all his lungs, in shape by living somewhere high in the mountains. In fact, he seems by now to have had his future charted, and to be finally feeling a genuine homesickness for Japan. Even the hardiest of travelers runs down sooner or later, and the excitement and determination of youth can seldom be sustained through middle age. He would not, he decided, remain an exile forever.

After a New Year's party with the three other Japanese, he had a final audience with the Dalai Lama on January 3, 1915. Books for the Imperial University were forthcoming, but His Holiness went so far as to apologize for their quality—"few really good books were available in these degenerate times"—and suggest that he might find something better in Gyantse.

On January 19, a year to the day since he had arrived in Shigatse, he left Lhasa for the last time. Once more, though in a very different mood, he took the southern route along the Yamdruk Tso to Gyantse. In Gyantse he acted on the Dalai Lama's suggestion, and in three days was able to gather together some unusual books. Arriving in Shigatse on February 1, he found his other manuscripts ready at last and received them from the Panchen Lama.

As he waited for the snowbound passes on the border to clear, he followed up another rumor by making a detour to a small monastery southeast of Shigatse called Zhalu. Here he found thirty-nine volumes in

Sanskrit said to have been brought from India by Atisha, and was even presented with several originals. Leaving Shigatse finally on April 18, he followed a devious route, having heard that the British had not forgotten him and were offering a reward of five hundred rupees for his capture. Even so, he traveled quite quickly and arrived on May 4 in Darjeeling, where he again stayed with his old friend Chandra Das.

At this point he was laid low—rather ignominiously—by a serious case of hemorrhoids. The intrepid explorer can hardly have been happy about this (one is reminded of Sir Richard Burton's disgust when he contracted gout in old age), but since the hemorroids were bad enough to require surgery, it meant at least that he did not have to go to Gangtok and explain how he had eluded the authorities on his journey toward Tibet.

The delay also allowed time for one more, almost totally inexplicable, event. The governor of Bengal, who was in Darjeeling for a while—it being the height of the hot season on the plains—gave a banquet in Kawaguchi's honor. Was this just a shining example of the British willingness to give the enemy his due? Or was it the old game, perhaps, still being played? Had the British received, via the aging Das, enough valuable information on Lhasan affairs to persuade them to let bygones be bygones?. . .

Either way, the trip had rounded off that part of his life which had begun in 1897, when he left Kobe for Calcutta with five hundred yen and a head full of dreams. He was now ready to go home for good. Indeed, so anxious was he to start that he went down to Calcutta in the very midst of the steamy monsoon, arriving on July 4. On August 8, he boarded a ship for Kobe. Under circumstances left unexplained, Surat Chandra Das and his eldest son were also on board, thus giving Kawaguchi a last chance to say good-bye to the scholar/spy, who died only two years later, at the age of sixty-eight.

The Twilight Years

Kawaguchi's life falls roughly into four periods: his childhood in Sakai; his years of wandering and study in Japan; the eighteen years in India, Nepal, and Tibet; and the last thirty years of his life back in Japan. To anyone interested in intellectual history or obscure currents in Buddhist thought, the last period would probably be the most interesting. But this account has concentrated on the third, and though Kawaguchi was not quite done with traveling—he was to make three trips to China, the final one in 1933, when he was sixty-eight—we can content ourselves here with a brief look at his later life and at the recollections of some of the people who knew him best.

By his return to Japan in 1915 Kawaguchi was a confirmed eccentric. Remembering the problems he had always had with temple politics, he was wise not to try living in a monastery again; instead, he was taken in by his brother Hanzui and Yane, his sister-in-law, as a sort of permanent house guest in Nezu, in downtown Tokyo (and later in Daita, another suburb). Yet he was in no sense a sponger: he had his own income from articles and books, as well as from frequent lectures, and apparently received a number of donations, too. And since his own needs were as simple as ever—a place to sleep and two vegetarian meals in the morning—he could afford to be generous with whatever he had; so generous, in fact, that it was sometimes unclear whether he was host or guest.

During his first year in his brother's home, Hanzui's wife gave birth to a baby girl, Sumi, the first of three girls and two boys to be born over the next decade. Kawaguchi would be surrounded by children for the rest of his life. We have seen how much he enjoyed their company in Darjeeling, in the village where he spent the winter on his way to

Lhasa, and in Lhasa itself, so it is no surprise to find that he got on well with his brother's family, and is remembered fondly by them. With children he was never overbearing; even the Buddhist Sunday School he organized every week was a popular event. Realizing that the kids soon got bored with his religious lectures, he kept plenty of *sembei* (a type of rice cracker) on hand as rewards, and regularly invited a publisher friend to enliven the occasion with the latest picture books. About the only thing he insisted on was cleanliness, and grubby youngsters were made to take a bath before they were allowed in.

The only minor conflict that arose in the house was over cooking. The mornings were no problem, for then the family simply adhered to the same diet of tofu, seaweed, rice, miso, and sticky, mashed yams (*tororo*) as did the old man himself. But in the evening the rest of the family would occasionally have meat or fish, and whenever Uncle Ekai was at home they had to do any grilling out in the garden lest the smell offend him.

With adults as well as with children, or at least with laymen, he now showed an affectionate, tolerant attitude that would have been unimaginable in the young monk who had once demanded that his friends stop fishing and serving chicken in their restaurants. A well-known painter, who often lent Kawaguchi his villa in Niigata Prefecture as a retreat, remembers him as very strict with himself but uncommonly understanding toward ordinary people; he was particularly grateful that the aging monk never bothered him about his lady friends. The ladies, incidentally, continued to find Kawaguchi attractive, and according to a former student there were frequent gifts, such as homemade noodles, from various admirers. Regularly, too, he was asked to help people with their family problems, especially where wayward adolescents were concerned. His own niece Sumi remembers, above all, how popular he was—so popular that he could have been a successful politician if he had wanted to.

That, of course, was the last thing that would have occurred to him. In everything, his principal concern was Buddhism and how best to put the words of Buddha into practice. Of these he now had a huge collection in four languages—Japanese, Chinese, Sanskrit, and Tibetan—all of which he could read fluently. But as usual he was out of step with the ecclesiastical establishment, and sometime during these years he again renounced his priesthood, this time for good. However, this made so little difference to his way of life (he still wore his monk's robes and lived by *shojin* vows) that it is hard to tell exactly when it happened; he himself seems not to have considered it a particularly significant event.

In his bluntness and honesty, he was also increasingly at odds with the society he lived in. Social intercourse in Japan embodies an attitude to the truth, referred to as *tatemae*, which to foreigners (and Japanese who have long lived abroad) often appears as institutionalized

Kawaguchi in old age.

hypocrisy. At its best, it is simply a way of making society function smoothly by regularly expressing acceptable ideas and wishful generalizations rather than true, individual opinions and feelings. But it can all too easily be abused, and to Kawaguchi it seemed to contravene the Buddhist tenet of "Right Speech." He personally had been obliged to "adjust" the truth quite often on his travels—his disguise was itself a patent lie—and apparently he felt a lingering guilt about this. In later life, he disapproved strongly of *tatemae*, and taught the children of the household to feel the same way.

There is some speculation that Kawaguchi may have wanted to found his own group of Buddhist individualists, one unassociated with any established sect, but, as he has demonstrated repeatedly, he was a poor organization man. Moreover, he was too stern and uncompromising with his followers for the relationship to survive very long: while he had mellowed considerably toward laymen in general, he was unrelenting toward those who sought to emulate him. The renowned Zen writer, Yamada Mumon, later president of Hanazono University, recalls how as an idealistic teenager (reminiscent of Kawaguchi in his youth) he had run off to become a monk, against his parents' wishes; and, deeply impressed by a lecture given by Kawaguchi around this time, he had asked to be taken on as his student. Kawaguchi already had two other pupils by then, but they were soon to depart, for the master's dietary rules were so strict that they became seriously ill. In the same way, Yamada himself, for all his zeal, soon succumbed to malnutrition and exhaustion and was unable to go on.

Though these spiritual apprentices tended, understandably, to drift away, Kawaguchi was much more successful with people who wanted to learn Tibetan, and the courses he gave at two universities were well attended. One of his private students was a Shingon priest, head of the Kannonji in Hanno, at the foot of the Chichibu Hills west of Tokyo. In those days, Hanno was still a country town, but there was a quick and convenient rail connection, and Kawaguchi was a frequent guest at the temple there. Possibly the elaborate religious paraphernalia and ceremonies of the Esoteric Shingon sect reminded him of Tibet; in any case, he undoubtedly found it necessary at times to get away from his brother's crowded house in order to write or meditate, and this lovely

297

temple overlooking the river was an ideal refuge. In a room facing the garden and close to the main hall, he worked on his manuscripts. (Today, a sample of his calligraphy in Japanese and Sanskrit hangs there, and in the same room the annual meetings of the Kawaguchi Society are held.) The chief priest is now quite old, and if asked about Kawaguchi he invariably repeats: "He was a fine man—yes, a really fine man."

In 1925, 1929, and 1933 Kawaguchi went to China, and on each occasion he renewed acquaintance with the Panchen Lama. One of the saddest figures of twentieth-century Tibet before the Communist invasion, this man was now a virtual prisoner of the Chinese, unable to return home though both he and the Dalai Lama desired a reconciliation. The seeds of dissension sown by O'Connor, and tended at various times by the British and Chinese, had borne their bitter fruit. But in his visitor's case, age had made him, too, an exile from Tibet, unfit for the rigors of a return journey; and though their talk, like those first conversations so long ago in Bodh Gaya, no doubt dealt mainly with religious themes, they must also have reminisced about the country that neither would see again. Kawaguchi, in addition, proposed on his first visit that the Panchen Lama accompany him back to Japan. Yet the political implications would have been considerable, and the lama himself, already the focus of so many intrigues, was unwilling to get involved with yet another country. (A Tibetan friend called Rinchen did in fact return with Kawaguchi, and stayed for some time at the house in Nezu.)

In all, Kawaguchi knew the Panchen Lama for longer than any other Tibetan, having first seen him in 1900 and first met him personally in India in 1905. In 1915 and 1916 he was his guest in Shigatse; they then met again in China. It must have been a blow to him when this old friend finally died, alone and unhappy, in 1937. Kawaguchi himself was then almost seventy-two.

Remarkably, he began to get fat around this time. His health continued to be excellent, and no one ever remembers him being sick, but his twice-daily meals got larger and his belly grew so big that he could balance two small children on its shelf. By his final years, however, the war and accompanying hardships had thinned him down again.

The spark of individuality, even then, still burned bright in him.

Sometime in the late 1930s or early 1940s, he was approached by the military for assistance on undercover Tibetan policy. Kawaguchi, to his lasting credit, turned them down point-blank, liking neither their mentality nor their methods. He had settled an old score. Others, like Aoki Bunkyo, willingly cooperated, and even the gentle Tada Tokan was forced to comply.

His books, a large number of them, continued to be written, but most are now almost impossible to find. His style was difficult even in those days, and the written language in the meantime has undergone considerable change and simplification, so that his works—which, with the exception of the travel books, have not been reprinted since the war— are virtually incomprehensible to most younger Japanese. There was also a dictionary he had spent a long time compiling (a sign on his gate read: "Japanese-Tibetan Dictionary, Editorial Staff"). This was to have been one of the crowning achievements of his life, but the manuscript disappeared under mysterious circumstances, and has never come to light.

*   *   *

Today he is little remembered, and then mainly as a traveler: a courageous, solitary wanderer who dared and succeeded in the days when failure meant imprisonment and death; a sincere but unorthodox Buddhist who traveled for the sake of his religion. Those of us who have bothered to look into his life can still sense his presence on the old trails and in all the other places he knew. We can almost see him talking to beggars at the Boudhanath stupa, riding his white horse up the Kali Gandaki Valley, eavesdropping from the chapel of the Serchan mansion. . . . That ragged pilgrim seen resting in Sera's debating garden, with his beard and travel-stained clothes, could almost be him, and we feel him looking over our shoulder in the dark and mysterious chapels of the Jokhang—laughing gently at us, perhaps, for having it so easy.

In the end, as is the way of things, Tibet was not changed at all by his sojurn. Yet he himself changed a good deal, though the difference at first was barely perceptible. The kindly, popular old man who tolerated his friends' mistresses and gave dirty children a bath on Sunday morning bore little resemblance to the firebrand who left Japan with a chip on his shoulder and set off across Central Asia determined to disapprove of all that he saw. The people who befriended him—Serab Gyaltsen, Alchu Tulku and his wife, Gelong Rimpoche, the Ganden Tri Rimpoche, the Panchen Lama, even Chandra Das—all worked their magic on him. Indeed, it is a pity that an older and wiser Kawaguchi did not sit down and rewrite *Three Years in Tibet* in, say, 1925.

His final trip abroad was made at the age of sixty-eight, a more appropriate occasion with which to end this account than his death in 1945. A photograph from the time shows him smiling quizzically at the camera as if to say, "Well, here I am, still at it after all these years," while Chinese workmen in the background pack up yet more scriptures for him. It is the smile of a man whose achievement of inner peace, and whose ability to relate to the world around him, are due as much to his worldly as to his spiritual adventures. It is hard to imagine such a man disapproving very strongly of our human weaknesses; and we are left wishing we could have talked to him face to face, for the sake of what he might have taught us.

Appendix: On *Three Years in Tibet*

If an enemy—that reporter, say, from the *Yorozu Choho*—had set out systematically to destroy Kawaguchi's credibility and reputation forever, he could hardly have done a better job than Kawaguchi did himself; *Three Years in Tibet* is so seriously flawed a work that the reader is occasionally tempted to dismiss the book, the trip, and even the author himself as worthless.

That would be a pity, for it is by no means bad throughout. It is, in fact, much like Kawaguchi's own view of the Tibetan priesthood and its practices, which he describes as "containing a few precious gems in a heap of rubbish." The saddest thing is that while Kawaguchi could be a perceptive commentator and a man of sympathy and understanding, these aspects are too often smothered, in his 719 ponderous pages, by the prude, the iconoclast, and the unbending fundamentalist—just as his best observations are often blurred by his "poetic turn of mind."

The basic problem, of course, is that he did not take the time and trouble to actually write the book himself, but left the work to a few journalists who had every interest in playing up the spectacular. That his material, in all the confusion and excitement of his homecoming, should have wound up being published as a series of newspaper articles is scarcely surprising. What is very surprising, though, is that a more careful job of editing and rewriting was not done when it came to publishing the articles in book form. Again, when the Japanese version was translated, one would have expected both Kawaguchi and his friends to have wanted to present to the world a professional and polished work. What the world got in fact was a disturbingly disorganized tome that reads at times more like a stream-of-consciousness novel than an important record of travels in an unknown land. Apart from eliminating some of the repetitions in the original, the only real concession to the needs of the English version was the deletion of the entire story of Kawaguchi's humiliation by General Oku's staff in Delhi. This was presumably done in order to make the Japanese—who, it seems, can always be counted on to close ranks against the outside world when national face is at stake—appear in a more favorable light, but it leaves the reader completely in the dark.

What was needed to save both the Japanese and English editions was a good editor: a discreet, understanding person to sit down with the scatterbrained priest and help sift the gems from the rubbish. "Look, Mr. Kawaguchi," he might have said, "I realize that you were going through a difficult time at Retapuri, but is it really necessary to dismiss the entire Tibetan nation as 'devils that live on dung'? And don't you think it's just a bit hard on Tibetan women to say that all they're concerned about is 'their own selfish interests, and they do not care a straw for their husbands as long as they are satisfied'? What about the section where you list the four most serious faults of the Tibetans, then come up with nothing better to balance this than the weather in Lhasa and Shigatse? And how can you call a people that has gone to such lengths to preserve its national identity 'destitute of the sense of patriotism'? I know that some Tibetans robbed and cheated you, and they may not be quite like 'us Japanese'—but you also had good friends who saved your life more than once, and who kept quiet when they could have turned you in for a reward. If we don't tone some of this down, your readers may begin to doubt your powers of observation, not to mention your motives. . . ."

As indeed the reader does, for no such editor was at hand, and however likable this bumbling but determined traveler might appear at his best, one can hardly ignore the pettiness and one-sidedness of his complaints when he is at his worst. After a while, we begin to weary of them; it occurs to us that he sounds like nothing so much as the type of long-term foreign resident in Japan who has no intention of leaving yet grumbles constantly about the country and the people.

Inconsistency plagues the book as well. He can deliver a sweeping condemnation of all Tibetan monks (with the exception, of course, of his "warrior priests"), calling them "deceitful and crafty in seeking their own happiness," yet go on to praise the virtues of his own clerical friends. On one and the same page he can call the incarnation system "an incarnation of all vices and corruptions," and proceed to claim that eighty percent of all tulkus are men of high ability. Within the space of a single page, he first states that the only thing that can influence Tibetan foreign policy is bribery, then declares that bribes (which he suddenly associates with "rational conviction") are usually wasted because everything is determined by "sentiment" anyway.

Other glaring inconsistencies, such as his contempt for Tibetan medicine after it had repeatedly saved his life, have been pointed out earlier. Particularly odd is his amusement at the fact that most Tibetans (*bodpa* in their own language) seem unaware that the rest of the world knows them by a different name. He implies that this constitutes a special form of ignorance, yet forgets that the average *nihonjin* eighty years ago similarly had no idea that to the English-speaking world he was a "Japanese."

The geographer, traveler, and historian alike may well find themselves hopelessly confused over certain aspects of the book. Blithely ignoring such bothersome details as exchange rates, he flits back and forth between Japanese yen, Indian rupees, Tibetan tanka, and occasionally even American dollars, giving his reader no clue as to whether he is referring to large or small sums of money. Moreover, the routes he describes are more often than not—as is hardly surprising when one considers how often he got lost himself—vague and impossible to follow, with altitudes and distances based on hearsay rather than on any sort of scientific measurement, and distances given sometimes in miles and sometimes in "Japanese miles." Yet, while he has no reservations about criticizing existing maps, neither he nor the Tokyo Geographical Society seems to have thought it worth the effort to make a new one, as suggested by Chandra Das.

The vagueness and disorganization carries over into the central purpose of his trip, for though he was drawn to Tibet by the ancient texts and spent a good deal of time, effort, and money collecting them, he never bothers to tell us exactly what they were. "The Complete Texts" is a favorite term of his, but what does it mean? Presumably it refers either to the *Kangyur* (the actual words of the Buddha translated from Pali into Sanskrit, then Tibetan) or the *Kangyur* plus the *Tangyur* (the standard commentaries on it, some taken from Sanskrit, and some original works in Tibetan). Together they form a total of over three hundred volumes—sometimes called "the Tibetan Canon"—but since they were easy enough to find even in Darjeeling, he was presumably after a good deal more as well. There are any number of firsthand Tibetan writings as well as translations from Sanskrit that are not part of the *Kangyur* and *Tangyur*: commentaries, works by the Dalai Lamas, books on thanka painting, and so on, and while their contents tend to be obscure, Kawaguchi has an irritating way of avoiding explanations by saying that matters are "too technical for the general reader." He never seems to have considered that some of his audience might be scholars, or at least knowledgeable amateurs, for whose sake he could at least have supplied the titles and a simple account of what they contained.

Another irritant—one that can be blamed on the translator, the proofreader, and the absence of a competent editor—is the misleading choice of official titles (e.g. "Pope" and "second Pope" for the Dalai Lama and Panchen Lama). More formidable, however, are the transliteration problems his book presents. The difficulties involved in transliterating Tibetan have already been pointed out; but, although there was no generally accepted system of romanization at the time, some of the place names in *Three Years in Tibet* are so garbled as to defy the imagination. At the root of this problem is the total inadequacy of the Japanese phonetic system, with its relatively few, simple sounds, and the consonant-plus-vowel syllabary to which those sounds are tied, in rendering languages such as Nepali and Tibetan, which have complex consonant clusters. But, in addition, for someone who spoke Tibetan so well, Kawaguchi appears to have had an exceptionally bad ear for place names (unless—as may possibly have happened—the journalists simply put down what they thought they heard in the debriefing). And when the translator took over, instead of checking with whatever maps were available, he seems merely to have transcribed in roman script what he saw in the Japanese syllabary. Thus, the Terai appears as "Dalai"; "Malba" is meant to indicate the Nepalese village of Marpha; Dolpo becomes "Thorpo"; the Russian agent in Lhasa, Dorjieff (whom Kawaguchi usually refers to by the Tibetan title of Tsan-yi Kenbo—which is quite close, since Shakabpa calls him the "Tsenyi Khenpo"), mysteriously appears on page 497 as the "Zaune"; and so on, ad infinitum.

Confusing and annoying as this is, it is still relatively minor. Far more serious, and downright offensive to many readers, is Kawaguchi's unwarranted slander of the Tibetan Buddhist faith. One of the most attractive aspects of Buddhism has always been its tolerance, yet sometimes the Buddhist Kawaguchi seems to go out of his way to sound like a fundamentalist Christian. The chapter entitled "Lamaism" would have been far better left out, for while it tells us a great deal about the author's prejudices, it says next to nothing about Tibet's religion. These prejudices often lead him to ridiculous oversimplifications. Dislike of Padmasambhava, for example, was no reason to sum up his entire teachings by saying he "declared that the only secret of perfection for priests consisted in leading a jovial life." Again, while he was well aware of the underlying symbolism of the *yab-yum* figures he found in Tibetan temples ("father-mother" images of deities locked in sexual embrace), he refused to attempt really to understand it. Indeed, his distress at the sexual element in Tantric Buddhism made him at times lose all grip on reality. At one point he explains that he brought home a number of Nyingmapa texts, but was obliged to keep them in a closed box "for they are too full of obscene passages to allow of their being read by the many." Where, one wonders, were the "many" to be found? Was Japan suddenly overflowing with readers of classical Tibetan?

The tragedy of this is that Westerners had been churning out the same kind of nonsense for years. During the colonial period, it was assumed by most Europeans that Asians were inferior, and that Tibet's obscene religion was simply one more, amusing proof of this fact (for a long time the *yab-yum* figures in the Tibetan temple in Peking were covered by a cloth which, for a fee, was removed for the titillation of foreign visitors). Kawaguchi, however, was an Asian traveler, from whom new insights could be expected; yet his stale views are in fact disturbingly like those of a Victorian Englishman. Just who was he trying to impress? Was he trying to convince the more narrow-minded of his fellow countrymen of his own unbending moral standards, or was he hoping to persuade the rest of the world that the Japanese were capable of being just as bigoted as the most ethnocentric European, and thus worthy of joining the imperial club?

In all of this, Kawaguchi did a disservice not only to the Tibetans but to himself. If his work remains largely unread, it is because most contemporary readers cannot believe that this sort of ragbag of bias and conventional morality can have anything worthwhile to impart. Nevertheless, the jewels are there, hidden but worth searching for. In places, *Three Years in Tibet* has an irresistible charm. Take, for example, the description of his disastrous trek toward Kailash, or the return journey alone across the western plains; the equally disastrous romance with Dawa; or the comic suspense of his escape to Darjeeling. In such episodes he displays an endearing willingness to laugh at himself. Then there is his account of the trials and tribulations of Alchu Tulku and his beautiful wife, whom he happily assists in maintaining their "sinful" relationship; the affection he felt for his friends (including the ex-minister and his companion, who were also living in "sin"); and his moving descriptions of the lives of the warrior monks and the poor scholars of Sera. All are memorable vignettes that rank among the best in travel writing; and they give us a glimpse of the author in a very different, unofficial light.

"If a man turns to disguise as a way of life, it suggests a savage dissatisfaction with himself," says Fawn Brodie in her psychological portrait of England's greatest disguised traveler, Sir Richard Burton. The statement undoubtedly has some relevance to Kawaguchi, for, reading between the lines and remembering what we know of his early life, he sometimes comes across as a man of strong, if repressed, appetites. In his youth he was known to have gone on the occasional spree, and even after taking his vows he kept himself in check only with a certain effort. He was a warm friend, moreover, undeniably brave, and fond of children. Back in Japan after his second journey, he so endeared himself to his relatives and other people he knew well that even now, forty-four years after his death, there is still an annual meeting of the Kawaguchi Society at which his old acquaintances solemnly burn incense, then get royally drunk in his memory. All present seem to consider this a fitting tribute.

* * *

It is difficult to realize how little was known about Tibet in those days. Many of the things that Kawaguchi saw had not been seen by a foreigner well versed in the language since the time of Desideri. Moreover, he was not only an observer but a participant; unlike those Westerners today who shave their heads and wear monk's robes, he did not have the company of fellow countrymen, nor could he take refuge in the better restaurants of Kathmandu or Dharamsala. When he wrote about Tibetan weddings, it was because a friend's son or daughter got married; when he wrote about Tibetan schooling, he was repeating what children and their parents casually passed on; and when he reported on monastic life, he was describing his own experience of it.

The custom of "sky burial," which was certainly little known in the early 1900s (though Das had published a posed photograph complete with a smiling corpse in 1885), provided a good example of his vivid on-the-spot reporting. His disguise as a monk gave him a perfect vantage point from which to observe the practice close up—particularly when a friend died—and to note things that no one else seems to have noticed before. The work of chopping up the body, cutting the flesh from the bones, and pounding the bones to powder is tiring and necessarily rather messy, and as the "grave diggers" and priests proceed with the task, they of course get hungry and thirsty:

> ... [They] prepare tea, or help themselves to baked flour, with their hands splashed over with a mash of human flesh and bones, for they never wash their hands before they prepare tea or take food, the most they do being to clap their hands, so as to get rid of the coarser fragments. And thus they take a good deal of minced human flesh, bones or brain, mixed with their tea or flour. They do so with perfect nonchalance. ... When I suggested that they might wash their hands before taking refreshment, they looked at me with an air of surprise. They scoffed at my suggestion, and even observed that eating with unwashed hands really added relish to food; besides, the spirit of the dead man would be satisfied when he saw them take fragments of his mortal remains with their food without aversion.

Kawaguchi also spent a good deal of time practicing Tibetan-style debating. Even today, when it has been widely filmed and photographed, this remains an astonishing spectacle, with its stamping, posturing, and hand-clapping. No outsider since Desideri had regularly taken part in this activity, and his description makes it come alive even for those who have never seen it:

> ... When he [one of the participants] utters the words of a question, he beats time with hands and feet. The teacher always teaches the catechists that the foot must come down so strongly that the door of hell [will] be broken open, and that the hands must make so great a noise that the voice of knowledge [will] frighten the devils all over the world. ...

Another, darker aspect of the scene was one that Kawaguchi, like Das, was unable to ignore: Tibetan methods of punishment. There is a particular intensity to his descriptions of such customs as public exposure by pillory in the Barkhor, flogging, tortures such as the placing of stone "bonnets" on people's heads until the weight forced their eyeballs out of the sockets, and death by drowning, not to mention the sheer horror of sunless Tibetan jails, where the prisoner as likely as not starved to death unless food was sent by his family. And though mutilation, even for minor crimes, had been outlawed in 1898, plenty of blind and handless beggars in Lhasa still bore witness to this savage practice. Kawaguchi can perhaps be forgiven for dwelling at length on all this, as it was only too easy to imagine himself or his friends in a similar predicament (and in the end, of course, a number of acquaintances did suffer for his sake). It is also worth bearing in mind that, though such punishments were out of character in a Buddhist country, they were no worse than those then commonly applied in China; Japan, too, had used similar methods until about the time of Kawaguchi's birth.

Some of Kawaguchi's best pieces of observation are those that might have got him into most trouble, as he devotes long chapters to the government, to the relationship between British India and Tibet, and to Russia's Tibetan policy. These political chapters form one of the notable incongruities of the book, in that he frequently protests that as a simple monk he had no interest in politics and other worldly affairs. In fact, he seems to have been a bit of a busybody and gossip, reveling in his command of the language and his ability to pick up elusive bits of information. His impressions, as he freely admits, were pieced together from rumor, hearsay, and conversations with the ex-minister, a current minister of finance, and other influential friends. These, of course, are the classical methods of the secret agent. Many of his assumptions, moreover, have stood the test of time remarkably well, leading people to the quite natural conclusion that he was spying. Ultimately, as we have seen, the available evidence neither proves nor disproves anything. The fact that it was the Japanese government itself that sent Narita should, in principle, suggest that Kawaguchi was not its agent. And while there is more than an even chance that Das was picking his brains, nothing has turned up to indicate that the British ever took him particularly seriously.

During his fourteen months in Lhasa, he detected a good deal of Russian influence—probably, as he says himself, more potential than real. The central fact of the situation, one that everyone always seemed to ignore, was that the Tibetans wanted to keep their territory and their religion independent, and that the way the British had gobbled up India had induced justifiable fears for their southern border. If the Dalai Lama and his ministers—notably Paljor Dorji Shatra, whom Kawaguchi believed to be the most powerful man in the country after the Dalai Lama—looked hopefully to St. Petersburg, it was essentially because Russia, for all its spectacular expansion in the nineteenth century, remained a distant power. The nearest station on the Trans-Siberian Railway was a five to six months' march over extremely hostile terrain, which made supply lines for an occupying force virtually impossible to maintain.

But if occupation was impractical, Russia could still bring pressure to bear. Their main agent in Tibet was a Mongolian of the Buriat tribe, which was both Buddhist and Russian, the Czar having sensibly bought their loyalty by allowing them to retain their religion. His name was Aguang Dorji, Russianized as Dorjieff, and his activities attracted considerable attention in London and Calcutta. It was largely on his account, in fact, that the Younghusband expedition had taken place at all. Kawaguchi learned a fair amount about him, the capital being full of gossip, and wrote it all down. But in the end, despite discovering some interesting facts about his behind-the-scenes movements, he came up with little more than what British diplomats could find out for themselves in the St. Petersburg newspapers.

As a young man, Dorjieff had insinuated himself into the Dalai Lama's court, and, being an immensely learned Buddhist, had become a trusted tutor to the new incarnation. When the latter came of age and outgrew his services, Dorjieff disappeared for a time, only to return mysteriously wealthy. This impressed the Tibetans no end. Later, he even led a delegation of Tibetans to the Russian capital. This much was well known, and the British probably felt that they were up against a Russian version of a Pundit: better financed, though, with a more definite object in mind, and conspicuously more successful.

Kawaguchi did, however, pick up two bits of information that seem to have escaped the notice of the British, though neither would have caused more than a mild raising of eyebrows in London or Calcutta. One was that Dorjieff had written a book which rather convincingly (at least in the eyes of a fairly credulous people) equated Russia, and the Czar's palace in particular, with the mythical Buddhist kingdom of Shambala, which some day was to win the world for Buddhism. The other—and Kawaguchi undoubtedly made too much of it—was that the Czar had sent the Dalai Lama, via Dorjieff, a set of "Episcopal" robes.

More impressive, perhaps, was his claim to have seen, on a ride north of Lhasa, a caravan carrying Russian arms. Most Lhasans thought the sealed boxes had contained silver or gold, but Kawaguchi made a point of seeking out a talkative member of the government, who confided to him that the boxes really contained guns. Significantly, Kawaguchi had not inspected the caravan himself, though he was later shown what he took to be an American-made, rather inferior rifle which was supposed to have come from it. But why anyone should take the word of a peace-loving, vegetarian Buddhist as an armaments specialist he does not bother to explain, and it is worth noting that Younghusband was to find no evidence of Russian or American arms—inferior or otherwise—in Lhasa.

The real advantage Russia enjoyed in Tibet had nothing to do with guns or bullets. It derived partly from the shrewd diplomacy of Dorjieff, and partly from the fact that the Russian goods that found their way to Tibet were of a far higher quality than those from British India. The reason, as Kawaguchi pointed out, was simple: Russia sent superior goods as gifts, while British India sent cheap, mass-produced things. The result was that the average Tibetan thought of Russia as a country vastly richer than its European counterpart. Information such as this was at least as important as any wild speculation about armaments, especially to a trading nation like Britain. And, again, the fact that no one seems to have paid much attention to this argues strongly that Kawaguchi was an independent observer.

*   *   *

The full translation and proofreading of *Three Years in Tibet* were not completed until the British journalists Landon and Chandler had begun publishing their accounts of entering Lhasa with Younghusband. Because of this, Kawaguchi seems to have undergone a crisis of confidence and stopped the book's publication, feeling that it "would not be of any use to the English-reading public." This was probably just as well, since Takahashi's original translation was *Chibetto Ryoko Ki* rendered into English as it stood, less satisfactory even than what eventually saw print.

Several years later, in India, he was convinced by Annie Besant, president of the Theosophical Society, that his book put forward a point of view different from anything else in English. Thus in 1909 it was issued by the Theosophical Publishing House in Madras, and later reprinted in London. It seems that he spent some time going over the manuscript with both Annie Besant and Professor Jamshedi Unwalla; and it is to the latter presumably we owe the more stirring passages of dated prose.

By 1909, Tibet was no longer much in the public eye. Although *Three Years in Tibet* was read—and, in fact, warmly appreciated by people like Younghusband—early in the century, it had been long out of print when in 1979 a limited edition of a thousand copies was published by Ratna Pustak Bhandar in Kathmandu as part of the Bibliotheca Himalayica series. This edition was printed from photocopies sent from London by Mrs. Miyata Emi, daughter of Kawaguchi's brother Hanzui.

Today he is little read, and appreciated even less. The one Tibetan historian to mention him, W. D. Shakabpa (who was under the impression that Kawaguchi went disguised as a Ladakhi), dismisses him as a spy who sent misleading information to the British. Western followers of the Dharma, who ought surely to look up to him as a forerunner, tend to reject him for his extreme views on Tibetan Buddhism. Yet, as we have tried to show, there was more to him than these hasty judgments would allow, and his life, one feels, deserves a better legacy than the inadequate record he left behind.

Selected Bibliography

Books

Allen, Charles. *A Mountain in Tibet*. London, Macdonald, 1983.

Auboyer, Jeannine. *Daily Life in Ancient India: From Approximately 200 B.C. to 700 A.D.* New York, Macmillan, 1965.

Avedon, John F. *In Exile from the Land of the Snows*. London, Michael Joseph, 1984.

Batchelor, Stephen. *The Tibet Guide*. London, Wisdom Publications, 1987.

Bell, Sir Charles. *Portrait of a Dalai Lama: The Life and Times of the Great Thirteenth*. London, Wisdom Publications, 1987. (First published in 1946.)

Blofeld, John. *The Wheel of Life*. Boulder, Shambala, 1978.

——*The Tantric Mysticism of Tibet*. New York, Dutton, 1970.

Chandler, Edmund. *The Unveiling of Lhasa*. New Delhi, Cosmo Publications, 1981. (First published in 1905.)

Das, Surat Chandra. *Journey to Lhasa and Central Tibet*. New Delhi, Manjusri Publishing House, 1970. (First published in 1902.)

David-Neel, Alexandra. *Initiations and Initiates in Tibet*. London, Rider, 1931 and 1970.

Desideri, Ippolito. *An Account of Tibet: The Travels of Ippolito Desideri of Pistoia, S.J., 1712–1727*. Edited by Filippo de Filippi. Introduction by C. Wessels, S.J. London, Rutledge, 1931.

Dowman, Keith (translator). *The Legend of the Great Stupa of Boudhanath*. Kathmandu, Diamond Sow Publications, 1973.

Eliot, Sir Charles. *Japanese Buddhism*. New York, Barnes and Noble, 1959.

Evans-Wentz, W. Y. *The Tibetan Book of the Great Liberation*. Oxford University Press, 1954 and 1972.

——*Tibet's Great Yogi, Milarepa*. Oxford University Press, 1972.

Fleming, Peter. *Bayonets to Lhasa*. Oxford University Press, 1984. (First published in 1961.)

Furer-Haimendorf, Christoph von. *Himalayan Traders: Life in Highland Nepal*. London, John Murray, 1975.

Hagen, Toni. *Nepal: The Kingdom in the Himalayas*. Chicago, Rand McNally, 1971.

Harrer, Heinrich. *Seven Years in Tibet*. London, Pan Books, 1965.

Hopkirk, Peter. *Trespassers on the Roof of the World: The Secret Exploration of Tibet*. Oxford University Press, 1983.

Humphreys, Christmas. *Zen Buddhism*. London, Mandala Books, 1981.

Jackson, David P. *The Mollas of Mustang*. Dharamsala, Library of Tibetan Works and Archives, 1984.

Kawaguchi, Ekai. *Three Years in Tibet*. Kathmandu, Ratna Pustak Bhandar, 1979.

Lamb, Alastair. *British India and Tibet*. London, Methuen, 1987.

Mattheissen, Peter. *The Snow Leopard*. New York, Viking, 1978.

Norbu, Thubten Jigme, and Colin M. Turnbull. *Tibet: Its History, Religion, and People*. London, Penguin, 1972.

Pallis, Marco. *Peaks and Lamas*. London, Woburn Press, 1974.

Peissel, Michel. *Mustang, the Forbidden Kingdom: Exploring a Lost Himalayan Land*. New York, Dutton, 1967. (A few insights are contained in this otherwise pretentious and self-centered travel book.)

Picken, Stuart D. B. *Buddhism: Japan's Cultural Identity*. Tokyo, Kodansha International, 1982.

Rana, Pramode Shamshere. *Rana Nepal: An Insider's View*. Kathmandu, 1978.

Regmi, D. R. *Modern Nepal: Rise and Growth in the Eighteenth Century*. Calcutta, Firma K. L. Mukhopadhyay, 1975.

Richardson, Hugh. *Tibet and Its History*. Boston, Shambala, 1984.

Richardson, Hugh, and David Snellgrove. *A Cultural History of Tibet*. Boston, Shambala, 1986.

Shakabpa, W. D. *Tibet: A Political History*. New York, Potala Publications, 1984.

Snelling, John. *The Sacred Mountain*. London, East West Publications, 1983.

Thapa, Netra B. *A Short History of Nepal.* Kathmandu, Ratna Pustak Bhandar, 1981.

Tohoku University. *Tibetan Materials in the Collection of Kawaguchi Ekai.* Sendai, Tohoku University, 1986.

Tucci, Giuseppe. *Tibet: Land of the Snows.* New York, Stein and Day, 1967.

——*Journey to Mustang, 1952.* Kathmandu, Ratna Pustak Bhandar, 1977.

Waddell, L. Austine. *The Buddhism of Tibet or Lamaism.* Cambridge, W. Heffer, 1959.

Younghusband, Francis. *India and Tibet.* Oxford University Press, 1985. (First published in 1910.)

Periodicals

Dowman, Keith. "A Buddhist Guide to the Power Places of the Kathmandu Valley." *Kailash—A Journal of Himalayan Studies,* Vol. VIII, Nos. 3–4, 1981, pp. 183–292.

Gauchan, Surendra, and Michael Vinding. "The History of the Thakali According to the Thakali Tradition." *Kailash—A Journal of Himalayan Studies,* Vol. V, No. 2, 1977, pp. 97–184.

Hyer, Paul. "Narita Yasuteru: First Japanese to Enter Tibet." *The Tibet Journal,* Vol. IV, No. 3, Autumn 1979, pp. 12–19.

——"The Dalai Lamas and the Mongols." *The Tibet Journal,* Vol. VI, No. 4, Winter 1981, pp. 3–12. (His slightly dated but valuable dissertation is "Japan and the Lamaist World: Japanese Relations with Tibet." University of California, Berkeley, 1960.)

Peissel, Michel. "Mustang, Nepal's Lost Kingdom." *National Geographic,* Vol. 128, No. 4, Oct. 1965.

In Japanese

Kawaguchi, Akira. *Kawaguchi Ekai, Nihon Saisho no Chibetto Nyukokusha.* Tokyo, Shunjusha, 1961.

Kawaguchi, Ekai. *Daini-kai Chibetto Ryoko Ki.* Tokyo, Kodansha, 1981.

——*Chibetto Ryoko Ki.* Tokyo, Kodansha, 1978.

Teramoto, Enga. *Zomo Tabi Nikki.* Tokyo, Fuyo Shobo, 1974.

Yamada, Mumon. *Bodaishin o Hasshimasho.* Hakujusha, 1970.